797,885 Books
are available to read at

Forgotten Books

www.ForgottenBooks.com

Forgotten Books' App
Available for mobile, tablet & eReader

ISBN 978-1-331-69125-9
PIBN 10222059

This book is a reproduction of an important historical work. Forgotten Books uses state-of-the-art technology to digitally reconstruct the work, preserving the original format whilst repairing imperfections present in the aged copy. In rare cases, an imperfection in the original, such as a blemish or missing page, may be replicated in our edition. We do, however, repair the vast majority of imperfections successfully; any imperfections that remain are intentionally left to preserve the state of such historical works.

Forgotten Books is a registered trademark of FB &c Ltd.
Copyright © 2017 FB &c Ltd.
FB &c Ltd, Dalton House, 60 Windsor Avenue, London, SW19 2RR.
Company number 08720141. Registered in England and Wales.

For support please visit www.forgottenbooks.com

1 MONTH OF FREE READING

at

www.ForgottenBooks.com

By purchasing this book you are eligible for one month membership to ForgottenBooks.com, giving you unlimited access to our entire collection of over 700,000 titles via our web site and mobile apps.

To claim your free month visit: www.forgottenbooks.com/free222059

* Offer is valid for 45 days from date of purchase. Terms and conditions apply.

English
Français
Deutsche
Italiano
Español
Português

www.forgottenbooks.com

Mythology Photography **Fiction**
Fishing Christianity **Art** Cooking
Essays Buddhism Freemasonry
Medicine **Biology** Music **Ancient Egypt** Evolution Carpentry Physics
Dance Geology **Mathematics** Fitness
Shakespeare **Folklore** Yoga Marketing
Confidence Immortality Biographies
Poetry **Psychology** Witchcraft
Electronics Chemistry History **Law**
Accounting **Philosophy** Anthropology
Alchemy Drama Quantum Mechanics
Atheism Sexual Health **Ancient History**
Entrepreneurship Languages Sport
Paleontology Needlework Islam
Metaphysics Investment Archaeology
Parenting Statistics Criminology
Motivational

SERMONS

BY

REV. CHARLES E. JEFFERSON, D.D., LL.D.

Author of
"*The Character of Jesus,*" "*Congregationalism,*"
"*Things Fundamental,*" etc.

THE PILGRIM PRESS
BOSTON   CHICAGO

Copyright 1917
By FRANK M. SHELDON

THE PILGRIM PRESS
BOSTON

CONTENTS

		PAGE
I	THE CLOUD AND THE SEA	1
II	THE PILGRIMS	17
III	THE PURITANS OF NEW ENGLAND	32
IV	THE PLACE OF THE PURITAN IN HISTORY	60
V	THE PURITAN TYPE	78
VI	THE PURITAN AND THE CAVALIER	91
VII	THE UNPOPULARITY OF THE PURITAN	104
VIII	THE STRENGTH AND WEAKNESS OF PURITANISM	127
IX	THE PURITAN THEOLOGY	146
X	THE PURITAN CONSCIENCE	168
XI	THE PURITAN AND THE HOME	183
XII	THE PURITAN SABBATH AND OURS	203
XIII	CONGREGATIONALISM	225
XIV	THE CONTRIBUTION OF CONGREGATIONALISM TO EDUCATION	250
XV	FUNDAMENTAL TRAITS OF PURITAN CHARACTERS AS ILLUSTRATED BY JOHN MILTON	268

FOREFATHERS' DAY
SERMONS

FOREFATHERS' DAY SERMONS

I

THE CLOUD AND THE SEA

"I would not, brethren, have you ignorant, how that our fathers were all under the cloud, and all passed through the sea." — 1 Cor. 10 : 1.

This is Forefathers' Sunday[1] — a day on which every year I ask you to look back. It is a good thing to look back, not always, but sometimes. Many of us do not look back often enough. The present engrosses us, the passing moment absorbs us. The duties and engagements and pleasures and tasks of the day crowd in upon us and blind our eyes to everything but the thing that now is.

We look back a little — as far as yesterday. We read the morning paper. That is a record of yesterday. But we do not care to go further back. We are not interested in day before yesterday, or the day before that. Nothing is so dreary and stale as a daily paper two days old. But we ought to look back to last year, and to the last century, and still further. It is a good thing to take long views. We need a long view backward and a long view forward. It is the long view which gives us poise, and courage, and patience, and hope. It is the long view which enables us to quit ourselves like men.

We do well when we look back to Abraham Lincoln — fifty years back. We are helped by looking back to George

[1] Dec. 17, 1916.

FOREFATHERS' DAY SERMONS

Washington — more than a hundred years back. This year we were edified by looking back to William Shakespeare — three hundred years back. Next year we shall be strengthened by looking back to Martin Luther — four hundred years back. It is an inspiration to look back to the days of Peter and John and Paul. Sunday is a memorial day, reminding us of something which took place nearly two thousand years ago. The long view gives us balance, and the power of seeing the things immediately around us in their correct proportion and in their true relations.

The Hebrews had a genius for looking back, and also a genius for looking ahead. The two capacities went together, and seemed to feed each other. The Hebrew poets and orators and statesmen and teachers were always talking about the great men of history. They never wearied of chanting the praises of Abraham and Isaac and Jacob, of Moses and Joshua and Samuel, of Gideon and Jephthah and Samson, of Elijah and Elisha, of David and Solomon. They were always bringing to bear upon the heart the lifting force of bygone days, always flashing on the mind the splendor of some regal soul who had led the way.

Paul was a Hebrew of the Hebrews when he wrote to the Corinthian Christians: "I would not have you ignorant how that our fathers were all under the cloud and all passed through the sea." He found inspiration in men who had been in their graves fourteen hundred years. Why does he say "our fathers"? He is writing to a Gentile church. The majority of the members were Greeks. There were no doubt Jews among them, but they were probably in a minority. He says a little later in this letter: "Ye know that when ye were Gentiles, ye were led away unto

THE CLOUD AND THE SEA

those dumb idols, howsoever ye might be led." But nevertheless Paul speaks of " our fathers." This is not surprising to any one acquainted with Paul's mind. He always moved in the realm of the spirit, and it was spiritual realities which interested him. He knew that there is a physical lineage and also a spiritual lineage, a physical ancestry and also a spiritual ancestry. He was surrounded by religious teachers who could understand nothing but physical descent. They were always shouting in his ears: " We are the sons of Abraham ! " But he denied it. Outwardly indeed they were Jews, but inwardly they were not. They had the blood of Abraham in their veins, but not the spirit of Abraham in their heart. To Paul, a man is a Hebrew, not when he has the blood of Abraham in his body, but when he has the faith of Abraham in his soul. It is faith which saves, and not blood. In his second letter to the Corinthians Paul makes the bold assertion: " Henceforth we know no man after the flesh: even though we have known Christ after the flesh, yet now we know him so no more." There was a time when Paul was interested in Jesus as a descendant of David, but that time passed, and he became interested in him solely as the Son of God. It was not the ancestry of Jesus, but the mind of Jesus, which became the object of supreme importance. These Greek Christians in Corinth had been baptized into the spirit of the patriarchs and prophets. They had come to accept the Hebrew attitude to God. They had embraced the ideas and ideals of the Jew of Nazareth, and therefore the heroes and saints of the Hebrew people became their spiritual ancestors. It was proper for Paul to say " our fathers."

So today let me speak to you about " our fathers." Some of you were brought up in the Methodist Com-

FOREFATHERS' DAY SERMONS

munion, and some in the Baptist, and some in the Presbyterian, and some in the Episcopal, and some in the Lutheran, and some in the Dutch Reformed, and some in the Roman Catholic, and others in some still different branch of the great church of God, but we can all think about "our fathers." The Pilgrims are our ancestors if we have accepted their ideals and been baptized into their spirit. It is not necessary to be related to any one who came over in the *Mayflower* to be a son of the Pilgrims. To be a descendant of the Puritans it is not necessary to have a drop of Puritan blood in one's veins. A man is a child of the Pilgrims not because he has in his house a piece of furniture that came down from the early settlers of New England, but because he has in his heart some of the furniture which was in the Pilgrim's soul. We Americans are all in a sense the descendants of the Pilgrims. They have influenced us all. Our life is different because they lived and labored. We can no more escape the influence of their ideals than we can escape the pressure of the physical atmosphere. Those immigrants of 1620 were our fathers. It would be egregious egotism for the Congregationalists to claim them as their exclusive property, and it would be sheer bigotry for any American to turn his back upon the Pilgrims, saying: "I take no interest in them, I care nothing whatever for them, because I am a communicant in a different branch of the church of Christ." As many as have been baptized into the spirit of the Pilgrims, they are the sons of the Pilgrims.

I would not have you ignorant, says Paul, of the experiences of our fathers. They were all under the cloud — the mystical cloud — the cloud that symbolized God's protection and guidance. They all passed through the sea, they made their way through inextricable difficulties, they sur-

THE CLOUD AND THE SEA

mounted insurmountable obstacles. They had extraordinary privileges. They were all baptized unto Moses. They all ate of the same spiritual meat. They all drank of the same spiritual drink. But notwithstanding their blessings and mercies, many of them never reached the goal. Most of them fell by the way. Only a few reached the land which had been promised. And why? Because they slipped down into the idolatrous feast which was spread around them. They slid down into the popular way of thinking and feeling. They sank down into the current practices and customs. They tumbled plump down into the old ways of living, and hence hardly any of them reached the promised goal. Therefore, Corinthian Christians, let me sound a note of warning. If any one of you thinks he stands, let him take heed lest he fall. For the idolatrous feast is spread at your door, and it is easy to fall out of the life to which you are called. I would not have you ignorant of the experiences of the men who have gone before you. Extraordinary privileges are no guarantee against the divine judgments. Wonderful mercies do not safeguard men against moral catastrophies and awful penalties. Men can be under the cloud and pass through the sea, and at the same time come to irretrievable ruin. Paul gathered together the failings of his fathers, and out of them drew a warning for the admonition of his fellow-Christians, and I this morning wish to roll together the virtues of our fathers, and out of them draw a lesson for our encouragement and strengthening.

I would not have you ignorant, brethren; I would not have you forget. I would not have the fact slip into the back of your mind, that our fathers were all under the cloud, the cloud of the divine guidance and protection,

[5]

FOREFATHERS' DAY SERMONS

and also the cloud of popular suspicion and disapprobation. They all passed through the sea, the Atlantic Ocean which rolled between the old world and the new, and also the ocean of hardship and peril, of persecution and tribulation. It is easy to forget that the Pilgrims were once despised and forsaken. They are now everywhere eulogized and exalted. Even men who do not praise the Puritans praise the Pilgrims, and men who speak sarcastically of the Puritans speak eulogistically of the Pilgrims. The Pilgrims were one species of Puritans, a sweet-spirited and tolerant and hospitable species. The Pilgrim stands on a pedestal in circles which have not yet become willing to put a wreath on the Puritan's brow. The Pilgrim has won golden opinions from all sorts of people. Churches are called Pilgrim Churches, halls are called Pilgrim Halls, presses are called Pilgrim Presses. Poems are written about the Pilgrims, and songs are sung about them, and a perpetual stream of eloquence eddies around their name.

But the Pilgrims were not always admired and lauded. They were once the most unpopular of all the people in England. Men looked upon them much as we now look upon anarchists. They were alleged to be the destroyers of public order and security. A very clever and Christian king — James I — declared that he would compel them to conform, or else he would harry them out of the land. They refused to conform, and so they were harried out of the land. They crossed over to Holland. They were all under the cloud and they all passed through the sea. In Holland they were ignored. Holland paid no attention to them. Holland met them with no bands of music. Holland uttered no eulogy over their virtues. Holland bade them no official farewell. Their coming and going did not cause a ripple on the placid surface of Dutch life.

THE CLOUD AND THE SEA

They were in Holland eleven years, but no statues were erected in their honor, and no tablets were put up to mark the spot where they had lived. They were nobodies. A company of a hundred Dukhobors living on the lower East side in New York City would cause about as much sensation as the Pilgrims caused in Leyden during their eleven years sojourn there. When they started for the New World there were no tears save on the cheeks of a few people as poor and socially obscure as themselves.

In the New World they were forsaken. New England was in 1620 one of the most God-forsaken corners in the world. Various companies of daring pioneers had tried to settle there, and every colony had ended in failure. Half of the Pilgrims died the first winter. The next year thirty-five new immigrants arrived, all desperately poor. There was not a biscuit left on the wretched little craft that brought them. They had no cooking utensils, and their clothing and bedding were scanty. Two years later sixty more came — also poor and needy. During the first three years the Plymouth colonists were obliged again and again to face starvation. It seemed at times they must inevitably succumb. In summer they dug shell-fish out of the sand, in winter they lived on ground-nuts and wild fowl. Nobody sent them donations. Europe was indifferent to their sufferings. Very few Englishmen could be induced to join them. At the end of twenty-five years they were still only a handful in number. When in 1628 and 1630 Englishmen began to settle at Salem and around Massachusetts Bay, these newcomers looked upon the Plymouth colonists askance. They had no desire to join hands with them. It was not till a number of them fell sick, that they were willing to send to Plymouth for a physician. I would not have you forget, brethren, that these Pilgrims

[7]

FOREFATHERS' DAY SERMONS

were all under the cloud of the world's condemnation, and that all passed through the sea of misunderstanding and neglect.

Why were these men so unpopular? Because they were Non-conformists. They refused to conform to things that had been established. They were Separatists. Rather than violate their conscience, they separated themselves from the crowd. The mediæval church compelled men to conform. It told them how they must act, and how they must pray, and how they must think. Many chafed under the bondage, and resented the tyranny, and again and again there were insurrections against the despotisms of the ecclesiastical hierarchy which had gathered all power into its hands, but all these insurrections were crushed. It was not till 1517 that a man appeared who was strong enough to lead a rebellion which was successful. Martin Luther tore Northern Europe away from the Roman See, and a little later Henry VIII wrested England also from the grip of Rome. The Pope was succeeded by the English King, and the Roman Curia was superseded by the English Parliament, and the civil hierarchy assumed the right to say who the officers of the church should be, and how the followers of Christ should worship God.

Multitudes resented this infringement of their rights. Thousands resisted the usurpers in their minds, hundreds with their tongues, only a few in act. A handful of radicals said: "We will not submit to this! We will go out! We will go out at once! We will go out alone! We will go out at any cost! It matters not what others think, or say, or do, our duty is clear. It matters not what King or Prince may say, or what Bishop or Archbishop may threaten, our allegiance is to the King of Kings, and him only will we serve." These men became the Pilgrim Fathers. They

THE CLOUD AND THE SEA

got their early inspiration from a man who wrote a little book entitled "Reformation Without Tarrying for Any." The keynote of the Pilgrim movement is sounded in that title. The Pilgrims refused to conform to an established thing which they believed was wrong. They went out alone. They went out at the risk of losing their fortunes and their lives. That is the Pilgrim spirit. When men ask you what is the distinctive trait of the Pilgrim spirit, this is the answer: "The distinctive trait of the Pilgrim spirit is willingness to depart alone from the established order, even at the cost of one's fortune and one's life." Many persons are willing to cast off an established custom when the time is ripe for such action, or in other words, when it is safe, when the public mind has been prepared, when the environment offers promise of success, but only a few are ready to go on ahead of their time, to march forward without waiting for any. It is the refusal to wait for the crowd that constitutes the essence of the Pilgrim spirit. There are many who are ready to depart from the established order when such departure involves no risk. There are times when it is easy enough to refuse to conform, and in such times non-conformists are many. But there are only a few who are willing to go out alone in the support of any great cause, if the going out involves the risk of losing one's friends and one's fortune and one's life. It is this willingness to stake everything on one's course of action which constitutes the crowning glory of the Pilgrim spirit. The Pilgrim went out alone, carrying his life in his hand. That is why the world today bows before him.

Now if any man thinks he stands in the line of the Pilgrim succession, let him take heed lest he fall. The Pilgrims of the 17th century were few in number, and there are only a handful in any age who are ready to do what

FOREFATHERS' DAY SERMONS

the Pilgrims did. The idolatrous feast is always spread, and men and women sit down at the table. It is easy to think the thing which others are thinking. It is natural to feel the thing that the crowd is feeling. It is comfortable to do the thing which the multitude is doing. The reason the world gets on so slowly is because the number of Pilgrims is small. Mankind is determined to do the thing that is customary, to bow down before the thing which is established, and that is why the world creeps on with many a delay toward the promised land.

If you were one of six persons who happened to come together on Sunday morning before church time, and all the other five said they were not going to church, what would you do? If you were a Pilgrim, you would go. A Pilgrim goes out alone. It is hard to retain the Pilgrim spirit in a great city. If you were one of a dozen persons discussing the subject of prayer, and one after another should say disparaging things about it, one advancing a scientific argument against it, another quoting a great name against it, still another scoffing at it as an effete superstition, what would you do? If you were a Pilgrim, you would stand up and confess yourself a believer in prayer. You would say that you had been in the habit of praying from childhood, and that you hoped that by God's grace you might be strong enough to continue praying to the end. It is difficult to be a Pilgrim among unbelievers. If you chanced to find yourself in a company of acquaintances or friends, and all of them proceeded one after the other to kick the church, each one vying with the others to see who could kick it hardest, what would you do? If you were a Pilgrim, you would defend the church, and tell the company that in your judgment the church is an institution indispensable to the well-being of mankind,

THE CLOUD AND THE SEA

and that without the church, civilization would go to pieces and society would rot. It is not easy in the midst of a scoffing generation to be a Pilgrim. If you were seated at a great dinner and everybody at the table was drinking champagne, and if you were convinced that at the present time it is not wise for men who wish to set the highest example to young men and young women to drink alcoholic drinks, what would you do? If you were a Pilgrim, you would refuse to taste the champagne. A Pilgrim is not afraid to be alone. In society, either high or low, it is not easy to be a Pilgrim. To be a Pilgim you must be willing to be buffeted, and criticised and scorned. You must be ready to stand alone. You must not hesitate to pay the price.

Already the Tercentenary of the Landing of the Pilgrims is in sight, and the question is up for discussion: How can we most fittingly celebrate the three hundredth anniversary of that great event? Various suggestions have been offered. Of course, there will be sermons preached, and orations delivered, and poems recited, and songs sung. The Pilgrims will be eulogized, and glorified, and vociferously applauded. This is well. It is proper that these things should be done. But these things are not an adequate celebration of an epoch-making event. It is easy to shout the praises of heroes who are dead. It is pleasant to cast flowers on the graves of men whom we could not live with were they alive. It is easy to extol courage and sacrifice when doing it costs us nothing. Building the sepulchers of the prophets and garnishing the tombs of the righteous has been a favorite pastime of all generations. There was nothing which so disgusted the heart of Jesus as the prattling of his contemporaries about the virtues of the prophets, when the spirit which

FOREFATHERS' DAY SERMONS

had made the prophets great had entirely departed from the hearts of those who were loudest in their praises. We want the eulogies, but let us remember that these are not enough.

It has been suggested that a concerted effort be made to increase the membership of our denomination. Nearing the end of three hundred years we discover that in numbers we have lagged behind, and that notwithstanding an early start and our multitudinous privileges, we have not made the most of our opportunity. We are now urged to endeavor to add a half million communicants to our membership within the next four years. This also is good, but it is not sufficient. Increasing the size of a denomination is not necessarily a blessing to the world. Everything depends on what the denomination stands for and what it is trying to do. There are institutions whose increase of bulk would mean an impoverishment of mankind. The Christian church increased its size enormously in the reign of Constantine, and the Christian cause was poorer ever afterward. What this world most needs is not larger numbers, but a finer spirit. The effort to increase the membership of our churches is not to be discouraged, but that is not the first thing which we have to consider. We cannot celebrate properly the Landing of the Pilgrims simply by adding members to our churches. That is too easy.

Some one has suggested that an immense sum of money be collected, several millions of dollars, and that great endowments be established for the support of our work. This also is excellent, but it is not all. The raising of money has become the customary American way of celebrating. All the denominations have adopted it. Nothing could be more popular or more easy. Somebody offers the suggestion, committees are at once appointed, a few

THE CLOUD AND THE SEA

rich men give large sums, and the thing is done. The celebration is a success.

We are not to toss aside the suggested effort to raise several millions of dollars, but raising money is not an adequate celebration of the Landing of the Pilgrims. We must do something more difficult than that. We must face a problem more fundamental than the problem of money-raising. We must not overlook the tremendous fact that our fathers were all under the cloud, and all passed through the sea, and that if we desire to praise them we must imitate them, if we are going to honor them we must be like them, if we are to celebrate them in any real and worthy manner, then we must become Pilgrims ourselves. We must refuse to conform to the established things that are wrong. We must dare to stand alone. We must go out from the world at the risk of losing our reputation and the world's acclamations. We must commit ourselves to some unpopular reform. We must dedicate ourselves to some impossible task. We must strike with all our might some colossal wrong. We must strive to break the bonds of some ancient tyranny. We are living in momentous times. The idolatrous feast was never so magnificent and inviting as today. The world is full of false philosophies, low ideals, materialistic ambitions, and if we wish to celebrate the achievements of the Pilgrims, we must come boldly out from the tame and timorous crowd, and audaciously stand up for the principles for which Christ died on the cross!

All this was finely said over seventy years ago by James Russell Lowell, in his little poem, "The Present Crisis." He wrote it at the age of twenty-six. It has in it the glow and virility of youth. Parents ought to teach it to their children. Such a poem dropped into the bottom of the heart acts like radium, it radiates energy into the will

FOREFATHERS' DAY SERMONS

through all the years. The poet begins, as you know, by glancing over the past. He is appalled by the apparent carelessness of the Almighty in avenging awful wrongs:

> " History's pages but record
> One death-grapple in the darkness 'twixt old systems and the Word ";

But this does not daunt him, for he hastens on to declare in lines which have been more frequently quoted, perhaps, than any other lines written by an American:

> " Truth forever on the scaffold, Wrong forever on the throne, —
> Yet that scaffold sways the future, and, behind the dim unknown,
> Standeth God within the shadow, keeping watch above his own."

He then falls to meditating on the deeds of the great men who have made the world what it is. He describes the spirit which made them great:

> " Count me o'er earth's chosen heroes, they were souls that stood alone,
> While the men they agonized for hurled the contumelious stone,
> Stood serene, and down the future saw the golden beam incline
> To the side of perfect justice, mastered by their faith divine,
> By one man's plain truth to manhood and to God's supreme design."

He notes how these heroes have been obliged to toil up calvaries at the top of which they were crucified, but their tragic end does not block the way of Progress, or overturn the plans of God:

> " For Humanity sweeps onward: where to-day the martyr stands,
> On the morrow crouches Judas with the silver in his hands;
> Far in front the cross stands ready and the crackling fagots burn,
> While the hooting mob of yesterday in silent awe return
> To glean up the scattered ashes into History's golden urn."

And from this he draws a lesson and a warning. The Pilgrims have set us an example, and we are reluctant to follow it:

THE CLOUD AND THE SEA

" 'Tis as easy to be heroes as to sit the idle slaves
　Of a legendary virtue carved upon our fathers' graves,
　Worshippers of light ancestral make the present light a crime; —
　Was the *Mayflower* launched by cowards, steered by men behind their time?
　Turn those tracks toward Past or Future that make Plymouth Rock sublime?
　They were men of present valor, stalwart old iconoclasts,
　Unconvinced by axe or gibbet that all virtue was the Past's;
　But we make their truth our falsehood, thinking that hath made us free,
　Hoarding it in mouldy parchments, while our tender spirits flee
　The rude grasp of that great Impulse which drove them across the sea."

The sum of the whole matter is this. It is expressed in lines which should be written on every American mind and heart:

" New occasions teach new duties; Time makes ancient good uncouth;
　They must upward still, and onward, who would keep abreast of Truth;
　Lo, before us gleam her camp-fires! we ourselves must Pilgrims be,
　Launch our *Mayflower*, and steer boldly through the desperate winter sea,
　Nor attempt the Future's portal with the Past's blood-rusted key."

Lowell has told us how to celebrate the three hundredth anniversary of the Landing of the Pilgrims.

Whence did the Pilgrims get their spirit? From the Bible. They loved to read exhortations like this: " Be not conformed to this world: but be ye transformed by the renewing of your mind, that ye may prove what is that good, and acceptable, and perfect will of God." And also this: " Come out from among them, and be ye separate, saith the Lord, and touch not the unclean thing; and I will receive you, and will be a Father unto you, and ye shall be my sons and daughters, saith the Lord Almighty."

Jesus himself was a Pilgrim, an example and a guide for all Pilgrims to the end of time. He refused to conform to

FOREFATHERS' DAY SERMONS

a wrong that had been established. He dared to defy custom and tradition. He was willing to walk alone. He understood the risk he took. He knew that non-conformity would bring him to the cross. But he did not falter. The learned men of his country forsook him. The influential men turned against him. The so-called good people arrayed themselves against him. At last the crowd became venomously hostile to him, and he was left alone with twelve intimate friends. The State was against him, the Church was against him, his own family was against him, the whole world was against him. Only twelve humble peasants were with him. He met them in an upper room. One of these twelve deserted him. He knew what the others would do. He told them plainly: "You shall be scattered, every man to his own, and shall leave me alone." But he was not dismayed. He did not quail. He was ready to pay the full price. This was his consolation: "I am not alone, because the Father is with me." The Pilgrims were what they were because they had been with Jesus. He, before them, was under the cloud, he passed through the sea.

II

THE PILGRIMS[1]

"*Being destitute, afflicted, tormented.*" — HEB. 11 : 37.

A distinctive feature of the system of Hebrew education was the tremendous emphasis which was laid upon the illustrious deeds of the immortal dead. The religious teachers of Israel made the past live in the mind of Hebrew youth. It was made to live in great personalities. The Hebrew mind had no liking for abstractions. It was not interested as we are in the analysis of virtues. It did not interest itself in pale ideas. It was fond of the concrete, the personal. It took little interest in the graces and virtues of character unless they were embodied in a living man. And so, Hebrew teachers were always dealing with the past. They were constantly picking up some chapter of history and asking the people to read it. In order to show what God is like and what God wants, they were always studying the experiences of their ancestors. It was only in experience that they found inspiration to make the future better than the past. Parents were always talking to their children about Abraham, Isaac, and Jacob, or if not about these, then about Moses and Joshua. They related again and again the wonderful experiences that attended the exodus from Egypt, and also the wonderful experiences attending the conquest of Canaan. They never grew weary of telling about Gideon and Samson and Jephthah and Barak. They spoke often of David and Solomon, Elijah and Elisha, of Isaiah and Jeremiah. It

[1] Dec. 19, 1915.

was by concentrating the mind upon the character and achievements of the mighty dead that the Hebrew mind was trained and the Hebrew spirit was strengthened. Thus in the course of the centuries there was built up what is known as the Hebraic mind, the Hebraic disposition, the Hebraic attitude to life. And out of this Hebrew stock there came in the fulness of time one who was the fairest of ten thousand and who was altogether lovely; the Son of Man, and as we Christians think, the Son of God.

We Americans might adopt with profit the method of the ancient Hebrew teachers. To be sure, we follow their method more or less already. We use it probably more in the public schools than we do as yet in our churches. In our churches we have gone only a little way. No preacher would hesitate to preach a sermon on George Washington or Abraham Lincoln, but most preachers do not go beyond that. The average preacher would not think of preaching about any great American poet or philosopher or scholar, or any distinguished American lawyer or doctor or merchant. Yet a great company of noble and great-hearted men have contributed to the building of this republic, and it is only because of their heroic service and sacrifice that our nation is today what it is. We do not think of these men as often as we should. We should be braver and stronger if we made a larger use of the past. It is absurd to suppose that God is a God of the Jews only; he is a God of Americans, too. It is unthinkable that God inspired men in olden times and that his inspiration ceased something like 1900 years ago. It is a fundamental teaching of the Christian religion that God's inspiration is continuous, that he is always guiding and teaching men, and we are to believe that all the virtues and graces which are exhibited in our American people are the outflowering of

THE PILGRIMS

his Eternal Spirit. We impoverish our life, therefore, if we do not hold communion with our mighty dead. We should be better Americans and better Christians if we went back more frequently to ponder the characters and the deeds of our ancestors. Let us think this morning about the Pilgrims. In the roll of American immortals they must hold forever a conspicuous place.

When we think of the Pilgrims we think of them as a group, a body, a family. There is no one Pilgrim who stands out head and shoulders above all the others. There is no one of them who shines with a peculiar glory as a central sun round which the others revolve. No one ever got the start of the rest so as to bear the palm alone. They constitute a sort of constellation which shines in our American sky. We are not so much interested in the particular stars as in the entire constellation. Indeed they hardly form a constellation, but rather a piece of the milky way. The stars have lost their individual splendor, and their light has melted to form a patch of fleecy whiteness. Many of us would find it difficult to give the names of a score of the Pilgrims, others of us could not name a dozen. Some of us are more or less familiar with William Brewster and William Bradford, John Carver, John Alden, Samuel Fuller, Isaac Allerton and Edward Winslow. Probably most of us know Miles Standish better than any of the rest because the poet Longfellow has thrown upon Standish's face the light of his poetic genius. But I am not to speak this morning about any one or two or three of these men — my subject is the Pilgrims, the whole body of the people who came over in the *Mayflower*. I want simply to tell the story of their coming to America. There are different kinds of sermons. There are explanatory sermons in which the purpose of the preacher is unfolding

FOREFATHERS' DAY SERMONS

some principle or idea, explaining its contents, and applying it to the affairs of every-day life. There are hortatory sermons in which the preacher exhorts his congregation to believe some truth, or to perform some duty. There are story sermons in which nothing is explained, and where there is no exhortation, the simple narrative being allowed to make what impression it will. For instance, the story of Joseph and his brethren is a sermon; it contains no explanation or exhortation, but from first to last it makes a mighty appeal to the heart. The story of Gideon and his exploits lays a strong hand on the soul. Various missionaries have told us that they have never been able to preach a sermon so moving as the simple story of Jesus' death on the cross. By the repetition of the facts as they are related by the evangelists, the missionary is able to get deeper into the human heart than by any other sermon which he is able to create. Let me tell you this morning, in a simple, unadorned manner, the story of the Pilgrims.

In the northern part of England, about 140 miles from London, in the county of Nottinghamshire, there is a little village with the unattractive name of Scrooby. It is a very old town, with a history running back to the twelfth century. At the beginning of the seventeenth century there lived in this village a man by the name of William Brewster. He was a graduate of Cambridge University. After graduating he became the private secretary to a distinguished English diplomat. Later on he succeeded his father as the postmaster in Scrooby, where he lived in a large manor house belonging to the Bishop of York. In the hall of this manor house a company of English men and women were in the habit of meeting every Sunday to worship God in a way that was different from the worship prescribed by the State church.

THE PILGRIMS

Some of them came from Scrooby and others from small hamlets round about. Among them there was a boy seventeen years of age, William Bradford, who came from Austerfield, three miles away. The one thing peculiar about these people who met in William Brewster's house was that they believed it was their right, as believers in Jesus Christ, to worship God in the way which they believed God had ordained. This belief, however, was contrary to the general belief of that time. Englishmen, on the whole, believed in uniformity. Queen Elizabeth had always insisted upon it, and now her successor, James I, insisted upon it still more strongly. James I was the son of Lord Darnley and Mary, Queen of Scots. Somebody once said that he was the wisest fool in Europe. He was not without a certain kind of ability, but he was very narrow and very stubborn, always insisting stoutly on the divine right of kings, and believing that the State has a right to determine all the forms of religious worship. Andrew Melville once drove him to fury, almost, by telling him that there were two kings in Scotland — James and Jesus Christ, and that in the church, Christ was king, and that James was his subject. Near the beginning of his reign the king called a conference at Hampton Court, where he heard so many distasteful things that he finally broke up the conference, saying of the Non-conformists: "I will make them conform or else harry them out of the land."

Things became more and more unpleasant for all non-conforming Englishmen, and the little company in Scrooby began at last to think of emigrating to the continent. Holland was at that time the place of refuge for all persecuted people, and so to Holland they decided to go. The first attempt was made in the year 1607. They hired an Eng-

FOREFATHERS' DAY SERMONS

lish captain to take them to Holland, but the rascal having gotten them all on board, turned them over to the English officers, who threw them into jail. There they were kept for a month. At the end of the month all were released except seven, who were held over until the next session of the court. Not at all, however, dismayed by this unhappy outcome of their effort, they made the attempt in the spring of the next year. This time they hired a Dutch captain, telling him of their former experience, and urging him to be true to them. On the day appointed he met them according to his promise, on a lonely stretch of shore, but after the first boat load had been put aboard, English officers appeared on the shore, and the Dutch captain, fearful of losing his liberty and his ship, immediately set sail, leaving most of the company behind. It is not easy to conceive of the consternation of those on the ship, or the distress of those on the land. Most of those who had been put on board the ship were women and children, only a few men being carried in the first boat. They had nothing with them but the clothes on their backs. What little money belonged to the company was in the hands of those who remained on the shore. In some cases husbands and wives were separated, and the outlook for all was dismal. I cannot do better at this point than simply to quote a few sentences from the history written by William Bradford.

"But pitiful it was to see ye heavie case of these poore women in this distress; what weeping and crying on every side, some for their husbands, that were carried away in ye ship as is before related; others not knowing what should become of them, and their little ones; others againe melted in teares, seeing their poore little ones aboute them, crying for feare, and quaking with could.

THE PILGRIMS

"They were hurried from one place to another, and from one justice to another, till in ye ende they knew not what to doe with them; for to imprison so many women and innocent children for no other cause (many of them) but that they must goe with their husbands, seemed to be unreasonable and all would crie out of them; and to send them home againe was as difficult, for they aledged, as ye trueth was, they had no homes to goe to, for they had either sould, or otherwise disposed of their houses and livings. To be shorte, after they had been thus turmoyled a good while, and conveyed from one constable to another, they were glad to be ridd of them in ye end upon any terms; for all were wearied and tired with them. Though in ye mean time they (poore soules) indured miserie enough; and thus in ye end necesitie forste a way for them."

Men and women of such grit and pluck could not be finally thwarted in the accomplishment of their purpose. And again quoting the words of Bradford: "In ye end, notwithstanding all these stormes of opposition, they all gatt over at length, some at one time and some at another, and some in one place and some in another, and mette togeather againe according to their desires, with no small rejoycing."

And so in the year 1608 a goodly number of these Pilgrims found themselves in the city of Amsterdam, to which city there had already come a number of English exiles, also seeking liberty. These exiles, however, were far from happy even in Holland, for fierce and irreconcilable differences had broken out among them, and the atmosphere of the English colony was so torn with storm that after living there for nearly a year the Scrooby Pilgrims deemed it wise to go on to Leyden. It was in the summer of 1609 that the change was made. And here for eleven years they

FOREFATHERS' DAY SERMONS

enjoyed, as Brewster says, "much sweet and delightful society, and spiritual comfort together in the ways of God." We do not know a great deal about those eleven years, and it is not necessary to dwell at this time on the little that we know. It is enough to remember that their minister was John Robinson, one of the most learned and spiritual and noble of men, and that his congregation numbered about three hundred. Most of the members were quite poor and were compelled to work hard. William Brewster at first taught English, and later on set up a printing office. Bradford was a fustian worker. The life of all of them was discouraging and exhausting, and after they had been there a few years they began to make inquiries as to a possible refuge elsewhere. In the first place, they were afraid that their colony might become extinct. They had hoped on coming to Holland that many of their English friends would follow them, but in these expectations they had been disappointed. Moreover, Leyden was at that time a city of a hundred thousand, and like all large cities had in it many bad boys and girls, and these boys and girls were constantly leading the children of the Pilgrims astray. Because they were so poor, and because they had to work so hard, and because their children were in danger, they became convinced that they had not yet found a permanent home. Moreover, they had in them the genuine missionary spirit. They had heard much of a great new world lying on the other side of the Atlantic whose inhabitants had never been taught the gospel of Jesus Christ, and when they began to think of seeking a new home, it was natural that their thoughts should run across the sea. Bradford tells us that "they had a great hope that they might lay some good foundation for advancing the gospel in those remote parts of the world,

THE PILGRIMS

even though they should be only as stepping stones to others for the performing of so great a work."

But it was not easy for them to decide in what part of the new world to settle. At one time they thought of going to Guiana, but reports from that quarter being so discouraging, they decided not to go. Virginia was strongly recommended by some, but Virginia was at last voted down. At one time an effort was made to induce them to come to New Amsterdam, at the mouth of the Hudson, but this also did not permanently appeal to them. New England was considered undesirable because of its extremely cold winters. It was finally decided that they should settle somewhere near the mouth of the Delaware.

We should pause at this point to ponder the magnitude of the courage of the men who decided to cross the Atlantic ocean in the year of our Lord 1620. The Atlantic was far wider in those days than it is now. You must measure the width of an ocean not by a yardstick, but by the clock. Measuring it in that way, the Atlantic ocean in the time of the Pilgrims was 30,000 miles wide. It required nine weeks to cross it. Moreover it was a mysterious and forbidding land. One is surprised in reading the history of the early seventeenth century to find how many settlements were attempted, only to end in failure. The difficulties were so numerous and the hardships were so awful, and the perils were so daunting, that only the stoutest-hearted of men and women were equal to so great an undertaking. A few years before the Pilgrims sailed a company of Englishmen under George Popham had made a settlement near the mouth of the Kennebunk river, but some of the company having died, the rest became discouraged, and they all hastened back to England again. Of a hundred and

FOREFATHERS' DAY SERMONS

fifty Englishmen who sailed in a ship for Virginia, a hundred and thirty died on the voyage. Stories of these disasters all reached Holland, but none of these things moved the Pilgrims. Having decided to emigrate to the new world, their hearts did not fail them.

One of their greatest difficulties was to secure means of transportation. It was not easy to get anybody to finance the trip. Finally they succeeded in interesting a body of London merchants, and through their assistance a little vessel called the *Speedwell* was bought, and a larger vessel called the *Mayflower* was chartered. Nobody knows how the *Mayflower* looked, no painter thought it worth while to paint her, no artist took the trouble to sketch her. All the pictures of the *Mayflower* which you have seen are nothing more than the creations of some artist's imagination. And yet, we know, in general, her appearance. We know that she was small, having a tonnage of only 180 tons; we know that she must have looked very much like many other ships of her own size, descriptions of which have been preserved for us. She deserves a place in the list of ships that might rightly be called immortal. One of the others was the ship that carried Columbus from the old world to the new; another one was the little ship that carried Paul from Asia into Europe; and shall we name also the little boat on which Jesus of Nazareth slept one day in the midst of a storm?

We need not dwell upon the departure from Leyden. It is enough to know that the parting was a sad one. Only those were to go to America who had volunteered, and a majority of the church decided to stay in Leyden. The pastor staid with the majority. The Pilgrims came to America without a minister. It was the *Speedwell* that carried the members of the Leyden church to Southamp-

THE PILGRIMS

ton, and there it was joined by the *Mayflower*. After a long controversy with the merchants in regard to financial matters, the two ships finally set sail on August fifteenth. Before they had proceeded far, the *Speedwell* began to leak, and so it was necessary that both ships should return to England, putting in at the little Devonshire harbor of Dartmouth. The repairs having been completed, on September second, they sailed again. After proceeding about three hundred miles, the *Speedwell* began to leak again, and it was necessary for both ships to return to England, this time anchoring in the harbor at Plymouth. It is not surprising that the hearts of some of the company began to fail, and that twenty returned to London. It was now decided not to take the *Speedwell* again, and so all the Pilgrims — a hundred and two in number — boarded the *Mayflower*. In this continuous sifting of the settlers of New England one is reminded of the sifting of the army of Gideon. In the first place, only the bravest of Englishmen ventured to cross into Holland, only the bravest of the Holland company decided to sail for America, and only the bravest of this company outlived the disheartenment caused by the leaking of the *Speedwell*. They were indeed a company of heroes who sailed on September sixteenth on the *Mayflower*.

It is singular how, again and again in human history, nature has done its utmost to thwart the efforts of men in great movements which were evidently according to the will of God. No sooner was the *Mayflower* in mid-Atlantic than a series of fierce storms broke upon her, and in one of these storms one of her main beams became sprung and cracked. So imminent was the danger that a conference was held for the purpose of considering the advisability of giving up the whole undertaking. On investigation it

FOREFATHERS' DAY SERMONS

was discovered that the cracked beam could be forced back into its place again, and this repair having been made, the little vessel once more proceeded on her way. It was on November nineteenth, more than nine weeks after leaving Plymouth, that the *Mayflower* cast anchor near Cape Cod. It had been their intention to make a settlement somewhere south of the mouth of the Hudson, but finding that they had gotten far out of their course they turned the prow of the *Mayflower* to the south. But here again nature seemed to be determined to resist them. Not only did the Atlantic become shallow, but a fierce storm threw itself across their way, and turning back they cast anchor, this time in the harbor of what is now called Provincetown. William Bradford says that "they fell upon their knees and blessed ye God of heaven, who had brought them over ye vast and furious ocean, and delivered them from all ye periles and miseries thereof, againe to set their feete on ye firme and stable earth, their proper elemente."

It was on a Saturday while the *Mayflower* was at anchor in the harbor of Provincetown that the men of the *Mayflower* drew up and signed their famous compact. For the information of all the boys and girls who are listening to this sermon, let me present the compact entire:

"In the name of God, Amen. We whose names are underwritten, the loyall Subjects of our dread soveraigne Lord King James, by the grace of God of Great Britaine, France, and Ireland King, Defender of the Faith, &c.

Having undertaken for the glory of God, and advancement of the Christian Faith, and honour of our King and Countrey, a Voyage to plant the first Colony in the Northerne parts of Virginia, doe by these presents solemnly and mutually in the presence of God and one of another,

THE PILGRIMS

covenant, and combine ourselves together into a civill body politike, for our better ordering and preservation, and furtherance of the ends aforesaid; and by vertue hereof to enact, constitute and frame such just and equall Lawes, Ordinances, acts, constitutions, offices from time to time, as shall be thought most meet and convenient for the generall good of the Colony; unto which we promise all due submission and obedience.

In witness whereof we have, hereunder subscribed our names, Cape Cod, 11 of November, in the yeare of the raigne of our soveraigne Lord King James, of England, France, and Ireland 18, and of Scotland 54. Anno Domini 1620."

About a month was now spent in making explorations. On Monday, December twenty-first, they set foot on the mainland where Plymouth now is.

It is not my purpose at this time to tell the chapter of the hardships and sufferings which now opened. The tribulations of the first winter were never forgotten by anybody who passed through them. In the months of January and February, 51 of their number died. Sometimes two and three died in a single day. At one time there were only six or seven of the entire colony that were able to be up and around. It looked as though possibly not one of them would survive. They used to bury their dead at night, and carefully smooth over the soil where the graves had been made in order that the Indians prowling round might not discover how great were their losses. But as William Brewster once said: " It is not with us as with men whom small things can discourage, or small discontentments cause to wish themselves home again."

These men and women could not be disheartened, they had come to America, and they had come to stay They

FOREFATHERS' DAY SERMONS

had come to this country for the sake of religion; it was for the liberty to worship God in a way that they felt sure God had ordained that they were willing to face all dangers. We are in the habit of speaking much about our political liberty; we have a right to rejoice in it, but it should never be forgotten that our political liberty came out of a passion for religious liberty. It was because men were determined to worship God free from the dictates of the State that by and by there was liberty both in the Church and in the State. It is sometimes said that the love of money is the mightiest force in the world. We are told that men are willing to endure every hardship for the sake of making money, but the experience of the Pilgrims proves that there is a mightier force in human nature than love of money, and that is the love of God. The colonies planted as commercial enterprises on the coast of New England in the early seventeenth century all went to pieces, unable to stand the strain of the terrific forces which played upon them. But the Plymouth colony, composed of men who were dominated by the spirit of religion, endured. It is devotion to God and to his Son, Jesus Christ, that is able to bear all things, believe all things, hope all things and endure all things.

It was on the fifth day of April that the *Mayflower* started on its return voyage. There were only about fifty of the original company left; twenty-one of these were men, and six were lads old enough to work. The remainder were women and children. When the time came for the *Mayflower* to depart, not one of the Pilgrims expressed a desire to return, not a man was dismayed, not a woman was afraid. I love to think of them as they stood there on the shore watching the *Mayflower* sail out to sea, I love to fancy the wistful look in their eyes as they saw

THE PILGRIMS

the ship grow smaller and smaller until at last it was only a speck on the horizon, and then finally disappeared altogether. If I were a painter I should paint that picture. It is one of the great scenes in the history of the world.

III

THE PURITANS OF NEW ENGLAND [1]

"*These are not drunken.*" — ACTS 2 : 15.

It is noteworthy that the first sermon of the first Christian preacher began with an apology. A strange thing had happened in Jerusalem. One hundred and twenty men and women, for many days sad and glum, had suddenly become radiant and vocal. A phenomenon so unusual demanded an explanation. An explanation was immediately forthcoming. Men were at hand ready to say that all this hilarity and boisterousness were due to an excitation of the nerves, induced by a free indulgence in alcoholic liquors. " These men are drunk ! " the scoffers said, and Peter took hold of the black lie and strangled it. " These are not drunken," he declared, and then went on to prove the truth of his assertion by an argument which, however weak to the occidental mind in a changed environment, was altogether convincing to the men to whom it was delivered. The crowd, which began with thinking that the Apostolic company were drunk, went away with the conviction that these men and women had been indeed baptized with the spirit of the Eternal.

Why did Peter pay attention to a sneer? Why did he not ignore the calumny and go on and proclaim his truth? Because he was in dead earnest to make room in Jerusalem for a message of vast significance, and he knew that truth can gain no admittance into hearts filled with prejudice

[1] Dec. 20, 1903.

and scorn. Spiritual influences cannot flow through souls which are choked with hate. A teacher of religion must not only possess a truth, but he himself must have a reputation which will incline the ears of men to listen. A man supposedly drunk, even though entirely sober, can teach the world nothing about God. Men shut themselves out from the influence of any teacher against whom they cherish a fixed dislike. We are reached and moulded only by those in whom we have confidence and for whom we feel a genuine respect. Peter knew that the progress of the Christian church could be blocked by false ideas of the character and spirit of its members, and so, before he delivers his message of Jesus and the resurrection, he tears to tatters a falsehood concerning himself and his companions. Having once opened the minds and hearts of those before him by freeing them from the grip of a false impression, he proceeded to sow the seed which brought forth a glorious harvest.

The Apostles have had their successors in many lands and times, and the experiences of Apostolic days are again and again repeated. Whenever and wherever a company of men, baptized from on high, have entered on the work of battering down customs which were wrong and changing standards which were low, and have given themselves to the task of turning life into new channels and establishing in society loftier ideals, the world has gnashed its teeth at them, and all the air about them has been darkened by great swarms of calumnies and slanders. If a hero cannot be struck down by a dagger, he is certain at least to be pelted and covered with mud. Just in proportion to the strength of the reformers, and the radical thoroughness of their proposed reformation, is the vituperation abundant and the hatred intense.

FOREFATHERS' DAY SERMONS

Now, of all the men who have played a part in history since the days of the Apostles, the Puritans were the loftiest in their ideals, and the most vigorous and uncompromising in their action. They gripped the world so tightly that the prints of their fingers are on it still. The English reformation under Henry VIII was a superficial and halfhearted thing. Henry VIII was born a Roman Catholic, and a Catholic he remained to the day of his death. He hated Martin Luther, his doctrines and his followers, and so fiercely did he attack the German heretic that the Pope called him the Defender of the Faith. But one day the will of the King and the will of the Pope clashed, and the King in hot wrath declared, " I will be henceforth the head of the English church." Various modifications of the ecclesiastical machinery were introduced, and England became nominally Protestant under a reputedly Protestant king. But Henry VIII, even when called a Protestant, held to the great mass of Roman Catholic traditions and dogmas, discarding for the most part those only which denied his supremacy as the head of the English church. What was true of Henry VIII was true, under limitations, of his illustrious daughter Elizabeth. She figures in history as a Protestant, but her religion was not deep. She was unscrupulous and profane, conservative in her tastes and church practices, looking with mingled fear and disgust upon a body of Englishmen, who having started upon the work of reform were determined to carry it through. For however conservative and worldly wise were the rulers of England, there was an increasing class of Christian English men and women who had in them the old Teutonic love of veracity and thoroughness. They went to the roots of things. They saw that the disease of Christendom could not be cured by sundry changes in the ecclesiastical

THE PURITANS OF NEW ENGLAND

machine. They went to the Bible and from its pages learned that no man, be he called priest or Bishop or Pope or King, has a right to come between the human soul and God. Thrilled by this great vision, they dared to array themselves against the world. England in the sixteenth century was frightfully corrupt. Polite society was full of drunkenness and debauchery. The nobility were in many cases unspeakably unclean. The court was, at least in spots, rotten. The stage was sometimes blasphemous and always foul. Art was often vile and degrading. Fiction was for the most part vulgar and obscene. Conversation, even in high circles, was profane and nasty. The church, like the nation, was laden with iniquity. The whole head was sick and the whole heart was faint. From the sole of the foot even unto the head, there were wounds and bruises and festering sores. Laymen in appalling numbers knew nothing of the spirit of Christ, and even church officials were in many cases ignorant and dissolute. Against all this a growing band of enthusiastic reformers made ceaseless and uncompromising war. With astounding audacity they spurned the world, the flesh, and the devil. They turned their back upon the stage, the novel, the pictures, the fashion and pride of society; yea, they resisted priest and prelate and Pope, spurned courtier and noble, and called in question the alleged rights of Parliaments and kings. Against the flood of worldliness and vice they set themselves like rock. In an age of widespread corruption they cried, " The church of God on earth must be clean ! " To them all ceremonies were sham and mummery so long as the heart was estranged from God. To cleanse the church and keep it clean, to free it from doctrinal accretions and debasing superstitions and the sins which had robbed it of its power, this was their steadfast and

FOREFATHERS' DAY SERMONS

passionate endeavor. "Puritans!" men cried in derision, because they worked tirelessly for purity. "Puritan!" The word was coined on lips of scorn, and had in it the heat of a hot disdain. Even today, when the word is spoken in certain circles, the old fire of contempt bursts into flame again.

Some of these men were sent to heaven robed in flames in the reign of bloody Mary; a few were hung, and more were driven into exile in the reign of good Queen Bess. A much larger number were driven into Holland in the reign of James I, and a great host left the country in the reign of the first Charles. Of the refugees from the tyranny of Charles and his relentless ministers, twenty-six thousand came to New England, and it is of these to which your thought is now directed.

No other set of men who ever came to the New World have been so much written about and talked about as these twenty-six thousand Englishmen. More books and pamphlets have been published about the Puritan commonwealth of Massachusetts Bay than about the entire eighteenth century with its great revolutionary war. More orations and addresses and lectures have been delivered dealing with the Puritans than have been spoken about all the other classes of our population put together. For some reason the world cannot let these men alone. For over two hundred years pens and tongues have been busy, eager to tell the story of what they attempted and accomplished. Even now new books appear each succeeding year, exploiting their blunders or eulogizing their virtues. Everything they ever did or said, or felt or thought, has been analyzed and critically inspected. Every feature of their conduct has been subjected to the X-rays of historical criticism. No light that ever

THE PURITANS OF NEW ENGLAND

beat upon a throne was so fierce as that which for two hundred years has beaten on the heads of these New England exiles.

What men have been so praised, eulogized, exalted as these have been? They have been placed on pedestals, lifted far above the heads of ordinary mortals, until at times they have seemed more than human, and to belong rather to a race of demigods. They have been painted often with halos round their heads. By men who have lost the sense of true proportion they have been pictured as so many colossuses bestriding the narrow world, while all other men are dwarfed into insignificance in the shadow of their huge legs. They have been represented as paragons of virtue, examples of wisdom, patterns of piety, the incarnation and quintessence of all human excellence. Even their blunders have been decked with laurel, their perversities covered over with leaves of roses, and their crimson sins washed white in the flowing breath of indiscriminating praise.

But the praise has been more than matched by the abuse. What men have been so egregiously misunderstood, so outrageously misrepresented, so persistently maligned, caricatured and hated? They have been pictured as coarse and cruel and despicable; as narrow-hearted persecutors and narrow-headed fanatics; as barbarians, destitute of taste and affection; as crabbed and crooked cranks; as glum-faced, sour-eyed Pharisees and hypocrites, unhappy themselves and rendering miserable everybody with whom they had to do. This stream of vituperation has flowed in a steady stream through two hundred years; and even today there are men so exceeding mad against them that they dig up the skeletons of these vanished culprits and hang them on the gibbet for

FOREFATHERS' DAY SERMONS

public execration. Anonymous scribblers in various papers still pelt them with scurrilous and flippant things, and after-dinner speakers provoke applause by publicly thanking God that the Puritans are dead. In divers ways the idea is kept alive that these men were drunk, soaked with bigotry and fanaticism, beside themselves with superstitious frenzy, intoxicated to the verge of madness by a spirit from the pit. There are Americans now alive to whom the entire seventeenth century of New England history is a vast Sahara desert, with scarcely an oasis in it to cheer the eye or warm the heart; a cold and dreary age of ice, in which titanic and ungovernable forces wrought a widespread desolation.

This is much to be regretted. It matters nothing to the Puritans what the twentieth century thinks of them, but it matters much to the twentieth century. No men can influence us whom we despise, and they who scorn the Puritans and execrate their memory build a barrier between themselves and a company of God's elect. No man or nation can afford to ignore or despise any company of men who have honestly striven to serve God in their day and generation. Our republic needs all the strength and inspiration which bygone heroes have to give, and Puritanism, with all its limitations and deficiencies, is surely one of the springs at which America must drink, if like a strong man we are to run the race and reach the goal. There are great and critical times ahead of us. Vast problems loom up before us, and huge dangers hang ominous and black upon the horizon. What struggles, what tempests, what reformations, what revolutions, what agonies of strife and baptisms of blood may lie ahead of us no one can say, but this much is certain, we cannot afford to face the future and dare its perils without the princi-

THE PURITANS OF NEW ENGLAND

ples by which the Puritan lived and conquered. Much that was his we do not care for. His fashions and customs, his science and philosophy, his political economy and theology, all these have been outgrown and are forevermore discarded, but the Puritan *spirit*, his temper, courage, tenacity of will, and passionate and unconquerable devotion, all these we need and must have; without them the republic must inevitably perish. Woe unto us if through prejudice or stubborn pride we shut our hearts to the influence of the very men whose help we are most of all in need of.

These are not drunken! In order to prove them drunk, various stories have been circulated and divers calumnies have been handed down from generation to generation which, even to this day, are among the uninformed faithfully cherished and believed. What I purpose now saying is well known to every student of history, but for the information of our boys and girls, and for the strengthening of our young men and young women who have already heard many an anti-Puritan sneer, and for the benefit of older people who have not had the time for extended historical reading, let me take up seven pieces of mud which the world has kept on hurling at the Puritans of New England, and show you how readily they crumble under the touch of historic fact.

I. The first accusation is that the Puritans of New England were cruel to the Indians, an unpardonable sin, of course, in men making high professions of piety. This calumny is often expressed in the well-known line, " They fell on their knees and then on the aborigines." All of which is funny, but false. The first settlers of New England fell on their knees and then proceeded to make friends of the aborigines. On their first Thanksgiving day, Mas-

FOREFATHERS' DAY SERMONS

sasoit, the mightiest chieftain of all that region, and ninety of his braves were entertained and feasted, and with this Massasoit, Plymouth colony then and there made a treaty, offensive and defensive, which treaty was faithfully and sacredly kept, both by the red men and the white men, for more than fifty years. Fifty-six years after the landing at Plymouth Rock, Governor Winslow was able to say that the English did not possess one foot of land in Plymouth colony which was not fairly obtained by honest purchase of the Indian proprietors. Because there were then, as there are in every community, men who would take advantage of ignorance and weakness, white men were forbidden by law to purchase or receive by gift any land of the Indians without the knowledge and allowance of the court. The officials were frequently complained of because of the partiality shown to the Indians. All the New England colonies were both just and kind in their treatment of the red man. To Christianize the Indians had been one of the ambitions of the Puritans before they crossed the sea. To educate him was one of the dreams of the founders of Harvard College. One of the first buildings of the college was called "Indian Building," and great was the rejoicing of the people when, after years of effort, an Indian was induced to complete the prescribed course of study and receive a diploma. As early as 1643 missionaries were at work among the Indians along the coast and on Martha's Vineyard, and three years later Massachusetts enacted that two persons should be chosen annually to spread the Gospel among the Indians. Of all who engaged in that difficult work one man stands out supreme and immortal — John Eliot. Every American boy ought to read the story of his life. With dauntless patience and industry he mastered the Algonquin

THE PURITANS OF NEW ENGLAND

language, reducing its huge mass of grunts and snorts, its nasal sounds and guttural noises to grammatical science, writing at the end of the grammar this fine sentence, " Prayer and pains, through faith in Jesus Christ, will do anything." Eliot's greatest work was his translation of the entire Bible into the Algonquin tongue. How idle the prattle of the calumniators sounds in the presence of this huge book, a lasting and monumental testimony to Puritan patience and consecration, and an indestructible proof of his devotion to the welfare of the red man. When Dean Stanley, a high representative of the Anglican church, on a visit to this country, was asked what place he would like most of all to see, he replied, " Show me where the Pilgrims landed and where the Apostle Eliot preached."

But how about the Pequot and King Philip's wars? They were terrible, but they were both brought on by the follies and savagery of the red man. There are men with whom even kind and Christian men cannot live in peace, and such men were the Pequots and the Narragansets. By depredations inexcusable and oft repeated, and by murders numerous and unprovoked, these tribes drove the Puritan to fight for his continued existence on New England soil. But the Puritan was, on the whole, as kind in his feeling for, and as just in his treatment of, the red man as William Penn himself; and if there were no Indian wars in Pennsylvania while William Penn was alive, it was because his neighbors were the weak and nerveless Delawares and the English-loving Iroquois, and not the murderous Pequots and the ferocious Narragansets.

II. Who has not heard of the awful cruelty of the Puritans in driving Roger Williams into the freezing forest in the depth of winter for no other reason than that he was a Baptist, and believed in freedom of conscience. The story, as commonly told, is from first to last a tissue of falsehood. In the first place, Roger Williams while a citizen of Massachusetts was not a Baptist. He was a Congregational minister, in thorough accord with his ministerial brethren in all doctrinal matters. It was not until he had been away from Massachusetts for two years that he began to have doubts as to the validity of baptism by sprinkling, and asked to be immersed by one of his friends. But his new convictions were not long satisfactory to him. In a few months he began to doubt the validity of his new baptism, and finally came to the conclusion that no one was then alive on earth who had a right to baptize another. He called himself a " seeker," and such he remained to the day of his death. His views of immersion had nothing whatever to do with his banishment.

Nor was he driven by the government into the forest in the middle of winter. His sentence was passed on the 3d day of September, and he was allowed six weeks in which to depart. He was free to go in any direction he might choose, either to England or to his former friends in Plymouth. At the end of the six weeks he was sick, and so the court allowed him to remain in Salem until spring, on condition that he desist from spreading his obnoxious views. But a man like Roger Williams could not keep still. He held meetings in his house, keeping the community in a ferment; and so, in the month of January, the patience of the officials having been exhausted, Williams was ordered to come to Boston and embark on a vessel about to sail for England. This he refused to do. He knew what English prisons were, and he preferred the

THE PURITANS OF NEW ENGLAND

forests of America. When, therefore, he heard that officers were coming to Salem to take him to Boston and send him to England, he and a dozen of his companions took to the woods, and came out at last at a place where the city of Providence now stands. He was not driven into the woods. He went there rather than return to England.

Why was he banished? Because he was a disturber of the peace. This he was from the beginning. On arriving in Boston in 1631, he at once reprimanded the church of that town because its members had not publicly repented for ever having had communion with the Anglican church. This seemed somewhat pert in a Welshman not yet thirty years old, and some of the Bostonians resented it. From Boston Williams went to Salem and thence to Plymouth. While at the latter place he wrote a book in which he denied the validity of the charter of the colony, called King James a liar and a blasphemer, and the reigning King Charles I a beast. He also used other unsavory epithets culled from the rich pages of the book of the Revelation. The appearance of this book filled the officials with alarm. Relations just then were much strained between the colony and the king. Men walked about on tiptoe and scarcely dared to draw a long breath for fear the charter might be withdrawn, and they proceeded to argue with the audacious Welshman and show him the error of his ways. He acknowledged his indiscretion and allowed the book to be burnt. But Roger Williams was not a man capable of keeping out of mischief. As Cotton Mather once said of him, he had a windmill in his head. A recent historian thinks that even this figure hardly does justice to all the facts in the case. He was, in the words of John Quincy Adams, conscientiously contentious. He was always on the off side. He never agreed with those around

FOREFATHERS' DAY SERMONS

him. He was sweetly but provokingly pugnacious. He railed against the magistrates because they punished men for breaking the Sabbath. This he said they had no right to do because the Fourth Commandment belongs to the first table, and civil authorities have to do only with breaches of the second table of the law.

Because times were troublous and many strange characters were coming into the colony, the General Court passed a law making it necessary for all men to take an oath of allegiance to the government. This law was immediately attacked by Williams, who claimed that an oath is an act of worship and that to compel an unregenerate man to engage in an act of worship is to compel him to take the name of God in vain. A little later, the General Court refusing to grant a certain petition of the people of Salem, Williams wrote to all the churches asking them to discipline the members of the court who had refused to do Salem justice. When these churches refused to act upon his advice, he wrote letters of defamation against them and asked the Salem church to withdraw fellowship from them. When the Salem church refused, he withdrew his fellowship from it, and when his wife persisted in still going to church he refused to pray with her. Like a hero, he stood alone against the world. He would be called to-day " cantankerous." Wherever he went he got the community into a turmoil. The leaders of Massachusetts became convinced that he was a dangerous man and they told him to go away. Whether this was wise or not, you must be judge. In passing judgment we must endeavor to put ourselves back into the seventeenth century into the mood and circumstances in which the men were who had to deal with Roger Williams. Such a man as he would cause us no concern to-day. The ship of state has become

THE PURITANS OF NEW ENGLAND

an ocean liner, and all sorts of Roger Williamses can jump and run upon the deck, and belch out their follies, insanities and blasphemies on the air, while the old ship drives steadily onward, unmoved by the antics of a few unbalanced passengers. But in 1635 Massachusetts was a little rowboat on an angry and dangerous sea. The wind was boisterous, and the billows were high, and the men who labored with desperate energy at the oars were in doubt as to their ability to reach the shore. In the boat there stood this obstreperous, incorrigible Welshman, jumping up and down, stamping here and there, threatening to upset the little vessel and toss all its occupants into the waves. The men who were rowing said to the Welshman, "Sit down." He would not do it. He took another jump. Again they cried, "Sit down." Again he refused to listen. Finding all their counsels and their prayers in vain, they told him he must get into another boat and allow them to go on without him. In saying this they may have acted unwisely, but I am sure they were not drunk.

III. Again it has been said in bitterness and indignation: "The Puritans persecuted and imprisoned and hung the quiet and inoffensive Quakers." Two words in this indictment must be altered. The Quakers of the seventeenth century with whom the authorities had to deal were not, as a rule, either quiet or inoffensive. We err when we think that the Quakers, as we know them, were always in all points what they are today. The very name of Quaker carries to us the atmosphere of gentleness and peace. The word calls up before us a serene-browed saint with broad-brimmed hat and coat of gray, and at his side a motherly, wholesome woman with the face of a Madonna and a smile which has in it a benediction, and with

FOREFATHERS' DAY SERMONS

these faces before us we grow indignant at the thought that such noble specimens of humanity should have been subjected to inhuman treatment at the hands of those who claimed to be servants of the Most High. But the Quakers of the seventeenth century, as they appeared to our forefathers, were anything but angels of light or apostles of peace. While they refused to fight with the sword, they made it up by fighting with their tongues. Quakerism had its birth in the seventeenth century, and like many another mighty movement it gathered in the earlier stages of its course a great mass of crude and ignorant humanity whose extravagances and eccentricities shocked those who looked on and hid from view the high and noble principles which the movement carried in its bosom. It was fundamental with the Quakers that a man must be guided by the " inner light." The one sentence of Scripture most highly prized by them was, " Where the spirit of the Lord is, there is liberty." As every Quaker felt himself to be in possession of the spirit of the Lord, he was free to indulge in liberties which were often distressing to his neighbors. This doctrine of the inner light was feared and opposed by all branches of the church in the seventeenth century, and it was especially abhorrent to the Puritans, who believed that the will of God is revealed in the Scriptures, and that as soon as men leave the Scriptures they are sure to fall victims to their own fancies and hallucinations. Surely there was good reason for this fear. Germany through the sixteenth century had been torn and cursed by bodies of fanatics who claimed to be following the inner light, and every nation had been visited by the same terrible and incurable plague. To the Quakers many of the essentials of the Christian church were an abomination. They did not believe in ministers. They called them

THE PURITANS OF NEW ENGLAND

seeds of the serpent, and other terms equally complimentary. They had no use for prepared sermons. These were to them man-made devices or inventions of the devil. They kicked over the communion table and tossed baptism behind their back. They stripped Christianity naked, and reduced the church to the movement of a spirit in the heart and conscience of man. After the religious training of fifteen hundred years, such revolutionary views must have been received with horror. To make matters worse, eccentric individuals did queer and outrageous things, confirming the suspicion in the minds of many that Quakers were in league with hell. Many zealous souls endeavored to imitate the example of Old Testament prophets. They would walk through the streets, bawling "The Lord is coming with sword and fire." They would go barefoot, and wear sackcloth and put ashes on their heads. Sometimes they would blacken their faces, and in a few cases they dispensed with their clothes. Religious meetings were sometimes disturbed by them. At the close of the sermon a Quaker would rise and overturn all the preacher had attempted to establish. One of them went into the Old South Church in Boston one Sunday and broke two bottles, saying to the minister as he did it, "Thus shall the Lord break you." Were any one to act thus in any of our churches to-day he would be promptly ejected. If he came back he would be arrested and sent to jail. If he persisted in his foolishness we should put him in an asylum. That is our way of dealing with people who act altogether from the "inner light." But in the seventeenth century men had not learned the trick of taking away responsibility by the plea of insanity. It was taken for granted that disturbers of the peace were in their right mind and therefore deserved punishment

[47]

FOREFATHERS' DAY SERMONS

for their misdemeanors. They were whipped, imprisoned, branded, mutilated, and if incorrigible, hung. The punishments of the seventeenth century were according to our standards shockingly severe. But the laws of the Puritans were not severer than the laws of other people. The laws of Catholics and of Lutherans and of Anglicans were fully as severe as those of the Puritans. There is no difference in severity between the laws of the Cavaliers of Virginia and the laws of the Puritans of Massachusetts. Even in the days of Blackstone, late in the eighteenth century, there were one hundred and sixty crimes punishable by death. The horrible picture of Charles Dickens in "The Tale of Two Cities" is true to English life as it existed a century after the tragic occurrences in New England.

The contest between the Puritan and Quaker would be ludicrous if it were not tragic. When Greek meets Greek then comes the tug of war. The Puritan had a conscience, so had the Quaker. The Puritan did not believe in bending, neither did the Quaker. Both men were inflexible as granite, and when they met a conflict was inevitable. The Puritan told the Quaker to keep out of Massachusetts, and he came promptly in. As soon as it became noised abroad that Quakers were not wanted in Massachusetts, many of them felt divinely impelled to hurry thither and bear their testimony before the New England unbelievers. The Puritan flung the first Quaker invaders from his borders, saying "Don't come back! If you do, I'll imprison you." And the Quaker, led by the inner light, came promptly back and went to prison. The Puritan cast him out, saying "If you come back again I'll whip you." The Quaker hurried back and got his whipping. Again the Puritan threw him out, saying "If you return

THE PURITANS OF NEW ENGLAND

I'll cut your ear off," and the Quaker, with great alacrity, came back and gave up his ear. At last the Puritan, enraged beyond endurance, said " If you come back again, I'll hang you," and the Quaker jubilantly came back and got hung. The Puritan could do nothing with such a man. At last he was obliged to yield. The only man in the seventeenth century who was able to conquer the Puritan was the Quaker.

In justice it ought to be said that the extreme measures against the Quakers did not have the sympathy of the people of Massachusetts. The law prescribing death as the penalty for the third offense was passed only after determined opposition, and then only by a majority of one. There would have been no majority at all had not one of the deputies been sick in bed. On hearing of the passage of the law he declared that rather than have had the law pass he would have crawled to Boston on his hands and knees. Those responsible for the law felt it necessary to apologize for it and hoped it would not be necessary to carry it into effect. When the time came for the first execution, so great was the popular indignation that soldiers were scattered through the town to suppress a possible insurrection. Four Quakers lost their lives, but they did not die in vain. They battered down the walls of Massachusetts exclusiveness and helped to prepare the way for the coming era of religious liberty. Probably the one man most responsible for the hanging of the Quakers was John Endicott. An official does not always represent the temper and wishes of the community which places him in office. We too often forget that there were various types of Puritans. We herd them all together, and by giving them a common name lose sight of the differences which distinguish them from one another. Men today sometimes speak and act as though all Democrats were alike, and yet Richard Croker is a Democrat and so also is Grover Cleveland. There are those who deem all Catholics alike, and yet Archbishop Ireland is a Catholic and so also was the last murderer who died on a Western gallows. Michael Wigglesworth and John Milton were both Puritan poets; one wrote doggerel, the other wrote one of the five greatest poems ever written. Thomas Dudley was a Puritan, so also was John Winthrop. John Endicott was a Puritan, so also was John Cotton. John Norton was a Puritan, so also was Thomas Hooker. William Stoughton was a Puritan, so also was Samuel Sewell, the man who had, as Whittier says,

> "A face which a child would climb to kiss,
> True and tender and brave and just,
> Whom man might honor and woman trust."

Because four Quakers died at the hands of the court of Massachusetts it does not follow that all Puritans were drunk with a thirst for blood.

IV. But did not New England Puritans burn witches? The question is often asked in a tone which gives an affirmative answer. There are men who speak of the burning of witches in New England as though it had been for a century an ordinary and almost daily occurrence. The fact is, no white man or woman was ever burned for belief or deed upon the soil of New England. Witches were burned in various parts of the world, but never in New England. It is true that probably thirty persons, between 1620 and 1692, lost their lives in Massachusetts because accused of witchcraft, but this is not a stigma on Puritanism. Puritanism had nothing to do with the witchcraft tragedy. Witches lost their lives in New England, not

THE PURITANS OF NEW ENGLAND

because the New Englanders were Puritans, but because they lived in the seventeenth century. In the seventeenth century everybody believed in witchcraft. That the human soul can be taken possession of by infernal spirits, and used to bring calamity on men's lives and homes, was one of the axioms of belief. Everybody believed this — all the great preachers and all the great lawyers, and all the great scholars and all the great reformers on both sides the sea. Nearly one hundred years after the tragedy at Salem, William Blackstone treated witchcraft as a terrible reality, and John Wesley declared that if men gave up belief in witchcraft they would have to surrender the Bible. Everybody in the seventeenth century believed that witches ought to be punished. The unhappy wretches accused of this crime were dealt with by a heavy hand by Catholics and Lutherans and Anglicans, and men of every class and name. The historians stagger us by their figures, telling us that in Germany alone, from first to last, one hundred thousand persons were put to death on the charge of witchcraft, seventy-five thousand in France, thirty thousand in Scotland and England. The wonder is that New England escaped with thirty. The tragedy came to an end in New England in 1692, but in old England it ran on to 1712, and in Scotland to 1722. The delusion in Massachusetts was confined to a small area, and shut up within narrow limits of time. Twenty of the victims lost their lives in one little village, and all within six months. Some lying children began to cut queer capers, and gave out as an explanation of their behavior that they had been bewitched by certain persons whom they named. These persons were tried and convicted, and, the panic increasing, still others were suspected, arraigned and executed. Salem for a season lost its head. A community can go insane as truly

FOREFATHERS' DAY SERMONS

as a man can. Salem was crazy. But she is not a sinner above all others. Even London on a well-known occasion lost its head. A liar named Oates told a great tale about a certain plot of the Roman Catholics to blow up the government buildings and burn the shipping on the Thames and take possession of London, and the city at once lost its senses. It was out of its head for a year. Catholics were dragged to prison, a few of them were hung, a law was passed shutting all Catholics out of Parliament. All sorts of wild and crazy things were done before sanity was restored. New York has more than once lost its head. A few lying women once caused a panic here by starting the story that the negroes were going to burn up the city and take possession of all the wealth they could rescue from its ruins. The story was preposterous, but by it the city was panic-stricken. Hundreds of negroes were seized, eleven of them were burned at the stake, twenty-two were hung, one was broken on the wheel, many were transported, and the sensible people of Manhattan acted like fools and demons until they recovered from their fright. Little Salem suffered from just such a frenzy. The paroxysm lasted for a few months only, and when men got cool again they repented of their folly. In the public fast day, held four years later, the people prayed for divine forgiveness for whatever mistakes they had fallen into. Judge Sewell, one of the judges at the trials, wrote out an humble confession and plea for divine forgiveness, standing in his pew in the Old South Church while the minister read his confession from the pulpit. The jurymen likewise made public acknowledgment of their error, and in 1711 pecuniary compensation to the heirs of the victims was voted out of the public treasury. And so of all the communities which under the witchcraft delusion have been guilty of the shedding of blood, the colony of Massachusetts is the only one which ever repented in sackcloth and ashes for the great evil which she had done.

V. But they say the Puritans disliked the Episcopalians and treated them most rudely, and condemned and despised their prayer-book. All of which must be acknowledged; and should you ask why this rudeness and dislike, let me suggest that you read the history of England and Scotland through the sixteenth and seventeenth centuries. The Puritans had received no mercy at the hands of the English church. Archbishop Laud, and others like him, had made it impossible for thousands of loyal Englishmen to live in England. Driven from home, deprived of most of the things which the human heart holds dear, by men who were determined that Christians should be ruled by Bishops, and that God should be worshipped under forms prescribed by the King, small wonder is it that when these persecutors followed the exiles across the sea they should be given but scant welcome and looked upon with aversion and fear. They remembered the fable of the coney, which, in a sentimental mood, allowed a hedgehog to come into his burrow, only to be crowded out by the hedgehog when the latter once got himself established. They could not forget her men whom Elizabeth had hung, or the scores whom Laud had fined and cast into prison; nor were they ignorant of the sufferings of the Scotch Presbyterians, who, driven from their churches, were arrested as traitors because they dared to worship God in the open fields. How can a man look with complacency on a foe who has hounded him out of his home, and then tracking him across an ocean persists in setting up the symbols and instruments of his tyranny under the front window of his victim? Having endured so much to escape the

FOREFATHERS' DAY SERMONS

bondage of a tyrant who never slept, the Puritan would have been more than human had he welcomed the incoming of a church which had persecuted his fathers and made him an exile in a strange land. And, as for his hatred of the prayer-book, that, too, was natural. The Puritans were not blind to the literary beauties of the Book of Common Prayer. They were not uncouth, illiterate barbarians, but men who were versed in the world's best literature, and whose libraries bear witness to the width of their sympathies and culture. Why then did they hate the prayer-book? Because Church and State officials had tried their best to ram it down their throats. Kings and Prelates had said, "Take this book and with this book approach the throne of grace; all other ways are by law forbidden." And the reply was, "We have no King but the Lord God Almighty. Take your hands off of our conscience!" And when officials persisted in thrusting this prayer-book upon them, our fathers trampled the book under their feet, to make it clear to the world that no man, no set of men, be the set of men Parliament or General Council, be the man Pope or King, has a right to dictate to a soul redeemed by Christ how it shall approach the throne of God. It is sometimes said that the descendants of the Puritans have changed, that they appreciate and prize the prayer-book, finding in it solace and inspiration. The fact is we have not changed at the core of our being one iota. Let any civil or ecclesiastical authority bring the prayer-book to us, saying "This is the book which you shall use. These are the prayers which you shall pray," and immediately we will tear the book to ribbons, and burn the ribbons in the fire. Let any man or set of men attempt to dictate to us our form of worship, and at once the Puritan in us rises up and says, "By the Eternal God, no!" In resisting the

THE PURITANS OF NEW ENGLAND

Episcopacy of the seventeenth century, the Puritans were not drunk.

VI. But surely the Puritans were narrow and morbid and tyrannical, else they could never have passed the "Blue Laws." Which Blue Laws? Men often speak of the Blue Laws of New England as though they were a definite and well-known historical institution. But all informed persons know that the most famous of the so-called Blue Laws never had any existence outside of the ingenious brain of that notorious liar, the Reverend Samuel Peters, who, driven out of this country during the Revolutionary War because of his Tory sympathies and conduct, took revenge upon his enemies on his return to England by publishing a pretended code of laws by which the new-world Puritans were governed. The law "No woman shall kiss her child on the Sabbath," and the law, "No one shall play on any instrument of music except the drum, trumpet, or jew's-harp," have been taken by many innocent and gullible people as features of actual New England legislation, even the most improbable fabrications of a slanderous Tory Munchausen being easily believed by those who are ready to think evil of the early settlers of New England. The early legislators of Massachusetts and Connecticut passed many quaint and curious laws; but they were never drunk.

VII. It is a charge often made that the Puritans were inconsistent; that whereas they came to America ostensibly to found a refuge where every one might enjoy perfect freedom of conscience, yet as soon as they got the reins of power in their own hands they became as tyrannical and exclusive as those from whom they had suffered beyond the sea. We give the Puritans too much credit when we claim for them a belief in full liberty of conscience.

[55]

FOREFATHERS' DAY SERMONS

Tolerance as we know it now did not exist in the seventeenth century. A few voices pleaded for soul liberty but the voices were few and far apart. The Puritans never for a moment believed that a man has a right to do as he pleases, nor did they ever profess such a belief. They claimed that God's will is expressed in the Bible, and that to that will we are bound to conform our worship, our church government and our life. The men of Massachusetts set up a theocracy after the fashion of the theocracy of the Old Testament, and the idea that men should be left free to do what was right in their own eyes, that never once entered their mind. They blundered in attempting to build a theocracy, but they were not inconsistent. They did not hold our views of tolerance, but they were not hypocrites. In fact there was little tolerance in the twentieth century sense in any of the colonies. The Cavaliers of Virginia drove out the New England preachers who went there, and three hundred Puritans in that colony were rendered so uncomfortable they were obliged to emigrate into Maryland. The toleration of Maryland has been often eulogized, and every now and then some one stands up in St. Patrick's Cathedral and reminds the faithful that while the Puritans of New England were persecutors, Catholic Maryland set a shining example of the spirit of toleration. But our Roman Catholic friends always fail to mention the fact that Lord Baltimore got his charter from a Protestant King, and that had the liberties of Protestants in Maryland been interfered with, the charter would have been straightway recalled. They forget also to state that wherever in the seventeenth century the Catholics were in supreme power they persecuted the Protestants and were indifferent to their rights. Even the reputation of Dutch New York is strained. Berke-

THE PURITANS OF NEW ENGLAND

ley in Virginia and Endicott in Massachusetts, and Stuyvesant in New York were all more narrow and severe than the masses of their fellow-citizens. Stuyvesant drove out the Lutherans and the Baptists and beat a poor Quaker almost to death. There was more room for heretics and dissenters in little Rhode Island than in any other colony in the land. But even Roger Williams came to believe it to be right to punish Quakers if their foolishness went too far. The Puritans did not know how far liberty might be extended without detriment to Church or State. They believed that the line must be drawn somewhere, and so do we. When the Mormon assures us that his conscience tells him he ought to have a dozen wives, we point him to the law and say, " It is a wise law, obey it or get out." When a Christian Scientist says that her conscience will not allow her to call a doctor when her child has diphtheria or smallpox, nor will it allow her to report such sickness to the Board of Health, we feel that the woman ought to be compelled to be sensible, and that, too, by law. When a man claims the right to denounce all government as a curse, and persists in stirring up men to set themselves against all magistrates and laws, some of us believe it to be well to hang up a placard, " No admittance," and tell the professional anarchist to pass on and find a home elsewhere. We believe in drawing the line, and so did the Puritans of two and a half centuries ago. Of course they drew the line far inside of ours, for we are older and more experienced and have with audacious faith drawn our line far out and dangerously near the ragged edge of license, but even if we in the twentieth century have drawn our line far beyond the reach of theirs, it does not follow that for their day and generation the line they drew was wrong. At any rate we may be sure they were not drunk.

FOREFATHERS' DAY SERMONS

And since they are clothed and in their right mind, let us get as close to them as we can, and learn from them the lessons which they have to teach. Their dress and fashions may amuse us.

> "The old three-cornered hat,
> And the breeches, and all that,
> Are so queer!"

But then we ourselves, with our funny tricks of dress, our uncomfortable and latest fashions, will look queer and antiquated to those who live three hundred years from now. They committed blunders, and we ourselves keep blundering right along. That is a frailty which our humanity does not readily slough off. They fumbled their problems, for their problems were complex and momentous, and so also are ours and we are fumbling, too. They made mistakes and committed sins of which their descendants are ashamed, and who dare claim that in our record there will be no blot to bring a blush to the cheeks of those who come after us? We see farther than they saw because we are standing on their shoulders. We do many things better than they did then, because we have the benefit of more than two centuries of experimentation and experience. Our eyes are no keener than theirs, but we have the use of a brighter light.

But superior though we are in some things to those who have gone before us, in others we are lacking and need a strength which they can give. These Puritans had ideas whose glory has not faded. They had beliefs whose perpetuation is the world's salvation. They believed in morality in public life and in private life, they believed that only the pure in heart shall see God. They believed in education, and wherever they built a church they also built a school. To the dream of giving all the children of the

THE PURITANS OF NEW ENGLAND

State an education they gave a local habitation and a name. They believed in the home, and in the wilderness built up a home life which poets love to picture and which will remain a priceless and imperishable possession. They believed in liberty, and they believed in it more and more. When the time came to break the chains by which two worlds were bound, Massachusetts made the largest contribution which was made. And above all else they believed in God. Plato had taught the doctrine that a man ought to live for the State. Mediæval thinkers had taught that man ought to live for the Church. The Tudors and the Stuarts had taught that man ought to live for the king. But these men grasped and held the idea that a man must live for God. Created in his image, the heir of immortality, he must serve him on the earth and enjoy him forever.

Because of his belief, the Puritan was able to do great things. He brought things long delayed to pass. He ushered in new eras. He laid the stepping-stones over which the race must pass in order to reach the golden age. He founded a commonwealth which became the corner-stone of the New England Confederacy, and this Confederacy became in time the corner-stone of a republic which, please God, shall be a blessing to all coming nations and ages. The Puritans are dead, but though dead they yet speak. They have ceased from their labors but their works follow with them. If you would see their monument, look round you!

IV

THE PLACE OF THE PURITAN IN HISTORY [1]

"I heard behind me a great voice as of a trumpet." — REV. 1 : 10.

It was the first day of the week, and the prisoner on Patmos was in the spirit of the day. His ears were open to the things which a man ought to hear, and suddenly he heard behind him a great voice as of a trumpet. He turned and looked, and beheld a sight which subdued him and brought from his heart a song of thanksgiving and praise. It is not my purpose this morning to inquire who it was that he saw, or what the person behind him said; I simply use his attitude as a suggestion to you, and my first question this morning is: Do you ever hear a voice like the voice of a trumpet behind you? It may be you do not. It is not uncommon for the voice behind us to be drowned out by the voices around us. We are living in an age of voices, multitudinous, myriad-toned voices, loud, shrill and discordant voices, soft, musical and appealing voices, jangling, scolding, shrieking voices, tender, pleading, thrilling voices — they roll in over us like a flood; no other generation has ever heard so many voices. The world has become a whispering gallery, every whisper reverberates around the world. The printing press is like a phonograph and catches all the vibrations, and we set up a phonograph on the breakfast table, and we hear the voices of the passing days. And right there lies a danger. We may listen too attentively to the voices of the present, we may become submerged in the voices of the *now* and be-

[1] Dec. 1906.

THE PLACE OF THE PURITAN IN HISTORY

come deaf to the voice that speaks to us out of the past.

Think what lies behind us: sixty generations of men between us and Jesus, sixty other generations between Jesus and Abraham. How many generations between Abraham and the first man who ever lifted his eyes toward God, it is impossible to say. And all those generations being dead, yet speak. They lived and toiled and suffered, they stamped the impress of their energy upon the earth before they left it. They created forces which have been working to the present hour. Because they were what they were, we are what we are. They have ceased from their labors, but their works follow after them. Their struggles, blunderings, anxieties, sinkings of heart, agonies are all ended, but the effects of their activity are alive in the world which is our home.

And it is a great privilege on the Lord's day, when wearied and fretted by the jangling voices of the present, to listen for the voice that speaks like a trumpet to us out of the caves of the years that have vanished and out of the sepulchres of the immortal dead. It was a great utterance of Napoleon Bonaparte which he spoke in Egypt to his soldiers: "Forty centuries look down on you." He braced the heart of every man in his army by telling him to listen to the voice that spoke behind him. Would we not all be stronger and saner and wiser than we are if we did our work conscious of the men into whose inheritance we have entered?

Every year at this season of December I try to help you hear a voice out of the past. This is the week that holds in it the day that commemorates the Landing of the Pilgrims on Plymouth Rock. I never allow the week to pass without asking you to think of some phase of the

FOREFATHERS' DAY SERMONS

mighty movement of which the *Mayflower* was a part, and without calling your attention to that company of broad-shouldered servants of the Lord of which the Pilgrims were shining representatives. The Puritan is a man of exhaustless interest. Sometimes we have thought about his virtues, at other times we have thought about his limitations, we have studied his contribution to religion, to education, to the life of the home, and now this morning let us think about his contribution to the cause of civil liberty.

In Pilgrim Hall, in the old town of Plymouth, Mass., there is a painting which many of you have already seen, and before which I wish that every American citizen might stand for at least an hour. The title of the picture is: " The Signing of the Compact in the Cabin of the *Mayflower*." The picture represents one of the most thrilling events in the history of the human race. It was on the 9th of November, 1620, that these Pilgrims came in sight of land. For sixty-four days they had been out upon a shoreless deep, cooped up in the little *Mayflower*. And now on the morning of November 9th their eyes look out upon the land. A miserable sort of land it is, — only the sand hills of Cape Cod and patches of scrubby woods — but to the hungry eyes of the Pilgrims even this land was paradise. The winds had blown them from their course, so that instead of landing somewhere near the mouth of the Hudson, as they had hoped, they had come out several hundred miles to the north. Turning the prow of their little vessel toward the south, they determined to make the mouth of the Hudson, but God threw a storm across their path and they were driven back into Cape Cod Bay. This was on November 10th. On the following day, realizing that they were soon to land, and that men on this

THE PLACE OF THE PURITAN IN HISTORY

earth cannot live together well without a government, a compact was drawn up embodying an agreement to form a State. The compact began thus: " In the name of God, Amen," and then it went on to say that the men whose names were written below had undertaken to form a body politic for the purpose of enacting such just and equal laws as should be found meet and convenient for the general welfare. The first man to sign his name was John Carver, then came William Bradford, then Edward Winslow, then William Brewster, then Isaac Allerton, then Miles Standish, followed by thirty-five others whose names the world will never allow to die.

That was in 1620; fourteen years later the men of Massachusetts colony were casting secret written ballots for a Governor, and five years after that the freemen of Connecticut gathered at Hartford and adopted the first written constitution known to human history which created a government. In 1776 Thomas Jefferson was drafting the Declaration of Independence, and in 1906 there stood upon the American continent a republic with windows looking out upon the Atlantic and the Pacific, its flag waving over the heads of millions of freemen determined under God that government of the people by the people and for the people shall never perish from the earth. And how did it all come about? So great a phenomenon must have an explanation. One explanation is that the dominant ideas of the American republic came from the heads of the French philosophers who lived in the latter part of the 18th century. According to this idea it was Rousseau and Voltaire and the encyclopædists who gave birth to the ideas upon which the republic has been built, and plausibility has been given to this explanation from the fact that Thomas Jefferson, the writer of the Declaration of Inde-

FOREFATHERS' DAY SERMONS

pendence, was imbued with the ideas of the French philosophers and got much of his inspiration from that quarter. But he does not look far enough who sees in the French history of the last part of the 18th century the beginning of the American republic. Back of Rousseau and Voltaire a man with eyes can see John Locke and John Milton, and back of John Milton can be seen the faces of John Knox and John Calvin. Rousseau and Voltaire and their contemporaries may have helped to light the fire which is warming the modern world, but they kindled their own torch at the hearts of men who were in their graves when these Frenchmen were born. You never can account for the American republic by tracing it to French infidelity.

There are those who think that the republic can be largely accounted for by its environment. "It is the product of a new world, such a thing would have been impossible in any other land than America, it grew up spontaneously, it came out of the unfettered heart of man, the exigencies of the time demanded it, the circumstances of the age compelled it. In America there were no entangling traditions, no institutions to oppress and retard. And because the heart was free from ancient ideas and all social and political conditions elastic, the American republic arose as a plant arises out of a soil which the rains of heaven have watered." It is a plausible theory, but will hardly stand examination. If the American republic was the product either of the air or the soil, how does it happen that no beginning was made until the Pilgrims landed at Plymouth? The Pilgrims were not the first men who arrived on these coasts. America had been discovered more than a century and a quarter before the Pilgrims sailed. For a hundred and twenty-five years men had been crossing the Atlantic, planting their settlements in different parts of

THE PLACE OF THE PURITAN IN HISTORY

the land. The Spanish had roamed over the country from Florida to California, the Frenchmen had made explorations from the mouth of the St. Lawrence to the mouth of the Mississippi, and yet in all of the land which the Spanish and the Frenchmen had settled there was not an institution different from that which was to be found in the old world, nor even a dream of a republic under which men should be free. The spirit of liberty did not come out of the soil, nor did it come out of the air.

Nor was the spirit of liberty peculiar to the new world. Samuel Adams and Patrick Henry in the 18th century stand up and defy George III, but they were not original in doing that. In the 17th century had not Oliver Cromwell stood up against Charles I, and even dared to cut off his head? And in the 16th century did not John Knox resist Mary, Queen of Scots, face to face and tell her without wincing that subjects had a right to resist their rulers when their rulers commanded that which was wrong? And had not Andrew Melville told James VI that he was not the head of the Church of Jesus Christ, but simply a member of it? And across the English channel had not the Huguenot Coligni stood up against Charles IX? and in the Netherlands had not William the Silent defied the rage of Philip II and all the generals which Philip II had sent into the field? The same sort of liberty which we find in America in the 18th century existed in England in the 17th, and was found in Holland in the 16th. It was not born of the air, neither did it come out of the soil. The people of America and Scotland and England and France and Holland and Switzerland had all drunk deep of the same fountain, and it is my purpose this morning to ascertain just what that fountain was.

For the last four hundred years there have been two

FOREFATHERS' DAY SERMONS

ideas struggling for the supremacy of the world: the idea of despotism and the idea of liberty, the Roman idea and the Teutonic idea. According to the Roman idea, supreme power is vested in the hands of a few men at the top, and this power is delegated to the men who stand below. That was the dominant idea of the Roman Empire. Upon that idea the Cæsars built their throne. They never admitted the principle of representation. The idea was unknown to the mind of the Roman statesman. When Christianity found its way to the city of the Cæsars, it lived at first in cellars and alleys, but with the conversion of Constantine it walked up the steps and sat down on the imperial throne, and on the day of its coronation in the Roman capital it was stamped with the impress of the Roman idea and passed into the spirit of the Cæsars. The Pope himself became a Cæsar, and round him was a group of councilors, and in the hands of Pope and councilors the supreme power of the Church of God was placed. The history of the mediæval ages is simply the history of the working out of that idea. The Pope became the monarch of the world, kings and potentates were subject unto him. He lorded it over parliaments and council chambers. He created and deposed kings at will, statesmen were glad to do his bidding. When Columbus announced he had discovered a new world, the Pope who then sat in St. Peter's chair calmly divided the new world into two parts, giving one part to the King of Spain, the other to the King of Portugal. In such a lordly manner did the Bishop of Rome deal with the treasures of this world. And not only did he lord it over the earthly treasures of men, but he lorded it over the mind. He and his councilors determined what men should think, what they should read and what they should write, and not content with assuming mastership over the things

THE PLACE OF THE PURITAN IN HISTORY

of this world, he laid his hand upon the heavens and claimed to be possessor of that. He held in his grip the keys of the Kingdom of Heaven and the kingdom of purgatory. He could shut men out of heaven, he could lift men out of purgatory, surpassing in the sweep of his power and the pride of his autocracy the boldest and loftiest of the Cæsars.

Of course there was a protest to all this. Not a century passed without a cry of opposition from some heart somewhere in love with liberty. In the 13th century there was a furious outcry in France from people known as Albigenses, but the revolt was trampled out in blood. For forty years the slaughter was continued, until almost the name of Albigenses was obliterated from the earth. In the 14th century there was another protest, louder still and more thrilling. In the 15th century the notes of opposition rose clearer still, but still the power of Rome remained unbroken. But in the 16th century the fulness of the times had come, the load of misery had reached its limit, tyranny had done its deadliest work, and when Martin Luther nailed his Theses to the old church door in Wittenberg, the nation rose to its feet. Modern history began with Martin Luther. It was a German who struck the decisive blow, but the blow awakened echoes in the hearts of men everywhere. England soon burst into a blaze. She tore herself loose from the Bishop of Rome. Henry VIII became head of the nation and head of the Church. But Henry VIII had the Roman idea. He accepted the theory that supreme power lies in the hands of a few men at the top, and that all power is delegated to the men who stand below. That was the theory of all the Tudors and all the Stuarts. The Tudors and the Stuarts not only had the Roman idea but they had the Roman

FOREFATHERS' DAY SERMONS

temper. They were lordly, domineering, unendurable. They claimed the right to dictate to men what ministers they should have, how they should worship, what they should believe. And little by little there grew in the hearts of Englishmen a conviction that kings have no divine right to govern wrong, and that under God men should be free. Up to this time kings had insisted upon the right to dictate to congregations who their ministers should be, but now the question arises, who gave the kings of the earth authority to decide who shall be the preachers in the Church of Christ? Kings had insisted upon the privilege of determining what should be the ceremonies and the order of worship, but now the question comes, who gave kings authority to dictate to the followers of Jesus in what manner they should approach the throne of God? Up to this time men had not been thinking about the State at all, they were thinking about the Church of Christ. They were asking themselves the measure of the liberty which Christ had given to his followers. It was a long and tremendous battle, but step by step they fought their way onward, winning their right to name their own ministers, framing their own church laws and formulating their own order of worship. First there came the vision of the King high and lifted up. The vision of his majesty blurred the glory of all earthly kings. In the presence of the Eternal all the potentates of the earth were only puppets, and in the light of eternal justice their usurpations became unendurable.

If every man has a right to enter the Holy of holies and commune directly with the King, then every man has a right to cast a vote in the choice of his minister, and to every man the privilege is granted of helping to shape the policy and program of the church of which he is a member.

THE PLACE OF THE PURITAN IN HISTORY

But in order to perform these duties well he must have an education, and so the common school arrived. Whereever the Puritans went they built two buildings, the church and the schoolhouse, from which twin fountains the rivers have proceeded which have made glad the earth. Wherever this vision of the King eternal was the most vivid, there did schoolhouses most abound, and there were men the bravest in the declaration of their rights. There were Puritans of course in every one of the thirteen colonies: Dutch Puritans in New York, Scotch-Irish Puritans in Pennsylvania, French Puritans in the Carolinas, English Puritans in New England. We are not true to history when we ascribe all the glory to the Puritans which came from England. Scotchmen were true to the sacred cause, and so were Hollanders and Frenchmen and Germans. Out of the veins of the five different nationalities came the blood which watered the sacred plant of freedom. But in boldness of aggression and in fiery energy of conviction, no Puritans surpassed the Puritans of New England. It is significant that Massachusetts alone sent more soldiers into the continental army which fought the battles of the Revolution than all the six southern states combined. And this becomes all the more remarkable when one remembers that the population of Virginia alone was as great as that of Massachusetts, and this is also noteworthy, that a large proportion of all the soldiers who came from the south were Scotch-Irish. These Scotch Irishmen bore upon their hearts the stamp of Oliver Cromwell and his Ironsides. Wherever they went they carried with them a flaming hatred against tyranny, an unquenchable love for freedom. During the Revolutionary period more than half of all the Governors outside of New England were Scotch Irishmen, and of the men who signed the

FOREFATHERS' DAY SERMONS

Declaration of Independence one quarter of them were either Scotchmen, Irishmen or Scotch Irishmen. Patrick Henry, the man whom Thomas Jefferson always acknowledged as the leader of the liberty party in the south, and who by his eloquent voice had silenced the voices of his aristocratic party, was himself the son of a Scotchman. Of course there were many men who threw their fortune and their energy into that tremendous contest who were neither Puritans nor the sons of Puritans, but impartial history declares that the men who bore the bulk of the burdens in the heat of the day were the men who traced their lineage back to the men who had fought the battles of freedom in the Old World.

Here then is a point never to be forgotten, that political liberty is the child of religion. The American Revolution was possible because of the political revolution of the 17th century, and the political revolution of the 17th century was possible because of the religious revolution of the 16th. The reason New England Pilgrims made the town meeting the corner-stone of their state was because already in the old world they had conceived of a church as a democracy in which all men were free in the Lord. It is not surprising that men fell at once to voting for their Governors when they had already learned to vote for their ministers. Six years before the men of Massachusetts colony voted for their Governors, Christian men in Salem had voted for the ministers of the Salem church. It never became clear to men that the common people have a right to curb and direct the power of kings in the State until they had grasped the conception that it is within the province of the people to manage their own affairs in the Church of the Son of God. There was no democracy in the State until there was democracy in the Church, and there was

THE PLACE OF THE PURITAN IN HISTORY

no democracy in the Church until the great vision of the Eternal.

I have spoken thus far of the conflict between the Roman and the Teutonic idea as though the victory had been long ago achieved, and so it is in the English-speaking world, but the age-long conflict still goes on in all countries over which the Roman Catholic church exercises lordship. We cannot understand current history until we understand the nature of this conflict and the causes of it. For several years an effort has been made among the members of the Roman Catholic church to secure another American Cardinal. There are at least eight million Roman Catholics in the United States, and yet these are represented in the sacred college by a single Cardinal. In the sacred college as it exists to-day there are 52 Cardinals, thirty-one of whom are Italians, Spain has five, and Austro-Hungary has five, Germany has three, the United States one, and Great Britain none at all. It seems quite surprising to our western eyes that Italy, a third-rate nation, should have thirty-one representatives in the body of men to whom supreme power is granted over the Roman Catholic church, that five Cardinals should be given to Spain, a decadent nation, and to Austro-Hungary, a second-rate nation, while this great republic of the West has but a single vote, and Great Britain, the mightiest empire on the earth, has no vote at all. It is all wrong from the American standpoint because we believe in the Teutonic or representative principle, but from the Roman standpoint it is entirely right. The representative principle has no place in Roman Catholic government. The men who belong to the sacred college say very distinctly and very boldly that no other nation outside of Italy has any claim whatsoever to a place in that august body. Everything that is granted to any other nation is granted not as a right but as a matter of grace and favor. American Catholics have one Cardinal not because they have a right to have one but simply because of the good nature of the Italians who sit on thrones in the city of Rome, and if the Roman Catholic church in America should swell to fifty millions, and if it should possess the greater part of the wealth and piety of the world, still it would have no legitimate claim to representation in the sacred college. But should the Italians so decree it, all these fifty millions would be obliged to remain dumb in the high council chambers of the church. That is Roman Catholic government according to the exposition of the very highest authorities in that church. The Roman Catholic hierarchy is always priding itself on the fact that the church never changes. It has indeed changed on a hundred points, but never has it changed in its idea of despotic government in the church.

The papers nowadays are filled with the tremendous commotion that is sweeping over France. A year ago the French government cut the bonds that had bound State and Church together, and just now the condition of affairs is more alarming than it has been for many years. What is the matter with France? It is torn asunder by this mighty conflict between the Roman and the Teutonic ideas. The conflict has been longer working itself out in France than in Germany, Holland, England or America, because France since the 16th century has been devoid of a body of Puritans. It was in the 13th century that the Albigenses uttered their protest, but they were ruthlessly slaughtered, and not until the 16th century did another body of French Puritans, the Huguenots, arrive. They were met with the same implacable hatred and the same incredible cruelty, the persecution culminating in that

THE PLACE OF THE PURITAN IN HISTORY

awful massacre of St. Bartholomew's, whose horrid butchery is still red before the eyes of the world. In the 16th century, one seventh — the best seventh of the population of France — was driven into exile, and from that time until this, France has had no Puritans. Through all this period the Roman church has perpetrated her usurpations, until some twenty-five years ago the movement began which has recently culminated in the separation of Church and State. Cardinal Gibbons has recently issued an appeal to the American people begging them to sympathize with the poor Catholics in France. His paper is plausible and also sophistical. What he says is true, but he leaves too many things unsaid. He dwells upon the fact that many of the French statesmen and ministers are infidels, that they hate not only the Roman Catholic church but religion itself, and even the name of Jesus. He quotes one of the ministers as having recently said that they had hunted the name of Jesus out of the schools, out of the asylums, out of the army, and that they now must hunt the name out of the kingdom altogether. But the question arises, why do French ministers talk after that fashion? How does it happen that the French government is so bitter against the Roman Catholic Church? It can be accounted for in precisely the same way in which you can account for Voltaire and the French Revolution of the 18th century. Why did Voltaire, one of the greatest of all Frenchmen, declare that the name of Jesus was infamous? It was because all the Christianity that he had anything to do with was execrable. The church in his day was rotten, many of its ministers' were vile. It was an engine of despotism forging fetters for the mind of man, and he hated the church with all the hot indignation of his great soul. That is the explanation of the opposition of the leading French-

FOREFATHERS' DAY SERMONS

men today. They have come to detest religion because the only religion they know anything about is the religion of Roman Catholicism — and with that they are disgusted. What Cardinal Gibbons says is true, but he forgot to tell us about the long series of intrigues and schemes and underhanded projects hatched in the fertile brains of the Roman politicians, extending through the last half of the century. The whole nefarious business culminated not long ago in the reprimand which the Vatican gave to the President of the French republic because he dared on a visit to Italy to call upon the King of that country. Is it to be wondered at that the blood of Frenchmen ran hot when that awful outrage was perpetrated? The Pope supposed he was living in the 16th century and forgot he was living in the 20th. Suppose that the Pope should attempt to reprimand our President for any act whatsoever, the country would at once burst into a blaze. He dare not do it. His advisers dare not do it. But they do just such things in every country in which they have the power. But in speaking of Roman Catholicism as something to be feared and resisted, it is important that certain clear-cut distinctions should be held firmly in the mind. We are always wrong and unchristian when we heap wholesale condemnation upon the members of the Roman Catholic church, for in that communion there are many of the truest and noblest saints which God has at present in this world. We are always wrong and inexcusably mean when we lump all Roman Catholic priests together and cover them with a common condemnation, for in the priesthood there are faithful followers of Christ who in the midst of privation and self-sacrificing toil are doing an amount of good which will never be known until the judgment day. We are always wrong and untrue to our traditions when-

THE PLACE OF THE PURITAN IN HISTORY

ever we condemn or make light of Roman Catholic forms of worship. We have no use for incense, candles, the rosary and the sanctus bell, but other people have, and they have a perfect right to use them if they wish. Because such things are not helpful to us, it does not follow they are not helpful to our brethren, and who are we, descendants of the Pilgrim Fathers, if we deny to any body of Christians the right to approach God in public worship in any way whatsoever that is pleasing to their souls? We are always unchristian and always mean when we pass sweeping condemnation upon the membership of Roman Catholic churches, upon the priesthood, or upon Catholic forms of worship, but we are always right when we fear and condemn and resist to the uttermost the Roman Catholic idea of government, for that idea is false and mischievous and dangerous. It has wrought havoc in every country in which it has been given full play. Unless checked, it would wreck the American republic.

I always take delight in speaking words of praise about the Puritan, thinking that possibly I may catch the ear of some man who has hitherto spoken of him with disrespect or scorn. There are many men who never speak the name " Puritan " except with a sneer. But sneers are ofttimes the very greatest eulogies. Some of the great names in human language were sneers at the beginning. The word " Quaker " was a sneer hurled at George Fox and his followers from lips curled in scorn. The word " Methodist " was a sneer, a very bitter and cutting sneer. " The friend of publicans and sinners " was a sneer, and so was also " He saved others, himself he cannot save." The cross of Jesus was a sneer, a bitter, piercing sneer, but God has changed it into the symbol of the love that is infinite. The

FOREFATHERS' DAY SERMONS

word "Puritan" was a sneer. It has been a sneer for three hundred years. But when men read history with their eyes, the world will become transfigured, and before the race has run its course there will be no sweeter, grander name than Puritan, for he was the man who at a crucial hour in the tremendous struggle for human liberty threw his blazing heart against the hosts of despotism and made it possible for nations to be free. Macaulay was no friend of the Puritans, but candor compelled him to confess that perhaps they were the most remarkable body of men that history had ever produced. Hallam was not prejudiced in favor of the Puritans, but he called them the depositaries of the sacred fire of liberty. Hume did not accept the religious belief of the Puritans: "The precious spark of liberty was preserved by the Puritans alone. To them the English owe the freedom of their constitution." John Richard Green was not biased when he stated that the history of English progress since the Restoration, on its moral and spiritual sides, has been the history of Puritanism. Carlyle rejected much of the Puritans' faith, but he declared Puritanism was the last of the world's heroisms. Whatever else then the Puritan may have been, or failed to be, he was the foe of despotism, the warrior by whose sweat and blood the principle of liberty was given a local habitation and a name. And when we, facing the problems and the dangers which confront us, grow despondent, or when we, submerged in business or immersed in pleasure, grow lukewarm in our adherence to the principles that are high, or when we, daunted by the excesses and extravagances of democracy, begin to question the wisdom of the principle upon which the modern world is built, let us on the Lord's day listen attentively to the voice behind us, the voice of those in-

THE PLACE OF THE PURITAN IN HISTORY

trepid servants of the Lord who with sacrifices multitudinous and indescribable won for us a larger place in which to do our work and flung over our heads a sky in which mighty thoughts shall burn forever.

V

THE PURITAN TYPE[1]

The world cannot dispense with its great men after they are dead. We cannot get on without the wisdom and insight of those who have inspired us, after a cloud has received them from our sight. It is a pathetic story which the Old Testament tells us of how King Saul at a critical time in his life felt an insatiable yearning for the prophet Samuel. Samuel was in his grave and Saul felt desolate and helpless without him. For years Samuel had been the leader of Israel. Even when his counsels had been despised, his greatness had been acknowledged. Saul, surrounded by his enemies, feels the need of the assistance which only the great-hearted prophet could render, and so he goes up and down the land in search of a wizard able to bring the prophet up from the realms of the dead. In Saul we see the image of humanity. That is what mankind has always been doing. In all of its difficulties and in the midst of its tribulations it has ever felt the need of the wisdom and strength of the prophet who has departed.

In the nineteenth century the cry breaks into voice on the lips of the poet Wordsworth. Wordsworth as he looks out over English society is appalled by its problems and disasters. He feels the need of the strength of men like Milton. In words which have become immortal he cries out:

> " Milton! thou should'st be living at this hour;
> England hath need of thee.

[1] Dec. 14, 1913.

THE PURITAN TYPE

<blockquote>
We are selfish men;
Oh! raise us up, return to us again;
And give us manners, virtue, freedom, power.
Thy soul was like a Star, and dwelt apart:
Thou hadst a voice whose sound was like the sea.
Pure as the naked heavens, majestic, free."
</blockquote>

Do not we Americans every February cry out for great men who have left us? Do we not say at our banquets, "O Washington, raise us up, and Lincoln, return to us again!" We who love our country and are most sensitive to its needs feel that we cannot get on without the brain of Washington, without the heart of Lincoln. Humanity always keeps calling out after its heroes who have vanished, its saints who have left it, its sepulchered deliverers and sufferers. The nations cannot live and conquer without fresh baptisms of the spirit of their immortal dead.

It is for this reason that I take delight on one Sunday of every December in standing in this pulpit and calling back the Puritan. I send my voice rolling through the nineteenth and eighteenth centuries back into the seventeenth, appealing to the central man of that century, its dominant hero, to come back and give us the blessing which he alone is able to bestow. I take all the more delight in doing this because there are many men now living who cannot appreciate the Puritan. Gallio does not understand him. Gallio is never able to interpret great spiritual movements. Gallio is always indifferent to the defenders of mighty causes. Festus does not understand him. Festus cannot comprehend the behavior of the man whose soul has been kindled by the fire from off God's altar. Festus always says to a leader of mankind, "Thou art beside thyself. Something or other has made thee mad." There are large sections of our American society so frivolous and so worldly-minded that they are incapaci-

FOREFATHERS' DAY SERMONS

tated for the understanding of the Puritan. Many of our young men and young women do not understand him. They have been prejudiced against him by things they have read and heard. In certain books of history, and in many a novel, and in not a few magazines and papers there are flings at the Puritan, gibes and jeers, sayings that are sarcastic. Society often pronounces the word "Puritan" with an intonation that has in it the sharp edge of a sneer. There are many who always think of the Puritan as an odd individual who cropped his hair short and talked through his nose. He was a narrow and benighted soul who did not believe in reading fiction and had no eye for beauty. He was a bigoted fanatic who broke the noses off the statues in the great English Cathedrals, and who in New England drove out of his community people who differed from him in opinion. He was a man with a hard and cruel heart who put culprits condemned for small offences into the stocks and hung women who were accused of witchcraft. That is the picture of the Puritan which hangs before many an American mind.

But we must remember that every man, as Lowell says, is the prisoner of his date. Every man is shut up inside the conceptions of his generation. For instance, all the men who wrote the Scriptures were the prisoners of their date in their scientific views. They were all imprisoned inside of the Ptolemaic astronomy. They all supposed that the sun moved round the earth, and that the earth was the center of the universe. How was it possible for them to get out? In their moral and spiritual conceptions, however, they transcended their age. They held views of God and man which have made them the teachers of all succeeding generations. The Puritans of the seventeenth century were prisoners of their date. They were shut up

THE PURITAN TYPE

inside the idea that there is such a thing as demoniacal possession, and that witchcraft is a crime which ought to feel the full rigors of the law. Every person of importance in the seventeenth century believed that. It was the conviction of all the great lawyers, the most learned doctors, the most famous teachers, and the most intelligent rulers and statesmen. Men and women were put to death by the thousands and by the tens of thousands all over Europe on the charge of witchcraft. Roman Catholics were responsible for these executions in Italy and Spain, Lutherans in Germany, Episcopalians in England, Presbyterians in Scotland, and Puritans in New England. It ought to be added that the Puritans were guilty of only a few such executions, and that they never on American soil burnt a solitary witch. When you hear people talking of the burning of witches in New England they are talking of something which never happened.

If you wish to measure the stature of men you must not judge them by the ideas which they shared with their generation, but by the ideas which were peculiar to them, to which they gave luster and vigor, and which they endowed with such tremendous vitality as to make them powerful and conquering through succeeding generations. So far as belief in witchcraft was concerned, the Puritans were like all the other people of their century, but the Puritans had a few ideas which were peculiar to them — advanced and radical ideas, wonderful and powerful ideas, and it is by those ideas that they are to be judged. What were these peculiar ideas? The first one was this: " Christ is the head of the church. The gentleman who claims to sit in the chair of St. Peter in Rome is not the head of the church in any such sense that he can dictate to all Christians what they are to believe and how they are to worship God.

FOREFATHERS' DAY SERMONS

Nor is the gentleman who sits on the throne of England the head of the church in such a sense as to give him authority over the worship and belief of Christian men. The charter of the Christian church is the Bible. The Pope cannot write the charter of the church, nor can the king, nor can parliament. The charter has already been written. It was written by holy men of old who spake as they were moved by the Holy Ghost. The state cannot dictate to the church. Christians are free men in Christ. Every man answers to God alone for his belief and looks to God alone for instructions as to the form of his worship."

All that sounds commonplace enough to us now, but it was not commonplace three hundred years ago. It was radical, quite revolutionary then, more radical and revolutionary than the very wildest of modern notions on political and religious subjects seem to us. To the men of their generation the Puritans were determined to turn the world upside down, they were undermining the very foundations of all ecclesiastical authority. They were certain to bring political institutions down in ruin on men's heads. Those were the ideas which were peculiar to the Puritan, and it is those ideas which he wrote indelibly on the life of the world.

To be sure the Puritans had their oddities, their eccentricities. All men have. When you want to caricature a man, you take up his idiosyncrasies. You do not seize upon things in which he resembles others, but the things in which he is peculiar. If you want to caricature socialism, you hold up as an example the most rabid and fanatical socialist you can find. If you wish to caricature woman suffrage, you hold up the crankiest of all the suffragettes. The men who have wished to caricature the Puritans have seized upon a few of the peculiarities of the oddest of them,

THE PURITAN TYPE

and have tried to make the world believe that all Puritans were bundles of disagreeable qualities. Macaulay, for instance, has painted us a portrait of the Puritan which has prejudiced thousands against him. He has called attention to his lank hair, his nasal twang, his peculiar dialect, his sanctimonious air. But we must remember that Macaulay was a rhetorician. He has had few peers as a word artist. He could paint the exterior of things, but he was sadly lacking in insight. He could not read character. He had no grasp of spiritual forces. He does not know how to interpret the important phenomena of history. You must lay your John Henry Greene down by the side of Macaulay if you would understand the history of England. It was not his lank hair and his nasal twang that made a Puritan what he was. Men do not climb to the seats of power by nasal twang or lank hair. It was because of what there was in him that made this man mighty. Instead of laughing at his peculiarities it is better worth our while to grasp the secret of his phenomenal energy and his perennial power. Our subject this morning is the Puritan Type.

That the Puritan is a distinct type in the portrait gallery of the world every one is bound to confess. The Puritan conscience was a spiritual creation. It did not exist in England before the Puritan came. He created it, and it exists to the present hour. It is not known as the Puritan conscience in England now, it is called the Non-conformist conscience. It is a power to be reckoned with in every English political campaign. For more than two hundred years English statesmen and politicians have been obliged to reckon with this invisible and mighty force. They have not dared to do things which they wanted to do, and they have been obliged to do things which they did not

FOREFATHERS' DAY SERMONS

desire to do, all because of their wholesome fear of the Puritan conscience. In our own country the Puritan conscience has been usually known as the New England conscience. It was created by the early New Englanders. It has been carried through the life of a belt of states extending across the continent. All over this country men speak either in praise or derision of the New England conscience. As there is a Puritan conscience so is there also a Puritan mind, a Puritan viewpoint, a Puritan attitude to life. There is such a thing as a Puritan face. You hear men saying, "He looks like a Puritan." There is such a thing as the Puritan poise, the Puritan bearing. You see in the distance a statue — you can see only the outlines, you do not know whom it represents — but you say to yourself, "That looks like a Puritan." There is such a thing as the Puritan type. It stands out clean-cut and distinct before the eyes of the world. It is a great thing for a set of men to be able to contribute to the spiritual wealth of the world a distinct and notable type of manhood.

In the portrait gallery of mankind there are different types of sainthood, one of the most striking of which is the mediæval type. This type is best represented, possibly, by Francis of Assisi and Thomas a Kempis. It is a beautiful type. The world would be poorer without it. It is the contemplative type of piety, it is the type of man who meditates and prays. The middle ages produced a kind of Christian who is so beautiful that his charm is still over the world. You are fascinated by the beauty in the faces of the mediæval saints. There is a look of gentleness, sweetness, submissiveness, patience which impresses us as divine. It is this image of sainthood which has been stamped indelibly upon the mind of the whole Christian world. This is the type of which we are thinking when we

THE PURITAN TYPE

say of a man or a woman, " O he is a saint! " We call him a saint because he is so calm, so unruffled, so patient, so sweet-spirited, so gentle. Only a man like that can be in our estimation a saint. It is probably because this is our idea of sainthood that it is generally conceded that there are more saints among women than among men. But in the fulness of time another type was added, another picture was hung by the side of the picture which the middle ages had painted, to the mediæval type of Puritan was added a type of an entirely different character. In the Puritan we have a saint of achievement, a militant saint, a saint endowed with a genius for action, a saint who gives himself to public service, who sets himself to the herculean task of reforming customs and institutions. This Puritan saint has a different look in his face from Francis of Assisi or Thomas a Kempis. He is not so gentle nor so sweet. There is something somber, almost severe, in his looks. At times he is almost grim. A Puritan is a fire, a man of action, a worker who brings things to pass, a hero who wrestles with the demons in the dusty arena of the world, covering himself with dust in his efforts to win the victory. Both types of sainthood are beautiful. We could not get on without either of them. We need the picture of the Catholic saint, and we likewise need the picture of the Puritan saint. Both of them can bless us if we will receive their blessing.

When one studies the Puritan portrait he discovers two prominent features. The first is seriousness. The Puritan was a serious man. From our standard he was quite too serious. His seriousness was rooted in his religion. His religion was dominated by his conception of God. The attribute of the deity which impressed him most profoundly was holiness. The music which thrilled him as no other

FOREFATHERS' DAY SERMONS

music did was the music which Isaiah heard in the Temple, the anthem of the seraphim, " Holy, holy, holy is the Lord God of Hosts!" The command in the scriptures which most arrested his attention was, " Be ye holy even as I am holy." Wherever he found the word holiness, he paused and meditated upon it. He believed that without holiness no one can see the Lord. " Come out from among them and be ye separate " was a text which he loved to hear expounded. " Touch not the unclean thing " was an exhortation which he tried to obey. The world in his day was frightfully corrupt. The Church was polluted and the State was rotten. With his vision of God and his conception of duty it was inevitable that the Puritan should be a serious man. His seriousness is one of the two chief features of the Puritan type of manhood.

His second most prominent feature is activity. This also was rooted in the Puritan's religion. He conceived of God as the Judge before whom every man must at last stand and render an account of the deeds done in the body. He was weighted down with the sense of responsibility. He was accountable not only for his own actions, but he was also accountable for the conduct of the state and the church. He believed that it was a part of a man's religion to secure a good government, a government whose policies should square with the principles of God. He believed that it is a man's business to do everything in his power to make the church worthy of the Lord Jesus Christ. It was this deep sense of responsibility which made the Puritan a reformer. A reformer is a man who fashions things over. He takes hold of things and reshapes them. He makes things over after a new ideal. The Puritan went furiously to work both in State and Church to make things over after the ideal which had been revealed in Christ. He

THE PURITAN TYPE

took hold of things with both hands, and with an energy almost superhuman he bent things to his will. He may be called a practical idealist. An idealist is a man who has a vision of a better world above the world which now is. There are two kinds of idealists — visionary and practical. The visionary idealist has a vision of a better world, but he does nothing to usher it in. He sees what ought to be, but he puts forth no effort to bring it to pass. A practical idealist is a man who not only has the vision, but he also puts forth efforts to work his vision into deed. The Puritan was an idealist who insisted upon reducing his visions to mundane facts.

It is at this point that we come to the explanation of his unpopularity. He was unpopular because he was a reformer. All reformers since the beginning of the world have been unpopular. It is impossible to reshape this world without stirring up opposition and hatred. No one can attempt to make things other than they are without lacerating men's feelings and incurring their ill will. You cannot take a splinter out of your finger without all the surrounding nerves shrieking out the moment you put the instrument in to pull the splinter away. You cannot remove an abnormal growth in the body without shedding blood. You cannot change any established feature of any earthly institution without arousing the antagonism of a host of men who want things to remain as they are. It is for this reason that all reformers have been hated and many of them have been killed. Elijah was a reformer, and Ahab hated him. Listen to the indignant king as he cries out to the meddlesome prophet, "O thou troubler of Israel." Jeremiah was a reformer, and so the Jews threw him into a cistern to get him out of their sight. John the Baptist was a reformer, and so Herod gave orders

FOREFATHERS' DAY SERMONS

to have his head cut off. Paul was a reformer, and so he was hounded from city to city by a pack of men who said he was trying to turn the world upside down. Jesus was a reformer, and that is why he was crucified. The Puritan was the most radical and vigorous reformer since the days of the apostles, and that accounts for the fact that his calumniators have pursued him with venomous words for more than two hundred years.

Here also we get an explanation of the severity of the Puritan's face. He has a wonderful face. You cannot forget it when you have once seen it. It is the face of a man who has fought and suffered. The Puritan lived in desperate times, and the mighty struggle in which he engaged left deep marks upon his face. What gave Lincoln that look of his which haunts us? It was the Civil War. It was the agony that he suffered through four years of bloodshed that deepened the melancholy in his eyes and stamped upon his face an expression which causes him to stand out unique among all the men America has produced. What gave Dante his grim and awe-inspiring look? The Italian women used to say to one another when Dante passed them in the street, "There goes the man who has been in hell." It was his tremendous struggle with his enemies and the anguish of long-continued exile which sculptured Dante's face. You never can forget it after you have looked upon it. Tennyson used to ponder the difference between Dante and Goethe, and he concluded that the difference between the two faces is that in Dante's face there is something of the divine. Goethe was a self-indulgent pagan. His mother brought him up to avert his eyes from everything that was disagreeable or painful. The kind of life he lived is pictured in his face. There is nothing of the divine there. The Puritan has a face which

THE PURITAN TYPE

haunts us. It has in it traces of the divine. It is a pathetic face because it tells of burdens which he bore for us, and the battles which he fought in order that we might be free.

What type of sainthood do you think the twentieth century is producing? I have been asking myself what sort of a saint is the church of our day building? What is our typical Christian like? Would we be willing to hang his picture by the side of the Catholic monk and the Puritan hero? Is there anything distinctively commanding in the type of manhood which the church to-day is forming? Many of the European scholars, from de Tocqueville down, who have written about America have called attention to our lack of distinction. They insist upon it that we are commonplace and prosaic, democracy has a down-pulling tendency and makes everyone too much like everybody else. This was the feature of our life which always impressed Matthew Arnold. He thought we were as flat as though a steam-roller had passed over us. Henry James, one of our own citizens, after he had lived in England for a few years, was wont on his return to our country to pass the same condemnation which had been passed by Matthew Arnold. We are too prosaic, too much inclined to echo one another's opinions and follow one another's example. We are not daring and original enough. Men do not venture to go ahead of their fellows and blaze a trail that is new. There is nothing America so much needs as a man who approaches the Puritan type. What we want is men who have a vision, and who do not hesitate to work for the conversion of that vision into fact. We need men who are intrepid and radical, aggressive and daring, who are not afraid to conceive bold schemes and stand up for them, no matter who sneers at them and stabs them in

FOREFATHERS' DAY SERMONS

the back. It is this type of man who makes history, and it is this type of man who will save our republic.

Of course we cannot reproduce the form of life that was lived by the Puritans. The world can never go back and slavishly imitate the men of preceding generations. We cannot think and feel and act as the Puritans did, or as the reformers did, or as Jesus and the apostles did. It is necessary that we should be ourselves. We must form a type of our own. We must build a manhood peculiar to ourselves. But so long as the world stands there are two features of manhood that will never become obsolete, there are two traits which each succeeding generation must admire and reproduce, and one is the trait of seriousness, and the other is loyalty to the heavenly vision. No man stands in history with a halo round his head except the man who is reverent toward his Maker, and who lives to fulfill his Maker's will.

VI

THE PURITAN AND THE CAVALIER [1]

"*Be not conformed to this world: but be ye transformed.*" — ROMANS 12 : 2.

William Wordsworth in one of the finest of his poems says:

> " There is
> One great society alone on earth:
> The noble living and the noble dead."

The poet sees that there are two sections of this great society, and he links the two together. In order to make ourselves members of this society, we must often commune with it, and draw from it into our lives fresh stores of inspiration.

We do not think frequently enough of the noble living. Do you find yourself thinking often of the noble men who are serving God in your day and generation, some in public office, others in the retirement of private life, some in our own country, others on far-off mission fields? Do you meditate now and again upon their words, their deeds, their characters, and let your heart go out to them in a tide of appreciation, thankfulness and praise? Alas, we too often forget the noble living, and we are still more prone to lose sight of the noble dead. The present like a hundred-handed giant lays all its hands upon us, and, held fast in their inexorable clutch, we have no time to think of the men who bore the burden in the heat of the day before we were born. Too seldom do we meditate upon the heroes and heroines who fought the good fight and kept the faith in

[1] Dec. 20, 1914.

FOREFATHERS' DAY SERMONS

other lands and far-off times, and too languidly do we enter into the sacrifices and sufferings of the dauntless spirits by whose fidelity to fine ideals the world was lifted to higher levels of thought and action. We cannot afford to allow a December to come and go without thinking for at least a few minutes about the little company of English men and women who landed on the coast of Massachusetts on December 21st, 1620, and without pondering afresh the great historic movement in which the landing of the *Mayflower* company was a picturesque and memorable incident. We should not fail to enrich ourselves every year by thinking of some scene or act of the mighty Puritan drama, and by studying again some particular aspect of the invaluable contribution which Puritanism made to the progress of mankind. Let us think today of the Puritan and the Cavalier, a study in contrasted types of character. We shall see the Puritan more distinctly if we look at him projected against a disposition and a temper the exact antithesis of his own.

English Puritanism had its rise, as you know, in the reign of Queen Elizabeth. At first it was a sort of ferment, a spirit of restlessness, dissatisfaction, discontent. It was an aspiration after larger liberty, a longing for deliverance from evils by which the church of Christ was plagued. In sundry isolated and humble circles, the spirit broke forth into articulate but ineffectual voice. In the reign of James I this spirit of dissatisfaction with things as they were deepened and stiffened, and here and there uttered itself in vehement protest. The protest took in many instances the form of exile. Hundreds of Englishmen were so dissatisfied with the condition of the church in their native land, that they crossed the English channel into Holland,

THE PURITAN AND THE CAVALIER

where they could enjoy a freedom denied them at home. In the reign of Charles I the dissatisfaction widened and became still more vigorous and aggressive. Men ceased to flee to Holland for a refuge. They stood up in the House of Commons and made the full story of their grievances and desires known. We have now arrived at the great times of John Eliot and John Pym and John Hampden and William Laud, of Oliver Cromwell and Prince Rupert and Sir Henry Vane. The ferment which started in little groups of obscure Christian men and women kept on working until it pervaded a large part of the nation. The questions which were at first discussed in religious meetings in private houses, worked their way in a single generation into the realm of political discussion, and became the cause of a fatal conflict between the Parliament and the King. The contention became fiercer and hotter until England was swept at last into the horrors of civil war.

It is in this fierce era of controversy and bloodshed that we come upon two names which will forever hold a prominent place in English history, the Roundhead and the Cavalier. In those two men the life and color of the seventeenth century became incarnate. Both names are nicknames, and, like many another nickname, they have become immortal. The men who opposed the old regime, and who were determined to wrest from the King reforms which he refused to grant, were for the most part from the middle classes. They were farmers, small traders, cobblers, tinkers, humble folk without family prestige, and with nothing noble about them but a spirit which was dissatisfied with the present and eager to build a better government and a purer church. Many of these men flocked to London to hear the debates in Parliament, and

FOREFATHERS' DAY SERMONS

were called derisively by the adherents of the King — "Roundheads." It was customary for gentlemen in the seventeenth century to wear their hair long. Often it was curled and the curls hung down sometimes to the shoulders. Long hair was a sign of noble blood, good breeding, social refinement. Men without social standing cut their hair short. Apprentices and servants cropped their hair so close that the exact contour of the head could be seen, and so they were often designated "Roundheads." The term was now taken up and applied to all men who opposed the King. The Roundheads retorted by calling their opponents, Cavaliers, literally horsemen, but on the lips of the Roundheads, it meant soldiers of fortune, gay and dashing courtiers, haughty and disdainful aristocrats.

England was thus split into two political parties — the Roundheads and the Cavaliers. The Cavaliers were loyal to the King, devoted to the church, supporters of things as they were; the Roundheads were loyal to Parliament, zealous for ecclesiastical reform, eager to sweep away things as they were, in order to make room for things as they ought to be. Each political party embodied a particular type of character. The Cavalier stands for one type, the Puritan or Roundhead for another type. The two types have often been held up side by side to furnish instruction, entertainment, and admonition.

The Cavaliers were the conservatives of England. They were loyal to the King. They loved the old traditions which had come down to them from their fathers. They were devoted to the church. They loved the old ceremonies, the old forms of worship, the old prayer-book, and the old ways of doing things. They were faithful to the past.

THE PURITAN AND THE CAVALIER

They loved the old customs, manners, festivals and feasts. They did not like innovation. They were fearful of the spirit of reform. This is the first mark of the Cavalier, he is everywhere and always a conservative, a devotee of the past, a conservator of things as they are. The Cavalier of the seventeenth century was a worshiper of the beautiful. He loved music and paintings and statues. He was fond of novels and the theater. He reveled in art. He had an eye for the artistic. He was more responsive to the æsthetic than to the ethical. The beautiful interested him more than the good. This is the Cavalier in all centuries. He is attuned to the beautiful. He prizes art more than morality. He becomes more enthusiastic over the lovely than over the true. The seventeenth century Cavalier was keenly alive in his sensuous nature. He was fond of sports. He took delight in amusements. He loved society, and was charmed by the gaieties of life. He looked upon the world out of joyous eyes. He believed that all things are given to us richly to enjoy. Pleasure was more often in his thoughts than duty. Conscience was not a cardinal word in his vocabulary. His constant tendency was to subordinate duty to pleasure, to convert life into a glorious feast. That has been counted one of the traits of the Cavalier character in all times and places.

Over against this man stands the Puritan — the Roundhead. He was the man who was not held tightly by the past. By nature he was a reformer. In temperament he was a radical. He was ready to change anything, no matter how sacred, in the hope of making it better. His heart was bent on progress. He was willing that the old royal prerogatives should go. He was not averse to radical changes in church government and worship. He had an

FOREFATHERS' DAY SERMONS

ideal. He found it in the Bible. He strove to bring the world up to that ideal, no matter how much of the old had to be sacrificed in the process. In every age the Puritan is a reformer.

The seventeenth century Puritan threw the emphasis on the good. Nothing but the good satisfied him. Holiness became to him the one thing to be aimed at. The quest after righteousness became a passion. Corruption was the one thing to be hated and gotten rid of. No matter how artistically evil was decked out, he could not be captivated. Artistic loveliness could never blind his eyes to moral ugliness. Much of the art of the seventeenth century was saturated with moral corruption, and the Puritan in his struggle for cleanness lost his appreciation for the beautiful. Art became to him a device of the devil to lead men astray. He felt that men when captivated by the beautiful ceased to care for the good and the true. And so he turned his back on pictures, and stopped his ears to music, and took no interest in statuary, and abhorred pictured windows in churches, and refused to read novels, and looked upon the theater as an open door to perdition. His passion for the ethical drove him into an irrational depreciation of the æsthetic. This is a weak point in the Puritan always. He is so engrossed in the battle for truth and righteousness, that he does not do full justice to the brighter and more artistic side of life.

The Puritan of three hundred years ago condemned the Cavalier for his general view of life. To the Cavalier life is a feast, to the Puritan life is a battle. The Cavalier liked to play. The Puritan had no time for play. The Cavalier asked himself what is pleasant, the Puritan had but one question: What is my duty? Life to him was not a jest,

THE PURITAN AND THE CAVALIER

a dance, a picnic; it was a difficult piece of work to be performed under the great Taskmaster's eye. While the Cavalier was reveling in his sports, the Puritan was reading his Bible or listening to sermons. The Puritan is everywhere the man whose tendency it is to cultivate the conscience overmuch, and to crowd recreation out of the curriculum of life.

We must bear in mind that it is never possible to describe by a single name a multitude of human beings. No one word will ever accurately describe the character of every member of a party to which it is applied. We speak sometimes of Republicans and Democrats as though all Republicans were alike, and all Democrats were alike. They are not alike. Republicans differ from one another in character, in disposition, in attitude, in outlook, in many doctrines of political belief and in preferences of program and method. And so also do the Democrats. We speak of Germans as though all Germans were alike. They differ in nature, in character, in opinion, as all other peoples do. When recently a distinguished Frenchman visited our city, it was a common remark: " Why, he does not look at all like a Frenchman!" Just as though all Frenchmen must look alike! When therefore we speak of Cavaliers and Roundheads, we must beware of being misled by the caricaturists, and must not be tyrannized over by general terms. Both the Cavalier and the Puritan had their excellences and their weaknesses. They both went to extremes and it is easy to caricature them both. It is possible so to picture the Cavalier as to make him out a dandy and a fop, a profligate and rake, a roysterer and debauchee. Some Cavaliers were all this, but many Cavaliers were not. There were among them true lovers, and faithful husbands, and tender fathers, and men of great and earnest souls, who

FOREFATHERS' DAY SERMONS

lived brave lives and died brave deaths. There were also Cavaliers who were curled and perfumed loafers, and some whose sentiments did not differ from those of Burns' "Jolly Beggars":

> "A fig for those by law protected;
> Liberty's a glorious feast:
> Courts for cowards were erected;
> Churches built to please the priest."

But there were other Cavaliers who were devoted to the things that are noble and true, who had deep-rooted convictions, and who met death with as much courage on the field of battle as the bravest of Cromwell's Ironsides. If it is easy to caricature the Cavalier, it is even easier to caricature the Roundhead. We can dwell on his peculiarities, and exaggerate his limitations, and emphasize his unlovable traits until he seems little more than sniveling hypocrite, a sour-eyed and narrow-headed bigot. There were Puritans of this type, but there were other types. John Milton was a Puritan — one of the most famous of them all — and yet he wore his hair long, and loved music and art, and even wrote plays, and Milton was by no means the only Puritan who loved the beautiful. Push Puritanism far enough and you get the ascetic and fanatic, push the spirit of the Cavalier to the limit and you get the roysterer and fop.

The fact is that we cannot draw a line by means of a label, and put all men of one type on one side, and all men of the opposite type on the other. Inside the Puritan lines the Cavalier type persists in appearing, and inside the Cavalier lines you will find many a man with the Puritan temper. We have often been reminded that Massachusetts was settled by the Puritans and that Virginia was settled

THE PURITAN AND THE CAVALIER

by the Cavaliers, and laborious efforts have been made to contrast the two. Sometimes it has been said that the South has been dominated by the Cavalier, and the North by the Puritan. But it must never be forgotten that all the people of New England are not Puritans, and that all the people of the South are not Cavaliers. Mr. Henry Watterson of Kentucky, in an oration delivered before the New England Society of this city in 1897, scorned the idea that you can draw a sectional line between the Cavaliers and Puritans in this country. He reminded his hearers that Daniel Webster had all the vices that are supposed to have signalized the Cavalier, and that John Calhoun had all the virtues that are claimed for the Puritan. He went on to say that the one typical Puritan soldier of the war was a southern, and not a northern, soldier, Stonewall Jackson of the Virginia line, and that Ethan Allen and John Stark were in reality Cavaliers.

What changes time brings! Men cannot live side by side upon our planet without influencing one another. The Puritan has transformed the appearance of the Cavalier. The Cavalier has cut off his curls, and has become a veritable Roundhead. All gentlemen in all lands are to-day Roundheads. The Cavalier has laid aside his ruff, and ribbons and laces, and gorgeous colors, and now dresses with the simplicity and quietness of a Roundhead. All men are Roundheads in their style of dress. But the Puritan has changed even more. He has come over to the Cavalier's view of art. The Puritan of our day likes pictures, and is fond of music, and believes in statuary, and is not averse to reading a good novel, or seeing a play. The Cavalier held fast to something which the world could not afford to lose, and now the Puritan accepts it and ac-

FOREFATHERS' DAY SERMONS

knowledges that it is good. Beauty and art no less than duty and conscience are words proceeding from the mouth of God.

The history of the world may be said to be the story of the eternal conflict between the Puritan and the Cavalier. Mr. Ferrero, the greatest living Italian historian, in his famous work on the Greatness and Decline of Rome, gives a graphic description of the way in which Puritanism in the Roman empire struggled generation after generation against existing conditions until finally the Puritan spirit was exhausted, and the Empire fell. To Ferrero the history of Rome is the story of the conflict between Roman Puritanism and the refined, corrupt, artistic civilization of the Hellenized East. "For centuries," he says, "the old Roman aristocracy sought through legislation and example and especially through religion to impose simple and pure customs upon all classes, to check the increase of luxury, to keep the family united and strong, to curb dissolute and perverse instincts, and to give a character of decency and propriety to all forms of amusement." Little by little, however, the old Puritan spirit fell into decay. It was still alive in the days of Nero and Tiberius, and that accounts, Ferrero thinks, for the terrible and lurid descriptions we have of the corruption of that time. The leading men are painted in appalling colors. They are all bad, depraved, and odious. They are all drunkards, gluttons, spendthrifts. When we pass on to the times of the Antonines, we hear little of corruption, although, in the judgment of Ferrero, the corruption then was deeper and more universal than in the days of Nero. Little is said about it, however, because the Puritan conscience of Rome was dead.

THE PURITAN AND THE CAVALIER

When a few years ago Mr. Ferrero visited our country, he told us some things which we should never forget. He confessed that before coming he had held the opinion of us which is held by most educated people in Europe, and which is derived from the lurid descriptions of our depravity published in our own papers. He supposed that our country was a sink of iniquity, that extravagance and luxury, and Babylonian display, and civic corruption, and demoralized family life were about all he would see. He was surprised to find here so much that is good. He was led to conclude that the reason we paint our own sins in such vivid colors is because the Puritan conscience in America is alive and awake. We are young enough yet to protest against the things that are bad, and to believe that the world can be made better. He said he did not believe that we are any worse than Europe, but that the Puritan conscience in Europe is dead, and that evils which cause us to cry out against them in pain, are in Europe taken as natural and ineradicable. He paid a fine tribute to New England, calling it the vital nucleus around which the rest of the country had been organized. He then proceeded to sound a note of warning. He said that the Puritan religion had stamped our society with a seriousness, austerity, and simplicity which was preserved without effort so long as men were satisfied with a modest, hard-earned competency, but now that wealth has increased, and luxury has grown, and we have been brought into closer contact with the old world, the temptation is to borrow from Europe those aspects of its civilization which are most ancient and most artistic — even if less pure morally — and that we have entered upon the same old struggle that was fought out in ancient Rome. The Puritan ideal has come to a hand to hand struggle against corruption, the breaking up of the family, and against those vices which are born in the slums of a great city. Just as the Puritanism of Rome was obliged to fight against the influence of the older and more artistic civilization of the East, so must the United States fight against the insidious and deadening influence of the more ancient and more artistic civilization of Europe.

The Broadway Tabernacle is a Puritan church. From the beginning until now it has been dominated by the Puritan ideal. It stands for simplicity and seriousness and cleanness. It is a radical church. It strikes great evils hard. It faces the future. It refuses to be shackled by the past. It believes in reform. It clings to the old only so far as the old having been tested has been proved to be good. It carries in its eye the vision of a better republic and a nobler church. In a city in which tens of thousands are content with things as they are, who cling to the old simply because it is old, the Tabernacle works in season and out of season to help make the world what it ought to be. It is a non-conformist church. It does not bend to the conventionalities of society or to the opinions of the times. It heeds the apostolic injunction: "Be not conformed to this world, but be ye transformed by the renewing of your mind that ye may prove what is that good and acceptable and perfect will of God." It is a church which lays the emphasis on the ethical. It is no foe of the beautiful. It makes no war upon art, provided art is clean. It is not indifferent to pictures and music and chiseled marble. It concedes a legitimate place for the novel and for the drama, provided they are clean. But its supreme emphasis is not on the beautiful but on the good, not on the artistic but on the true. In a city where thousands read literature that is foul, and where a section of the theater is always hover-

THE PURITAN AND THE CAVALIER

ing on the edge of the indecent, and where men and women talk much about art for art's sake, the Tabernacle lifts up its voice for whatsoever things are honest and just and pure. It glorifies the idea of duty. It gives lofty place to conscience. It refuses to admit that life is a feast only. Men are here for a purpose. The plan of their life has been formulated by God. To each one a great work has been given. In a city in which the love of amusement runs riot, and thousands live solely to have a good time, counting it the end of existence to see a thrilling play, to attend a good concert, to partake of a rich banquet, to dance life away, the Tabernacle speaks constantly of duty, of character, of destiny. It pleads for simplicity. It condemns extravagance. It calls a halt upon luxury. It summons men to seriousness. It denounces frivolity. It insists upon cleanness, cleanness in politics, cleanness in the drama, cleanness in the home, cleanness in the innermost recesses of the heart. In the metropolis of the new world where the forces of evil are insidious and mighty, and where the temptations to shirk the responsibility of working out social problems, to be indifferent to the demands of justice and truth, to follow expediency instead of principle, and to place pleasure above duty, are peculiarly subtle and often well-nigh irresistible, this old church stands as a representative of the spirit which made England great, endeavoring to strengthen the forces which are at work to curb dissolute and perverse instincts, to check the growth of luxury, to give a character of decency to all forms of amusement, and to keep the family united and strong, calling men and women through succeeding generations to simplicity, and seriousness and cleanness of living.

VII

THE UNPOPULARITY OF THE PURITAN: ITS CAUSES AND GLORY [1]

"And overthrew their tables." — JOHN 1 : 16

This is the Sunday on which for several years I have thought with you about those true benefactors of humanity and servants of God, who in the sixteenth and seventeenth centuries by their arduous labors and stupendous sacrifices turned the stream of history into a new channel and by their unparalleled victories created a fresh hope in the heart of the world. It was in the month of December, as everybody knows, when a little company of one hundred Englishmen landed on the coast of Massachusetts. These were the forerunners of a great company of twenty thousand Englishmen who came to New England within the next twenty years after the *Mayflower* had landed her immortal cargo on the Massachusetts sands. And these twenty thousand were representatives of a still greater company who in many countries, animated by the same spirit and engaged in the same work, wrought out greater blessings for humanity than any other company of mortals who have ever moved across the stage of the world's life. These men are known as Puritans. In preceding years we have thought together of their principles and achievements, their character and temper, their virtues and limitations. Let us think this morning about their unpopularity, its causes and its glory.

[1] Dec. 15, 1907.

[104]

THE UNPOPULARITY OF THE PURITAN

That the Puritans were unpopular is known to every boy and girl in the High School. The very name is a nickname, a term of derision and contempt, a word coined in the mint of obliquy, soaked in vitriol, hurled by slanderous tongues for the purpose of making blisters and inflicting wounds. It was a malodorous word, and even to-day when heated on a certain type of tongue it gives forth an unsavory odor. Do not men still say with a sneer and a leer, "He is a Puritan." To be puritanic is to be bigoted, narrow, cruel, pharisaical, and generally contemptible. To many of the men of their age the Puritans were disagreeable and exasperating; to some of their contemporaries they were loathsome and abominable. Through their lifetime they were hated, detested, execrated, and after they were dead their memory was held in abhorrence. For nearly three centuries they have been followed by continuous and pitiless abuse and vituperation, and in many circles of our modern world there is no one found willing to do them reverence. Schools of historians have vied with one another in exploiting their blunders and blackening their reputation, and literary artists have painted a picture of them calculated to draw out a hiss of contempt from the lips of succeeding generations. That they were unpopular, repellent, abhorrent to a large part of the world for which they labored and sacrificed is one of the best-known facts of history.

Have you ever asked yourself what was the cause of this deep-rooted dislike, this widespread and extraordinary detestation? Why were these men so pelted with invectives while they were still alive, and why have they been repeatedly taken from their graves, hung on the gibbet, and exposed to the contumely of generations who never saw their faces? An answer to this question is to be found

FOREFATHERS' DAY SERMONS

only by a careful study of history. Their unpopularity was due to their attitude to the world in the midst of which they lived, and what that attitude was it is worth our while to study and ponder.

What is the attitude which a Christian should take to the world of which he is a part? This is a question which confronts the follower of Jesus at the beginning and it pursues him to the end. Saint John in one of his letters says " Love not the world, neither the things that are in the world. If a man love the world, the love of the Father is not in him. For all that is in the world, the lust of the flesh, and the lust of the eyes, and the pride of life, is not of the Father, but is of the world." That the nature of man is evil and that the world is the center and seat of forces inimical to the will and purposes of God is one of the axioms of the Christian religion. What shall be the attitude of a man, consecrated to the ideal life, to this evil-thoughted, corrupt-hearted, mischief-working world? Two clean-cut and definite answers have been given to this question, and each has worked itself out into a specific type of character and a particular stamp of civilization.

The first and most natural answer is, " Flee from the world! Get away! Come out from among wicked men. Touch not the unclean thing. Are there evil customs, give them up and hide yourself from their injurious influence. Are there social relations which have become contaminated, then renounce them and live a life of self-abnegation. Are there institutions which have absorbed the poison of the world, escape from their defiling touch, and in a little world removed from the great world in which the devil does his work, give yourself up to holy contemplation and assiduous prayer." Here is an answer clear, simple, and consistent. Every mind can understand it. To thousands

THE UNPOPULARITY OF THE PURITAN

it has had a fascination too strong to be resisted. This answer is written large in the history of Christianity and is known as Monasticism. Under Monasticism men do not live in society, they live in monasteries. Their life is separated from the life of the world. The sexual instinct is the cause of boundless sin and woe, and therefore it should be crucified. Men take the vow of celibacy. Property is the channel through which a horde of temptations and burdens come to the heart, and therefore property must be surrendered. Men take the vow of poverty. Freedom is the spring from which flow streams of disorder, and therefore it must be given up. Men take the vow of obedience to some ecclesiastical superior whose surer judgment can be relied upon and whose more abundant wisdom will save the soul from foolish choices and fruitless wanderings.

Under the impulse of the great ambition to live a life acceptable to God, thousands of men who caught in Jesus the vision of a life high above the sordid level of the ordinary world, turned their backs upon society and gave themselves whole-heartedly to what they called the saving of their souls. There is something unspeakably sublime in this great act of renunciation. Society was frivolous, crazy for luxury and pleasure. Kings and nobles were dissolute, tyrannical, godless. Immorality like a mighty tide overflowed the world. In the breaking up of the Roman Empire it seemed as though the deep foundations of the world were melting, and that the universe was slipping back into the primeval chaos. In the midst of the wild welter of confusion Monasticism was the answer which came to devout souls crying out for peace and rescue. And so these homes for religious men were built by the thousand throughout the Christian world. They were located sometimes in the heart of trackless forests, some-

FOREFATHERS' DAY SERMONS

times high up on some well-nigh inaccessible crag, sometimes on an island in a river, sometimes on a rock surrounded by an angry sea, the main purpose being isolation, separation, sequestration from a world bent on evil and hostile to the highest interests of the soul.

We Protestants have not always been fair in our judgment of Monasticism. We have seen its evils and have not been careful to search out its blessings. When some of us think of a monk we think of a lazy and lecherous reprobate, who, too indolent to work, has crawled into a warm nest to be fed there by the labor of other men. When we think of a monastery we turn away from it with loathing as from a den of iniquity, a place filled with things that defile. But we ought to be careful to remember that if some of the laziest men in the middle ages were monks, some of the most industrious men were monks; that if some of the most selfish men were monks, some of the most self-sacrificing and charitable men were monks; that if some of the worst men were in monasteries, some of the best men were also there; and that if monastic life had its perils and corruptions, so also it had its opportunities and victories. Even though Monasticism separated men from the world, it aimed to keep alive a feeling for humanity. The monks when at their best were ever interested in the poor and the sick and the defenseless. Many a day the poor were fed at the monastery gate, and sick folks were carried there that they might feel upon their feverish brow the cooling touch of holy hands. In a wild and lawless world the monastery became a house of refuge to which the unprotected traveler was glad to flee. And in the monastery the flame of learning was never allowed to go completely out. The monks were lovers of books, and in an age when the treasures of bygone ages were at the mercy

THE UNPOPULARITY OF THE PURITAN

of savage men who cared nothing for literature or art, the monastery threw its sheltering protection over the masterpieces of Greek and Roman literature, and for the preservation of these priceless treasures the world will be indebted to the monks forever. Nor was the cultivation of the virtues and graces of Christian character left neglected. In many a monastery men were trained to work, giving lessons in industry to a world which had come to hold all labor in contempt, and setting an example which shone like a light in a dark night. Not only in the fields did the monks labor daily, but what endless toil did they bestow upon their books! What penmen many of them were, copying with patient fingers the books of Scripture and the masterpieces of antiquity, producing works of art at which all the world still marvels. It was in the monastery that men had time to think, brood, meditate, until there grew up in the heart an indestructible hope of immortality. If this world was evil, there was a world of light. If this life is stained and poisoned, the soul shall some day be radiant and free. Here and there throughout the middle ages there were men so true in their devotions and so high in their aspirations that there came into their faces something of the sweetness which we love to think of as belonging to the face of the beloved disciple, and something of the greatness which belonged to the Master himself. It is not without reason that some of the monks have been canonized, given a place among that shining company of immortal witnesses by whose sacrifices and achievements we are chastened and strengthened.

Such a man was Bernard of Cluny. In his writings you get Monasticism at its best. He was a Frenchman of the twelfth century, a member of the Benedictine Order. His greatest work is a poem entitled " De Contemptu Mundi."

FOREFATHERS' DAY SERMONS

The burden of the poem is that " This is a very evil world." That is the story of Monasticism always, the world is evil and therefore get away from it. But whither shall we turn? Turn to the Eternal City through whose gates you will, if faithful, some day pass. Bernard of Cluny impressed with the evil of this world, found delight in thinking of the world Eternal. The two loveliest of his hymns are included in our hymn-book and are sung by Protestants the world over. They point the soul heavenward with phrases which thrill and brace the heart.

> " For thee, O dear, dear country,
> Mine eyes their vigils keep;
> For very love, beholding
> Thy happy name, they weep.
> The mention of Thy Glory
> Is unction to the breast,
> And medicine in sickness,
> And love and life and rest."

Or what can be sweeter than this?

> " Jerusalem, the golden,
> With milk and honey blest,
> Beneath thy contemplation
> Sink heart and voice oppressed:
> I know not, oh, I know not,
> What joys await me there,
> What radiancy of glory,
> What light beyond compare."

In those hymns the inmost soul of Monasticism comes to expression. The man who sings them has turned his back on the world with its works and pleasures and is gazing steadfastly into heaven. As a second illustration take an Italian of the thirteenth century, Francis of Assisi, founder of the Order of Franciscans. He was a man of purest heart and loveliest spirit, and at the age of 37, retiring to a mountain, he spent the last seven years of his life meditat-

THE UNPOPULARITY OF THE PURITAN

ing on the passion and death of Jesus. So concentrated was his contemplation, so close his communion with the Lord, that there arose a rumor which has lived to the present hour, that in his hands and feet could be seen the very prints of the nails which held Jesus to the cross. I do not wonder that he was canonized two years after his death, and that for nearly seven hundred years his life has been commemorated every October by the faithful throughout the Roman Catholic world.

But while Monasticism was not altogether evil and produced many a useful and saintly man, Monasticism is not the correct answer to the question. What shall be the attitude of the soul to an evil and rebellious world? Monasticism was not without its influence for good, but it was not adequate to the demands of a world such as ours. It made the awful mistake of casting a slur on married life, and of teaching men to think that men and women can be holier unmarried than when married. By withdrawing thousands of the most gifted and best educated men from family life, Monasticism impoverished the ideal and crippled the influence of the home. By segregating men of principle and character in isolated places, cutting their connections with the race of which they were a part, Monasticism left society at the mercy of forces which tore it and threw it into chaos. By shutting men up in the cloister, some of them men of genius and many of them men of talent, freer rein was given to princes and potentates to work their autocratic will, and larger scope was allowed to ambitious ecclesiastics to spoil the church of which under Christ they were the stewards. Monasticism crowded men down into an existence which was abnormal, and in every kingdom of life disastrous effects began to make themselves manifest. While men were scourging their bodies and

FOREFATHERS' DAY SERMONS

dreaming of heaven, the burdens on men's backs grew heavier and humanity fell into even deeper depths of misery and despair. After a trial of Monasticism for a thousand years the world was going to wreck. An awful darkness fell on Europe. Society seemed to be falling to pieces. The world like a great ship was battered by a storm which threatened to submerge it. The monks looked at the tragic situation from the monastery window, but it never occurred to them that the world could be saved. All that they could do was to throw a rope from the cloister window in the hope that now and then some shipwrecked wretch might take hold of it and be drawn up to safety. That, then, is Monasticism! Look at it — an answer built in granite all the way from the western edge of Asia to the islands which lie off the coast of Scotland — an answer to the question, what shall be a Christian's attitude to an evil world?

But when the answer of Monasticism had shown itself to be mistaken, an Augustinian monk by the name of Luther came out to announce a message which flooded the world with light. The strokes of the hammer with which he nailed his theses to the old church door in Wittenberg awakened men everywhere. Once awake, they began to ask themselves, What should be the Christian attitude to a world which is filled with corruption? Here and there was a man who said, a Christian man must not run away from evil, he must fight it. He must not hide; let him stand out in the open. He must not separate himself from men, he must co-operate with them in the pulling down of strongholds. Let him not be afraid of the world, but let him take hold of it with both his hands and mould it into a shape which shall be pleasing unto God. If customs are bad, let him change them; if manners are evil, let him

THE UNPOPULARITY OF THE PURITAN

reform them; if social relations have become demoralizing, let them be cleansed; if institutions have grown corrupt, let the corruption be purged out; if the forces of evil are mighty, then let the children of light put on the whole armour of light, and fight, every man in his place, for humanity and God. If home has become defiled, then purify it; if the state has become corrupt, then purify it; if the church has become stained, then purify it. Men who spoke after this fashion became known as Puritans, because they were always talking of purity, and not only talked about it but started out at once to do the work which they saw had to be done. Society had grown frivolous and dissolute, and they took hold of it; the state had become tyrannical and oppressive, and they laid hands upon it; the church had grown superstitious and corrupt, and they began to strip her of her pagan finery and to clothe her in the robes of righteousness. These men were reformers. Calvin was a theologian, but he cleaned up Geneva. Knox was a preacher, but he defied and conquered a vain and untruthful Queen. Cromwell was a farmer, but he took off the head of a king. The Puritan is the antithesis of the monk. Puritanism is a flat contradiction of Monasticism. The monk runs and hides. The Puritan stands and fights. The monk prays and ministers to men who have been wounded and crippled by society, the Puritan also prays but works to change the structure and temper of society that men may not be wounded or crippled. The Puritan of the sixteenth and seventeenth centuries went at once into politics, determined to correct the abuses and usher in a new régime. He went into commerce, knowing that commerce brings wealth and that with wealth he would help forward the kingdom of God. He went into society, undaunted by its sneers and not

FOREFATHERS' DAY SERMONS

afraid of its threats, pulling down standards which were ancient and overthrowing customs which had had the sanction of many generations. By the might of his genius he created three worlds — a new world of politics, a new commercial world, and a new social world.

But he did it by the payment of an awful price. It was a furious battle, and at evening his face and hands were bleeding, his clothes were torn, and he was weary unto death. Do you ask why the Puritan was unpopular, my reply has already been suggested by my text — " He overthrew their tables." Why was Jesus unpopular? Seek the answer in my text. St. John says that at the very beginning of his ministry Jesus was deeply stirred by what he saw in the temple at Jerusalem. He saw men there selling cattle and doves, and changing money for the pilgrims who come to make their annual contribution to the Temple Treasury. But what was wrong in selling sheep or in exchanging money? Nothing. Business is always honorable when honorably conducted. It was not only right but a convenience that these things should be sold and that the money should be exchanged. No coin bearing the head of a pagan king was allowed to go into the Temple Treasury. Only the Jewish half-shekel could go into that sacred box. But the people in their homes, scattered as they were throughout the world, were obliged to use Roman coinage, and on coming to Jerusalem it was a convenience to have men nearby who could give them for their foreign coins the coins which the temple authorities demanded. But these money-changers had degenerated into robbers. They took advantage of the ignorant peasants, and charged exorbitant sums for making the necessary exchange. They did it inside a temple dedicated to the God of Mercy. It was right to sell cattle

THE UNPOPULARITY OF THE PURITAN

and doves, but it was wrong to sell them at exorbitant prices. These cattle dealers, taking advantage of the necessities of the pilgrims, asked many times too much for their animals, and even the sellers of doves, whose business it was to supply the needs of the very poor, driven on by the same mercenary spirit, also became robbers, demanding from the poor peasants sums which it was not right they should pay. And the great soul of Jesus burned like a furnace as he looked on the unspeakable outrage. How long it had been going on we do not know. It had no doubt grown up gradually as all abuses do, and men had grown accustomed to it and conscience had fallen asleep in the presence of it. It was within the province of any Jew to put an end to such a scandal, but no one cared to do it. What others refused to do the Son of God did. He made a whip. He drove the cattle out. He turned over the boxes which held the money. He overthrew the tables. No such scene had ever been witnessed within the memory of man like unto the scene which was now presented. You cannot imagine the bustle and confusion, the surprise and consternation. The bellowing cattle, the bleating sheep, the shouting, cursing men, the precious coins rolling under the feet of the crowd, the hearts blazing and flashing with indignation, who has words with which to paint the thrilling picture? John says that it was in that lurid hour Jesus caught a vision of the cross. When the angry crowd gathered round him, asking him for a sign, he said, "Destroy this temple, and in three days I will raise it up." That is his first intimation that he must die. It all flashed on him at the instant in which he overturned the tables. By upsetting the tables he kindled a fire which burned with an energy which could not be quenched. By interfering with vested interests he set every man of property against

FOREFATHERS' DAY SERMONS

him. It all seemed so impertinent, impudent, uncalled for, this interference of a teacher of religion with the practical affairs of men. There were monks all along the desert shore of the Dead Sea. These men prayed and sang and worshipped God continually. They were beloved and honored by all the people. The world always likes religious men who attend to their own business and do not interfere with its aims and doings.

Jesus by the overturning of the tables made his suffering and his crucifixion sure. And so it was with the Puritan. He put his hand upon the tables, he overturned them, he interfered with vested interests, he put an end to age-long abuses, he trampled upon the golden coins of men. What could the world do but hate him? The disciple must be as his Master, and the servant as his Lord! If men called the Perfect Man Beelzebub, do not marvel at the list of epithets which they hurl at his imperfect followers. In the great temple of society frivolous and selfish men and women had set up their tables piled high with absurd customs, foolish fashions, demoralizing practices, and the Puritan, burning with indignation at the profanation of human life, overthrew the tables and sent the accursed conventionalities rolling in the dust. He got hated for his trouble. In the temple of state, cruel and despotic kings had set up their tables and covered them over with precedents and arguments constructed by hireling lawyers, proving that kings have a divine right to govern wrong and that under no circumstances have subjects a right to resist their ruler, and the Puritan overthrew the tables and sent the lying legal documents rolling under the feet of men. Venomous vituperation was his reward. Ambitious and worldly men had set up their tables in the temple of religion and had weighted them down with

THE UNPOPULARITY OF THE PURITAN

interpretations and doctrines and ceremonies which made of no effect the law of God and corrupted the simple religion of the Son of Man into a superstition and a burden, and the Puritan, with hands hot with indignation, overthrew the tables and sent the claims and works of priestcraft rolling on the ground. Murderous, unrelenting detestation was the Puritan's compensation. Be not surprised that the Puritan was unpopular. He was a reformer, and when have reformers ever been popular among the people whose wicked thoughts they have rebuked and whose sinful ways they have resisted? The Puritan interfered with men's pleasures, he intruded into realms into which religious men had never gone, he pushed himself into circles in which kings and princes had reigned supreme, he threw himself across the track of the world's ambitions and endeavors, and that is why he has hung on the gibbet for well-nigh three hundred years. He saved others but himself he could not save.

But some one at this point interrupts me with the remark that the Puritans were too severe, entirely too grave and sober. That is because they were soldiers in the midst of a tremendous battle. I have noticed that no painter who has attempted to paint Pickett's charge at Gettysburg has painted a smile on the face of a single soldier. War is grim and earnest work, and the only smile that is seen on the battlefield is the smile that flits across the face of the wounded man, who, in the moment of death, thinks how glorious it is to die for one's country. But some one says, the Puritan made mistakes. So he did, because he was a man of action. Men of action always commit blunders. But no matter how many blunders a man of action is guilty of, he is a nobler and more useful man than he who attempts to do nothing. Simeon Stylites on his lofty pillar outside of the walls of Antioch never

FOREFATHERS' DAY SERMONS

committed any social or political blunders. For thirty years he lived upon his pillar, spending hours every day with his arms extended so that his body might stand out like a cross against the sky. Great crowds of admiring people gathered daily to see the holy man and to marvel at his unparalleled devotion. He was guilty of no social blunders because he was not in society. He made no political mistakes because he held aloof from politics. But his whole life was a stupid and disgusting and unpardonable blunder. The Puritan was not a perfect man. He had the defects of his qualities, and these became conspicuous and glaring because he acted in a wide and open field. A man with an unruly temper who stays at home may by his temper make things disagreeable for his wife and children, but his ugliness will not work havoc with interests outside his own domestic circle.

But if that same man comes out of his seclusion and attempts to deal with large affairs of church and state, then his temperamental infirmities, having a large sphere in which to work, may do mischief in divers directions and affect the comfort of many homes. The Puritan exposed himself to criticism by jumping into the arena and wrestling with the most complicated problems of earthly life, and if at many points he blundered, do not forget his numberless successes and immortal triumphs.

Some one says that the Puritan was too zealous. His manner was rough and not to be commended. The criticism is one to which every reformer is exposed. Men who saw Jesus in the act of cleansing the temple were scandalized by his action. He made a whip. When have men liked a whip? He poured out money on the ground. What a waste! He overthrew the tables. What needless violence! He said in a tone which frightened, " Take these things

THE UNPOPULARITY OF THE PURITAN

hence!" Why did he not go at this work with the poise and quietness of a gentleman? Why did he not in courteous tones invite the cattle-dealers to pass out? Why did he not give the men time to gather up their money, and why instead of turning the tables upside down did he not offer to help carry them out and set them up in a place both convenient and proper. The manner of Jesus was criticised by his contemporaries. It has been criticised continuously to the present time. And so also many men cannot understand the fury of the Puritans. Why did they pull down the monasteries, and tear the priests' robes to pieces, and trample on sacred ceremonies, and say in a savage tone to Cardinals and Princes, "Take these things hence!" If this is a mystery to you it is because you lack the Puritan heart and the Puritan fire. You can never understand the Puritan manner unless you are ablaze with the Puritan zeal. Do you catch fire at the sight of injustice? Do you flame with indignation when you see the weak and helpless abused? Do you love God and humanity enough to quiver and thrill in the presence of men who, haters of God and enemies of man, trample down with their cruel feet interests which are dear to all hearts which have not lost out of them the spark which comes from heaven? How can you hope to sympathize with the Puritan unless you hate tyranny and despise religious mummery and loathe the things which hurt and slay? You yourself must have the soul of the Puritan if your heart is to go out to him with a full tide of affection.

You say that you cannot love him, that you cannot even like him, because he is disagreeable to get on with and altogether too strenuous. Whom do you like? You like a monk, a mild-eyed, sweet-faced dreamer, whose soft hands have no knack for overthrowing tables! Hang these three

FOREFATHERS' DAY SERMONS

portraits on your right, Benedict, Bernard of Clairvaux and Francis of Assisi, and these three portraits on your left, Calvin, Knox and Cromwell. What a difference in the two types of faces. The eyes of the monks are soft, the expression of their face is sweet, the faces of the Puritans look as though they were made of iron. Why this difference? The monks were dreamers, the Puritans were men of action. The monks were shepherds in green pastures where the waters were very still. The Puritans were soldiers on a field swept by black tempests from hell. You like the monks and so do I, but these men with the iron faces bring from my heart a deeper reverence and from my soul a fuller homage. Down in the dust I prostrate myself before them, for by their bloody sweat the things which men now count dearest were made ours forevermore.

To come into closer sympathy with the Puritan is one of the ways of increasing the efficiency of the Twentieth Century Church. What is the matter with present day Christianity? We have too many monks. We Protestants do not believe in monks, but we have been diligent in cultivating them. The soul of Monasticism does not lie in holy buildings or strange ecclesiastical garbs, but in a certain temper and attitude, and this temper and attitude are not peculiar to Roman Catholicism but come up perennially out of the heart of man. Monasticism changes its form from century to century, but the essence of it remains forever the same. We smile at the quaint Monasticism of the medieval times and imagine that all Monasticism has vanished, whereas Protestantism in the twentieth century is swarming with monks, and how to convert them into Puritans is the outstanding problem of modern Christianity. The Protestant monk does not take any vows. He repudiates the vows of celibacy, poverty and obedience.

THE UNPOPULARITY OF THE PURITAN

He believes in marrying, he likes to make money, he obeys no man but does as he pleases. But a man can marry and make a fortune and do as he will and still be a monk. He may separate himself from the world which he was sent to help redeem. He may hold aloof from social reform, and keep out of politics, and never lift his finger to lighten the burdens of the men who are oppressed. Through the day he may shut himself in behind the solid walls of his office or place of business, and at night he may seclude himself in the privacy of his home, revelling in the luxury of reading his magazine and books, having the same sort of good time which the medieval monk had in his cloister when far away from the tumult of the world and its fever, he spent the long hours in poring over the pages of poets and philosophers, refreshing his soul by visions and fancies, undisturbed by the entanglements and exasperations of a world which had gone wrong and which was crying night and day for some one to set it right. Our modern monk is a courteous and agreeable gentleman. He cultivates the family virtues. He is temperate, honorable, kind. He does not like reform movements, for they are always noisy and stir up trouble. He loathes politics, for politics, you know, are dirty. But he is a good man. He says his prayers, and now and then he sings " Jerusalem the Golden." He is a first-class modern monk. And this is the type of Christians which have been too common in our world. The day for the Puritan is upon us. There are going to be lively times in this country during the next thirty years. We are going to clean up a lot of things and make a host of crooked things straight. We are going to have a new type of preacher, for the seminaries are sending out men awake to the social problem, and we are going to have a new type of layman, men who are not afraid to overthrow the tables

FOREFATHERS' DAY SERMONS

of the miscreants who by their practices defile the temple of human life. Christianity is going to be more virile, aggressive, radical. We have been monkish in our dealing with wickedness. We have not worked to transform the kingdoms of the world into the kingdom of God. How have we dealt with the saloon? It is a fountain sending out streams of woe and misery and death, and we have stood round it like so many monks picking up the drunkard, caring for his wife and children, striving to repair the awful damage, but seldom thinking of so bold a thing as overthrowing the tables. But that is what the new type of Christian is going to do. The good work has begun already. The most remarkable anti-saloon movement which this country has ever known is now in progress in the South and West. Men stand bewildered asking, " Why is this? How do you explain this rising tide? " The answer is that men are increasingly interested in the social problem. Instead of building monasteries on the top of mountains we are establishing social settlements in the slums. A host of workers are toiling to lift humanity up, and the cry that comes up from the men who are working down in the ooze and the slime is, " We have found a serpent down here — Alcohol — and we can make no progress until the serpent is cast out! " Moreover the saloon has been becoming more and more a social nuisance, oftentimes a menace and a curse. In the smaller towns it is the lounging place of loafers and foul-mouthed men and boys, while in the city it has become in many cases the rendezvous of thugs and cutthroats and harlots. The monk way of dealing with the liquor traffic is to bind up the wounds which it makes. The way of the Puritan is simply to overthrow the tables and say to the men who for the sake of gain send men to hell, " Take these things hence." That

THE UNPOPULARITY OF THE PURITAN

type of Christian is the type now needed, and he is sure to come.

Sunday desecration is another evil against which good men must be on their guard. Like all evils its approach is stealthy and its growth is gradual. The desecration of the Temple in Jerusalem did not spring up full statured in a day. The court of the Gentiles was a spacious place having an area of fourteen acres. Round its four sides there ran a colonnade with four rows of marble pillars and a roof of costly cedar. Many things were needed in the sacrifices of the temple and what place more convenient for the buying of them than this great, spacious court? One day, I imagine, a man stepped inside with a cage of pigeons. A bird so small and sweet voiced as a dove could not hurt the sacred place! By and by a man with a sheep to sell led it in. A sheep is the most innocent of all animals. No harm could come to God or man from the presence of a sheep. Still later the man with a steer to sell brought him in. "I have as much right here as you have," he said to the man with the sheep and the man with the pigeons, and soon there were a dozen steers. That is the way it all happened. The abuse grew up so gradually that nobody observed it, and before men knew it the sacredness of the place was gone. Just so does the desecration of the Day of Rest take place in great cities. One man steps into the Temple of Rest, saying: "Let me sing you a little song." His voice is sweet and the song is pretty, and what is so beautiful and innocent as a song? And a man outside hearing this song inside the temple says, "I think I'll come in and sing, too." His voice is harsh and his song is a different kind of song, but in he comes, and who is wise enough to draw the line and say this song is proper, that song will never do? And while these two men are singing, another

FOREFATHERS' DAY SERMONS

man who cannot sing at all and who can only use his feet decides that he too has a right to exercise his gifts inside the temple, and in he comes and after him a dozen others and after them a hundred others, some bringing doves, some sheep, some steers, until the whole day is trampled into sordidness and one of the most precious of all the privileges of man has been wrested from him. The monk stands by and does nothing. He is busy with his prayers. What is needed is the Puritan, the man who with the strength which was in the hands of Jesus will overthrow the tables.

Let no one deceive you on this question of Sunday desecration. Be not surprised if many papers befog the moral issue. Not all newspaper managers are noted for their fondness for anything that makes for righteousness. Many men are determined to make money at all hazards and at all costs, seven days in the week, no matter how many high interests of life are impaired or how many human beings are reduced to slaves. As long as there is one man in the community obliged to work seven days in the week so long will the Christian church have a wrong to redress and a soul to set free. If men do not blaze with indignation at the desecration of the Day of Rest, it is because they do not feel the awful and unspeakable tragedy of dooming human beings to the galling and soul-destroying slavery of toil which is unbroken. The Day of Rest must be cleansed and there will come, if not to-morrow, then sometime, a type of Christian who will overthrow the tables and drive the desecrators out.

How has the church up to date dealt with war? It has played the part of a monk. It has mitigated the horrors of war. It has established Red Cross Societies and other kind-hearted agencies for relieving suffering and making the dying hour less horrible. And while the monk has

THE UNPOPULARITY OF THE PURITAN

been busy devising ways of reducing the horrors of war other men have been just as busy in building new cruisers and battleships and torpedo boats, swallowing up the treasure of the nations, and keeping alive in men's hearts the thought of destruction and slaughter. Militarism is having a great day. It has deceived the very elect. It cries for millions and they are given, and then it cries for millions more and gets them. But some day there will come a type of Christian in England, France, Germany and America who will overthrow the tables of these monomaniacs who are always thinking and planning and getting ready for war, and will pour out the money which is now wasted in the enginery of slaughter into hospitals and schools and art galleries and other institutions which work for the uplifting and happiness of mankind. The church will some day overthrow the military tables.

But how can men overturn these tables or any others without stirring up the animosities of the men they interfere with, and bringing down on their heads the maledictions of all who are content with things as they are? Let a man in many parts of this country oppose the saloon in any effective way and he will meet with a storm of opposition and possibly be obliged to give up his life. Again and again within the last few years men who have overturned the tables of the liquor sellers have been shot down in the street or murdered in their beds. Let a man take hold of any of the tables owned by men who coin money by the desecration of the Day of Rest, and he will be laughed at by all of the sweet-faced monks of the community and hated by all with whose vested interests he has interfered. Let him stand up against the advocates of militarism tearing to tatters their arguments and blocking their way to still more colossal follies and madnesses, and

FOREFATHERS' DAY SERMONS

he will be smiled at as an impracticable ignoramus who does not understand the world in which he is living. How can a man in any land, at any time, overturn the tables, and still be popular? It is impossible. If a man is brave and true enough to do the Puritan's work let him expect to meet the Puritan's fate, but let him not forget that he shall from the hand of God receive the Puritan's unfading crown.

VIII

THE STRENGTH AND WEAKNESS OF PURITANISM[1]

AS ILLUSTRATED BY THE LIFE AND CHARACTER OF JOHN KNOX

"I know thy works, and charity, and service, and faith, and thy patience, and thy works; and the last to be more than the first. Notwithstanding I have a few things against thee." — REV. II: 19-20.

That is a wonderful picture with which the Book of the Revelation opens. Christendom stands before the throne of God for judgment. Seven churches selected from the mass of churches stand as the representatives of Christ's followers throughout the world, in the presence of the King to hear his words of approbation and of censure. To each one of them he utters words of praise: "I know you," he exclaims, "your history and your condition. I know your defeats and victories, your temptations and your burdens, all the sacrifices which you have made in my name and for my glory. I know your faith and hope and love, and all the graces which have blossomed in the garden of your soul." Thus do the words of praise run on, and then all at once there comes a change. The tide of praise is checked. A thrilling silence falls, and then the King goes on to say: " Nevertheless I have a few things against thee." Every church has done deeds worthy of commendation, and every church also brings down upon itself the censure of the Judge. "There is none righteous, no not one."

This picture is perennially pathetic because it represents an age-long experience. Walk down the Christian

[1] Dec. 17, 1905.

FOREFATHERS' DAY SERMONS

centuries and see the mighty movements which, inspired by the Eternal Spirit, have moved forward in the name of Christ for the extension of his kingdom. Wherever the Christian church has gone it has planted seeds in the hearts of men which have brought forth harvests oftentimes a hundred fold. And to every movement inspired by Christ in all the Christian centuries words of commendation are spoken by the King. We can hear him saying: " I know your origin and your history, your struggles and your triumphs. I have counted all your sacrifices, and I know what you have suffered in my name. But nevertheless I have a few things against thee!" There is none righteous, no not one.

And were you to picture the Christian world to-day, you would be obliged to picture it as the apostle painted it nineteen centuries ago. We can see in our imagination the great families of the Church of God standing before the throne. Each one of them comes up freighted with the trophies of a thousand battlefields, wearing the crowns of countless victories, proud of traditions descended through blessed years, and thankful for sacred memories of the saints. And to each and every branch of the church universal the King speaks high words of praise. " I know you, one and all," he says. " I know your ambitions and your conquests, your virtues and your graces, and all the lovely things which you have accomplished in my name and for my glory. Nevertheless I have a few things against you." To each and every one is given a word of commendation, upon each and every one a condemnation falls. There is a blemish on every forehead, a stain on every robe. There is none righteous, no not one.

This is Forefathers' Sunday, the Sunday that begins the week in which occurs the anniversary of the Landing

STRENGTH AND WEAKNESS OF PURITANISM

of the Pilgrims on Plymouth Rock. For many years it has been my custom on this Sunday to speak of some phase of the Puritan character and work, and having spoken to you in other years about the virtues and the graces of the Puritan spirit, let me this morning call your attention to a few of its defects and limitations. My theme is the strength and weakness of Puritanism; and as this is the four-hundredth anniversary of the birth of one of the three greatest men of the Reformation era, I want to light up my sermon by illustrations taken from the life and character of the greatest of all Scotchmen, John Knox.

The use of John Knox, by way of illustration, will not be without advantage to us because it will call up to our mind the world of heroes and mighty deeds which existed before the *Mayflower* sailed. Language has sometimes been used which would almost intimate that modern history began with the Pilgrim Fathers, that the Pilgrims were the pioneers in that great movement which has filled the world with glory. It is wholesome for us to remind ourselves that the Pilgrims were not the creators of the movement but the products of it, and that they came upon the stage of history in the afternoon of an illustrious day. We shall understand them all the better and appreciate them all the more if we first enter fully into the spirit of those intrepid servants of the Lord who, like an army of John the Baptists, cried in the wilderness and prepared the way. 1620 sounds like a far off date, but how comparatively recent it is when compared with 1505, the traditional date of John Knox's birth. John Knox lived a long life, and did his work and was in his grave almost ten years before the first Congregational church was organized. He was in his grave nearly a quarter of a century before the little church was organized in Scrooby, out of which Bradford and Brewster came.

FOREFATHERS' DAY SERMONS

He had been dead a quarter of a century before the Pilgrims left Scrooby for Holland, and almost fifty years elapsed after his death before the Pilgrims turned the prow of the *Mayflower* toward the West. As long a period lies between the cradle in Haddington in which the Scotch baby Knox was rocked, and the sailing of the *Mayflower* as lies between George Washington and Theodore Roosevelt. What a world of effort and achievement and of progress lies between our first President and our last. An equally great world of struggle and achievement lies between the birth of the Scotch Reformer and the sailing of the English Pilgrims. The winds that filled the *Mayflower's* sails had been set loose by the magic hand of heroes who were in their graves when the *Mayflower* sailed. I would not take any of the glory from the Pilgrims' faces, but it is only fair to remember that not a little of this luster is the reflected light from the faces of those tall statured saints of God who in the sixteenth century broke the power of Rome and turned the stream of history into a new channel. Nor did the heroes of the sixteenth century do their work without first receiving inspiration from those who went before them. They braced their hearts and increased their strength by drinking at the fountains which had been opened high up in the hills of God by Wycliffe, Huss and Savonarola.

We have heard much of the Puritan's idiosyncrasies and foibles, of his blemishes and limitations, and whenever such things are mentioned the mind runs naturally to the men of the English commonwealth and to the men of the New England theocracy in the first half of the seventeenth century. But these seventeenth century men were not a whit more peculiar nor was their temper any more defective than was the temper of the Puritans who lived a hun-

STRENGTH AND WEAKNESS OF PURITANISM

dred years before these were born. From the very beginning there were certain traits in the Puritan character which we must confess to be blemishes, and there were certain limitations in the Puritan mind and heart by which their efforts were handicapped and their influence lamentably curtailed. It may be helpful to consider briefly a few of these defects and limitations.

First of all must be mentioned a certain severity of disposition, a tendency to hardness and sternness of heart. Sometimes the sternness was accompanied with somberness, and the somberness not infrequently deepened into gloom. Much can be said, of course, on the other side. The Puritans were not so austere and gloomy as they have sometimes been painted. Life was much more pleasant to them than has been in many quarters imagined. John Knox, for instance, was severe, and yet the Scotchman had a tender heart, so tender that he could not punish his sons without shedding tears. And along with this tenderness there existed an overflowing humor which flashes out again and again in his History of the Reformation, and which illuminated his conversation with his friends down to the last week of his life. But after all has been said concerning the Puritan's sunniness and humor which can be legitimately said, the fact remains that the Puritan temper from first to last was sober, austere and stern. Whether you read the life of William the Silent or of John Calvin, of Coligny or of Cromwell or of John Milton, of Endicott or of Mather or of Sewall, you cannot escape the conviction that these were stern and abnormally sober men. Nor is it to be wondered at that they were, for they lived in sober times. The old world was going to pieces beneath their feet, and a new world was in the process of formation. The sky was filled with thunder clouds and lightning danced

FOREFATHERS' DAY SERMONS

incessantly about their heads. They were engaged in one of the most savage and bloody conflicts in which the human soul has ever put forth its powers. And strange indeed it would have been if with laughing faces they had danced jauntily along their way. No wonder with such a battlefield, beneath such a sky, their hearts lost something of the buoyancy that belongs to the heart, and that their faces took on a stern and somber look by which we are both attracted and repelled. But although we can measure the forces which produced their temper, we must acknowledge that the severity of it was no small defect. Our hearts are not warmed by the biographies of any of the greatest of the Puritans. We admire them but we do not love them, we eulogize them but we are glad that they are dead. It is a significant fact that neither of the two men whom America has seated on the highest thrones was either a Puritan or the son of a Puritan. Washington and Lincoln had a breadth and a sympathy, a mellowness of nature, a sweet and winning humanness which the Puritan character from first to last lacked.

And this hardness of temper was accompanied by a lack of sympathy not only with the larger part of the world that existed around the Puritans in their own day, but especially with the world of the great past. They underestimated the value of tradition and gave little place in their hearts to the sweet memories of the olden days. There had been many beautiful things in the past, but the Puritan turned his back upon them all. There was much that was true in tradition, but he scorned it with fiery scorn. His heart was unresponsive to all appeals from one of the great kingdoms of life. He cut himself off from one of the fountains at which wise men must forever drink. It is not difficult, however, for us to understand just how this came to be.

STRENGTH AND WEAKNESS OF PURITANISM

The immediate past was hideous to the Puritan heart, and rightly so. The church had become one vast sickening mass of hypocrisy and corruption. The priests were in appalling numbers ignorant and foul. Archbishops and Cardinals, not a few, were cruel and avaricious. The Pope was the head of a vast hierarchy of ignorance and superstition. No wonder the Puritans turned away from the sickening spectacle and gazed into the future. It was a common saying that things were bad in Germany, still worse in England, and worst of all in Scotland. In Scotland, therefore, we must expect to find a swift and terrible reaction against the world as it had been. In the consuming flame of fiery indignation the beautiful links by means of which generation is bound to the generation that preceded it were burned up and cast away to the serious impoverishment of the Puritan mind and heart.

And for three hundred years we have been suffering from this same infirmity of temper. The descendants of the Puritans have not yet learned to appreciate at its full value the centuries that have been. The result is a certain shallowness of feeling and a certain contractedness of vision which it should be our earnest ambition speedily to outgrow. It is surprising how little use many of us make of the history of the church universal. Some of us know hardly anything of the Christian church before our own generation. Some of us have read back as far as the Pilgrim Fathers, some of us have even gone back to the Reformation era, but how few of us have plunged into that great period known as the dark ages, and how little do we know of that vast stretch of fifteen hundred years which lies between the death of the apostle John and the nailing of the theses to the old church door in Wittenberg. We simply speak of it all as dark ages, taking it for granted

FOREFATHERS' DAY SERMONS

that it is unworthy of our study. If we should once walk through those distant times we should be amazed to find how much light there was even then. And this also would amaze us, the number of ideas that were thought out then which we ignorantly suppose to be modern. In every century since the days of the apostles God has had his heroes, martyrs, leaders, saints, and all the virtues and the graces have blossomed somewhere in every generation, and in every Christian land. How little we care for this past may be seen by our courses of study in the Bible School. We spend years in the study of the Hebrew church as that history is written for us in the Scriptures, and hardly give one hour to the study of the Christian church, notwithstanding we hold it true that the Holy Spirit was never granted in fullness until the day of Pentecost, and that the Church of Christ has enjoyed a fullness of guidance which was never given to the Church of the Jews. We should have sublimer ideas of the Christian church, and our hearts would be sweeter and more mellow if more frequently we walked down the great cathedral aisle nineteen centuries long, and allowed the subdued light to fall upon us from the pictured windows in which prophets and apostles, saints and heroes like a great cloud of witnesses, speak to us of the high things of the spirit, and encourage us to lay aside every weight and the sin which doth so easily beset us and to run with patience the race that is set before us.

Furthermore, there was in the Puritan disposition a native incapacity to be tolerant toward opinions and people which differed from him. He could never quite bring himself to acknowledge that there can be truth on both sides. To us this is an axiom and a commonplace. We now see that there is always truth on both sides, and that whenever large companies of men array themselves in opposition to

STRENGTH AND WEAKNESS OF PURITANISM

one another in regard to any important matter the truth is not monopolized by one party. In the contest, for instance, between labor and capital there is truth on both sides and error on both sides. In the contest over the tariff there is truth on both sides, otherwise the tariff question would have been settled long ago. In the realm of religion there is truth on both sides. The religions of the Orient are not totally false. There never has been a religion that has won the allegiance of large numbers of men that did not have in it a deposit of truth. But it was hard for the Puritan to see this. His inability to see, it is difficult for us to understand. In the sixteenth and seventeenth centuries he was arrayed against men who, although in possession of much truth, were in possession of such large quantities of falsehood that the truth was sadly overshadowed. There is no doubt that the Puritan was intolerant, and in order to understand his intolerance you must throw yourself back into the environment in the midst of which he lived. Mr. Andrew Lang has recently written a book in which he has given John Knox a bad preëminence in the sin of intolerance. Let us acknowledge the intolerance of the Scotchman, but do not let us forget the forces which contributed to make John Knox what he was. Bear in mind what he saw. Picture to yourself his opponents. Do not forget the things which his antagonists were doing. In England, Bloody Mary was burning men and women to death at the stake, and in the Netherlands the Duke of Alva like an incarnate fiend was subjecting Protestants to torture, the recital of which still causes the world to shudder. And in Spain, Philip II was carrying on his monstrous campaign against the saints of God who dared to lift their voices against the supremacy of the Pope. While in France the tragedy had already begun which culminated

FOREFATHERS' DAY SERMONS

at last in the horrible butchery of St. Bartholomew's. Is it any wonder that the Puritans thought that the truth was on their side and that the father of lies, and the father of lies only, was on the other side? Suppose that you had seen what John Knox saw and suffered what he was called upon to endure! He saw his dearest friend, the man who to him was the purest and noblest man that ever trod the soil of Scotland, burned at the stake. And while George Wishart's body was being consumed in the flames, Cardinal David Beaton and other ecclesiastical dignitaries looked out of their castle windows at the horrible spectacle with complacency and devout satisfaction. For eighteen months Knox had bent over the oars of a galley ship until his health was broken down and infirmities were contracted from which he suffered to the end of his days. He was an exile, he was driven from place to place on the continent, and when at last he came home he was the target of abuse — lied about, hounded, threatened, shot at, execrated. Can you wonder that he was an intolerant man? It is difficult for any one to be tolerant toward a highwayman that has him by the throat. But extenuate the intolerance of the Puritans as we will, this is one of the infirmities of their temper. In every generation they have been prone to feel that they have the truth, the whole truth and nothing but the truth, and to give scant recognition to those who hold diverse opinions and contradictory convictions. That is the Puritan temper all the way from John Endicott down to William Lloyd Garrison and Wendell Phillips.

Not a little of this spirit of intolerance came from the Puritan's conception of the Scriptures. According to the Puritan the Bible was a book of oracles, the oracles of God. God had spoken every word written in the Scriptures, and every word had in it meanings of immeasurable and ever-

STRENGTH AND WEAKNESS OF PURITANISM

lasting significance. It was a solid and an equal book, inspired in its every sentence and its every letter. All the books were on a level: Genesis as high as Matthew, Numbers as high as Mark, Leviticus as valuable as Luke, Ecclesiastes as good as John, Daniel equal to the letters of St. Paul. It was a book that contained in it the law of God. It was a statute book. The judicial regulations of Moses were the laws of the Eternal announced to the Jews and binding on all Christians to the end of time. Whatever was necessary for the human soul to know was contained in the Scriptures, and anything not written in the Scriptures was not worthy of man's serious concern. Such was the conception which the Puritan held of the Bible. How he came to hold this opinion it is not difficult to ascertain. The Roman Catholics drove him into this doctrine of the Bible. For a thousand years religious teachers had made the church the organ of God's will. Through the church and the church only came the divine voice to men. Through the hierarchy as through a channel flowed God's grace into human hearts. Outside the church there was no salvation, and without the church man could not know the will of the Eternal. But little by little the hierarchy became corrupt. Cardinals through their evil living lost the power of hearing the voice of God, and priests ignorant and superstitious mumbled out a message which had no meaning in it. Convinced that the church did not speak the voice of God, and that its sacraments were no longer the channels of his grace, the Puritans turned to the Scriptures, saying: " Here is the message that has come from heaven, to this voice let us pay earnest heed." Against the church of Rome the Puritans set up the Bible. Immediately the Roman Catholic doctors and leaders made war upon this dangerous heresy. " The church is one," they shouted;

and the Puritans replied, "So also is the Bible one, one solid book, every sentence in it equal to every other sentence." The Roman Catholic leaders declared that the church was inspired, that under the inspiration of the Almighty it did its work and carried on its teaching. The reply was: "This book is inspired in every sentence, every word, every syllable." The Roman Catholic leaders said "The church is infallible, it cannot err, it has never erred, it will never err." And the Puritan replied: "This book is infallible, there is no mistake in it, there cannot be one, it is inerrant from first to last." The Roman Catholic leaders declared that the church had authority, divine authority, authority direct from heaven. And the reply from the Puritan was that the Bible is the fountain of authority, that it and it alone can bind the consciences of men, and that from its decisions no soul can appeal and still be guiltless. The Roman Catholics declared that the church knows everything that it is necessary for man to know, and the reply was that the Bible contains everything which it is necessary for man to know. The Catholics said that the church is the appointed ruler and guide of men, ordering men's lives and directing them in their pleasures and their work. The Puritans replied: "The Bible is our guide and teacher, it regulates our coming in and our going out down to the minutest detail." This was the theory of the Scriptures which the Puritan built up in order to meet the audacious claims of the insolent and domineering hierarchy. But the Roman Catholic idea of the church was wrong. From large circles of thoughtful men it passed away long ago, amid explosions and wild terror. To many pious hearts it seemed as though the world was rushing to destruction when men began to question and attack that ancient and erroneous theory. Equally mistaken was the

STRENGTH AND WEAKNESS OF PURITANISM

Puritan conception of the Scriptures. Accept the Puritan conception, and there is no escape from many an absurdity and many a cruelty. Nearly every foolish and terrible thing which the Puritans did was the result of their erroneous conception of the Bible. Each generation brought forth a company of men to defend things that could not be defended, and to set up claims against which the human judgment arose in fiery-eyed opposition and rebellion. It was only about forty years ago that Puritan preachers all over the South and some of them in the North defended slavery as a divine institution, proving it from the Scriptures by citing the fact that God had pronounced a curse on Ham. All of us are completely emancipated from the Roman Catholic doctrine of the church. To us it seems unreasonable, preposterous and dangerous. Not all of us have yet outgrown the Puritan conception of the Scriptures. To many of us the Bible is a perplexity and a problem. We always feel uneasy when the book is mentioned. We do not know what to make of it, or just how much authority to grant unto it. We have never thought our way out into clearness concerning it. And the cause of all our trouble is the fact that we are still entangled in the meshes of the old Puritan conception. John Knox was a Puritan of the Puritans. In his reading of the Bible he took it all as truth and he took it all as law. When they remonstrated with him because of the insulting language which he applied to the Queen even in his prayers, he confidently pointed to the Scriptures, saying: " I have a warrant for my language in the word of God." There is no more pathetic scene in all Knox's life than that presented in the old church at St. Andrew's in the very year before the year of his death, when he stands in the pulpit hurling anathemas at a poor woman accused of witchcraft whom her accusers have placed at the other end of the church. The great reformer having covered her all over with the most scorching language that he could find in the pages of the Old Testament, allows her to be taken out on the following day and burned to death. To such cruelties have good men been led simply by holding wrong ideas of the Bible.

This erroneous conception of the Scriptures led to an impoverishment of public worship. It was an axiom of John Knox's that nothing is divinely sanctioned which was not established by the apostles, and nothing in worship is pleasing to the Eternal or lawful for man except what God has in express words commanded in his Holy Book. It was in this way that the Puritans got rid of the church year. Does the Bible, they said, tell you to keep Christmas? Then don't keep it. Does the Bible command you to observe Easter? Then don't observe it. Does the Bible tell you to commemorate the outpouring of the Holy Spirit? Then don't commemorate it. The whole church year with all its feasts and holy days was exorcised and banished. We can see just how this came about, for the church year had lost its beauty and significance. The Holy days had degenerated into holidays. The Christian calendar was weighted down by a mass of paraphernalia and rubbish blinding to the intelligence and demoralizing to the heart. There were so many saints to be remembered and prayed to that the Lord God of heaven was well-nigh lost sight of. And thus the church year had become a nuisance and a curse, and the Puritans put it boldly into the fire. But there is a use of the church year which is both legitimate and beneficial, and such a use is gradually coming back. The annual commemoration of the great truths and facts of the Christian revelation is a means of grace

STRENGTH AND WEAKNESS OF PURITANISM

to the Christian heart. The historical basis of the Christian religion is a series of colossal facts entirely independent of any theories or interpretations which may be woven around them, or of any theological systems which may be built upon them. The birth of Jesus, the temptation of Jesus, the passion of Jesus, the death of Jesus, the resurrection of Jesus, the ascension of Jesus, the coming at Pentecost of the Holy Ghost, these are the cardinal facts in the history of redemption. And before these facts a man should sit down once every year, and let them make upon his soul whatever impression they can and will. It is not well that a minister should be left on every Sunday to select his theme after his own caprice and inclination. Certain days of the year should have the right of dictation and should tell the minister what it is that he and his people are to think about. In this way he is saved from monotony, and his people are carried out through wider ranges of experience and of thought. And because this is true the church year after an exile of several hundred years is making its way back to the place which rightly exists for it. Christmas has come back and so has Easter. The Day of Pentecost will also come back, and so will Ascension Day, and so will Advent. Holy Week has already come back with its Palm Sunday and its Good Friday. Now that the Christian year has been cleansed and reconsecrated, why should it not come back to help us all in the way of life?

And it was the Puritans who banished kneeling also from the Christian church. Christians for centuries had been trained to kneel at the sacrament of the Lord's Supper. But the Lord's Supper in the course of time had become the mass, and the mass in the hands of sensual and ignorant men became idolatry, and to the Puritan mind and conscience it was idolatry in its most heinous form. They

FOREFATHERS' DAY SERMONS

would not kneel before the wafer, and little by little all kneeling vanished from the Puritan churches. Men and women stood up when they said their prayers, and later on they sat down with hushed hearts and bowed heads, and later on they sat boldly upright, the body refusing to show in its posture any consciousness of reverence and dependence. And so it has come to pass that the worst church manners in Christendom are to be found inside of Puritan churches. If the Roman Catholic church had no other blessing to give to the world but this, it would be rendering a service worthy of lasting gratitude if it did nothing more than train men to kneel. It is an inspiration to worship God in any church in which the spirit of reverence is still alive and manifests itself in the attitude and posture of those who pray.

But with all his limitations the Puritan was a mighty man. Make the list of his defects as long as you can and the list of his virtues is still longer. If we criticise him, let us never forget to praise him. The world will never forget him because his supreme desire on earth was to know the will of the Eternal. This was the passion that burned in his heart with fervent heat from first to last, making glorious the entire record of his life. "O that I knew where I might find him, that I might come even to his seat." This was the constant cry of his noble spirit, and the very loftiness of his aspiration separated him from other men. No one can ever understand him, or do justice to him, who has not known what it is to long to know the will of God. The idlers will never be able to understand him, nor the loafers, nor the shallow spectators of the world. Only men of earnest spirit and eager to understand the plan of the Almighty can ever come close enough to him to grasp the secret of his strength. Worldly-minded men in love with the surface of things have had much to say about the awful rudeness

STRENGTH AND WEAKNESS OF PURITANISM

of the Puritan, his barbarous destructiveness and the ferocity with which he destroyed works of art and trampled under his feet some fine specimens of noble architecture. But there are some things in this world more precious far than the colors of a picture or the carving of a doorway. The soul of man is worth infinitely more than anything which genius has ever yet created, and if in order to liberate the soul of man it becomes necessary to destroy the work of human hands, let the sacrifice be made without regret and without complaining. There are those who never think or speak of General Sherman without dwelling upon the barns which he burned and the dwellings which he destroyed on his march from Atlanta to the sea. But the men who loved the Union, and wished to save the Union from destruction, will never let the smoke of the burning buildings blind their eyes to the fact that Sherman cut the confederacy in two. He knew that war was hell, and said so, but sometimes gigantic evils cannot be crushed without the destruction of the temple in which the evils have built their shrine. John Knox was not responsible for all the iconoclasm in Scotland in the sixteenth century. Much of the destruction was carried on by what he called the "rascal multitude." Scotchmen, long deceived and abused by the Roman church, when once their eyes were opened, could not be restrained from acts which we in these cooler and gentler times find it impossible to justify. But while Knox did not create the spirit which broke the images to pieces, he shed no tears over the shattered granite, so deeply interested was he in the liberation of the soul. There was much truth in his famous saying: "If you do not want the rooks to return, you must pull down their nests."

But to the Puritan the end of life was not knowledge but action. His supreme ambition was not simply to know

FOREFATHERS' DAY SERMONS

the will of God, but to do it. He believed that it belongs to men to establish God's kingdom here upon the earth, and it was that belief of his which made him so exceedingly uncomfortable to many of his contemporaries. A man may desire to know the will of God and still be able to live at peace with his neighbors, but let a man start out to do God's will and to persuade other men to do it, and to build that will into the structure of the Church and State, and he kindles at once a conflagration on the earth. No more practical men than the Puritans ever lived. God is sovereign and it is his right to rule in private life and social life and political life. The State must be Christian. We sometimes speak of the Puritan preachers as being doctrinal — doctrinal they were as all the great preachers have ever been and must ever be. But they did not stop at doctrine; they went on to apply the doctrine to the institutions and people of their day. The thing that delighted John Knox in Geneva was not the doctrine preached, but the superb way in which the doctrine was expressed in the lives of the people. "I neither fear," he said, "nor am ashamed to say that Geneva is the most perfect school of Christ that ever was on the earth since the days of the apostles. In other places I confess Christ to be truly preached, but manners and religion so truly formed I have not yet seen in any other place." In his own preaching he was ever intensely practical. Like all the great Puritans he laid his strong hands on human institutions to mould them so far as possible into forms which would please the King. We have a description of his preaching when he was old and partially incapacitated by a stroke of paralysis. Near the close of his life he was exiled from Edinburgh, spending several months in St. Andrew's. He was weary of the world, and described himself as being half dead, but half dead

STRENGTH AND WEAKNESS OF PURITANISM

though he was he was still able to move the souls of men. James Melville was at that time a student in St. Andrew's and used to go to hear him preach. He has told us how two servants lifted the old preacher into the pulpit. " In the opening of his text," says Melville, " he was moderate for the space of half an hour, but when he entered to application, he made me so to thrill and tremble that I could not hold a pen to write." " God give me Scotland, or I die," — that was the great burning, thrilling cry that vibrated in every sermon. And because these men desired to know the will of God and did their utmost to do it on the earth, the laurel will never wither on their brow.

In one of the squares of the City of Edinburgh there stands a statue of Charles II, and near the pedestal there is a worn slab in the pavement of the street bearing the simple inscription: " J. K. 1572." The statue and the slab are not without pathos and suggestiveness. The statue of the English king catches and holds the eye. In his life he was handsome and picturesque, and the world will always take delight in looking at him. He was dressed in soft raiment and lived in kings' houses, and his laces and ribbons made him interesting to many people of his day, as to many people since. But the burning Scotchman was not a Potentate. He was nothing but a prophet of the Lord. It is fitting that Charles II should have the statue, and that Knox's only monument should be a worn slab in the pavement of the street. Let the old slab lie there. It is more eloquent than any statue. It speaks to us of one who along with others threw up the splendid highway upon whose granite slabs the hoofs of the steeds of the chariot of progress make music in our ears, and along whose upward slope civilization thunders and flashes in its surprising and glorious career.

IX

THE PURITAN THEOLOGY [1]

"*I saw the Lord sitting upon a throne, high and lifted up.*" — ISAIAH 5 : 1.

The Puritans had more to do with the building of our modern world than any other body of men who have lived since the days of the Apostles. The marks of their influence are everywhere. They have left their impress on the structure of our Republic, they have left a deeper imprint on the fiber of our church. Our exterior life bears witness to the force of their example. We men wear our hair short because of the fashion set by the Puritans. Before the day of the Puritans, English gentlemen wore their hair long and curled. We men prefer sober colors in our clothing because that was the taste of the Puritans. Before the Puritans set a quieter fashion, the gentlemen of England dressed in colors which were brilliant and gaudy. Upon our interior life the Puritans have left their stamp still more indelibly. They have moulded our vocabulary, giving certain words a luster which they have never lost. They have furnished us with many of our ideals and dominant conceptions. The pressure of their spirit is on our spirit. They are the men best worth knowing of all the men who have lived within the last thousand years.

We need to know them in order to appreciate and understand the world in which we are living. In many kingdoms of our life there are things which cannot be interpreted, or fairly dealt with, or profited by, unless we know something of the ideals, the temper and the achievements of

[1] Dec. 17, 1911.

THE PURITAN THEOLOGY

the seventeenth century Puritans. Let us think this morning about the Puritan Theology.

Theology is the science of religion. A science is the intellectual interpretation or exposition of a certain group of related phenomena. For instance, the starry heavens present a spectacle upon which the mind goes to work. Those moving points of light excite the curiosity. What are they? why do they move? why do they move with varying speeds? why do some of them change their relative positions while others do not? how are they related? and what are their magnitudes and distances? For all these questions, the mind seeks answers. The result of the study is a series of interpretations and conclusions, and this product of the intellect is known as the science of astronomy. The reality is the sidereal heavens, and the science of astronomy is the account which the mind gives to itself of its work among the stars.

We have round us a plant world. This world contains trees and shrubs, flowers and grasses and lichens and mosses. Upon this mass of growing things the mind goes to work. It analyzes, arranges, classifies. It traces processes and ferrets out relations. It writes a statement of what it finds, giving it a shape which will satisfy the reason. This intellectual presentation of what the mind thinks of the world of plants is called the science of botany. The plant world is the reality and botany is the intellectual interpretation of it.

Man turns his eye upon himself. He studies humanity. He notes that everywhere men are religious animals. Everywhere and in every time they feel after unseen powers. They have the sense of weakness and of guilt. They offer prayers, perform acts of penance, build temples, set up forms of worship. They obtain a sense of relief, and are conscious of augmented strength and joy. These are phenomena of religion, and the mind goes to work upon them in order to define them and relate them and ascertain their significance. The reaching after some one above himself, the hunger for something this world does not contain, the sense of sin and the assurance of forgiveness, these are data with which the intellect must deal, and the resulting conclusions constitute the science of theology. Christian theology is the exposition of the phenomena of religion viewed in the light of the consciousness of Jesus Christ, and using his words and deeds, his life and death, as primary media for obtaining a deeper insight into the nature and laws of the spiritual world. It is the intellectual statement of what God is and of what man is as seen through Jesus of Nazareth.

There is a prejudice against theology in many quarters, deep-rooted and sometimes bitter. One finds it not only among men who are experts in other sciences, but also in the man in the street. Not only do unbelievers jeer at theology, but so do also many professed disciples of Jesus Christ and members of his church. Theology, it is assumed, is a mischievous and debilitating science, quite unworthy of a place among the physical and social sciences which are the pride and glory of our generation.

By many intelligent persons it is assumed that theology is useless, and that time spent upon it is worse than wasted. "**Don't** bother yourself about theology, do your duty and let theology go," such is the brave advice often given, and many deem it wise. But is theology after all a needless science? How can man live without theology? He cannot go without a theology unless he refuses to think. Let him think, even a little, about the phenomena of religion and he begins at once to become a theologian. The product

THE PURITAN THEOLOGY

of his thinking is theology. If you think about the stars you are bound to have astronomy, and if you think about the flowers you are certain to have botany, and if you think about God and sin and duty and destiny you cannot escape theology. When men say, therefore, that they do not believe in theology they are really saying that they do not believe that men ought to think about the highest class of phenomena which comes within the scope of human observation. You may think about the stars, and about the flowers, about the rocks and about the beetles, but you need not think about prayer or the sense of sin or the efforts of the soul to find strength and peace. All thought about the highest experiences of human beings is altogether useless! How strange that men can bring themselves to so foolish a conclusion. I can imagine a frog sitting on a starry night on the edge of a pond, saying to himself: " I see no sense in the science of astronomy. Why do men worry themselves about nebulæ and eclipses and comets? What is the use of wasting time in trying to find out the cause of heat in the sun, or the character of the surface of the moon? As for me, I like to sit here bathed in starlight, never puzzling my head about the problems which torment the astronomer's brain. I think it is enough simply to sit here and croak!" I can imagine a cow, browsing contentedly in a field, saying to herself: " What care I for botany? The clover is sweet and I do not want it explained. If now and then I get a buttercup or daisy I gulp it down along with the clover. What interest do I take in sepals and petals, in stamens and pistils, or in any of these new-fangled notions about the functions of insects in the fertilization of flowers? I despise all your sciences. I just eat!" But man belongs to a different order of being. He is intrusted with a mind. He is capable of thinking

FOREFATHERS' DAY SERMONS

God's thoughts after him and entering into his plans. If he does not care to think about the highest objects of thought, then he has abdicated the position to which he was called and has thrown away one of the brightest jewels in his crown!

There are others who think that theology is an antiquated science. It may have been at one time the queen of the sciences, but its glory has departed. It is a belated and benighted science with which ages of progress can have nothing to do. That brilliant Frenchman, Auguste Comte, the founder of the Positivist Philosophy, was always saying that humanity passes through three stages in its mastery of the world. The first stage is theological, the second is metaphysical, the third is positive. In the theological stage, man searches for causes, while in the positive stage he is a student of laws. It is not until you outgrow the theological and pass into the positive that the world takes a leap forward. That is the opinion of many who have never read the books of Auguste Comte.

The reason why theology is counted by many a discredited science is because of the blunders and errors of theologians who lived long ago. It is easy to make a collection of absurd theories and ridiculous deductions and cruel doctrines, and by means of these prove that theology is a dangerous science and that theologians are rightfully classed among the foes of progress. But is this fair? Is theology the only science which has gone astray? Are theologians the only men who have been caught in error? What science can escape if we compel it to face its past? One of the noblest of modern sciences is astronomy, but what a record astronomy has to answer for. Astrological astronomy was full of superstition, farther from the truth

THE PURITAN THEOLOGY

than any system of Christian theology has been, but no one now looks askance at astronomy. Astrological astronomy was followed by Ptolemaic astronomy, which was a strange hodge-podge of fanciful conjectures and specious error. To make the earth the center of the universe and set all the stars revolving around it is riduculous enough to us now, but for thousands of years it was the best conception which the very noblest minds could attain. No one, I think, wants to stone the astronomers of our day because of what astronomers taught a thousand years ago. Why, then, pelt theologians with disparaging epithets because of blunders committed by their predecessors long since turned to dust in their graves?

Another count in the arraignment of theology is that it is an airy science, dealing in speculations and vagaries, and built largely on clouds. But this again is a misconception. Theology deals with facts, solid and incontrovertible as any of the facts with which other sciences have to do. The facts of the spiritual world are not a whit less substantial than are the facts of the physical world. The cravings and aspirations of the heart are as truly facts as the constellations. That man prays and finds satisfaction in prayer is as certain as it is that the oceans roll on their beds. That Jesus of Nazareth died on the cross is as incontrovertible as that Demosthenes stirred the Greeks to march against Philip, and that Cæsar conquered Gaul. To be sure there is a speculative element in theology as there is in every science. The hypothetical and the conjectural cannot be eliminated from any science. It is by means of hypothesis and observation and deduction that every science progresses. Again and again it happens that the hypothesis is not sustained, the observation is not wide enough, and the deduction is erroneous. For this

[151]

FOREFATHERS' DAY SERMONS

reason every science has two elements, the permanent and the transient. But all sciences alike deal with reality.

It is often tauntingly said that theology is autocratic and conceited, claiming to have reached conclusions, all of which are final, and therefore, theology, unlike other sciences, is stationary and cannot interest men who believe in everlasting progress. The accusation is a calumny. There have been theologians quite too dogmatic and omniscient, but this foible is not confined to the theologians. No science has had a monopoly of dogmatism and conceit. Everybody who reads church history knows that theology has never been stationary, and that from the nature of the case it never can be. Like all other sciences it is always changing, and progresses with the unfolding of human thought. A glance through the volume of Harnack's History of Dogma will satisfy any one that theology is not a stationary science, and a survey of New England theology reveals that Calvinism was always being restated, modified, improved, to meet the demands of the Christian conscience and reason. The theology of Jonathan Edwards is somewhat different as worked out by Samuel Hopkins, and different still in the writings of Nathaniel Emmons, and modified again in the volumes of Nathaniel William Taylor, and again recast in the lectures of Edward A. Park. That theology is a cast-iron thing, fixed and forevermore the same, cramping the mind of those who devote themselves to it, is one of the chimeras of the uninformed imagination. Like every other science, theology may, for a season, be arrested in its development, but soon or late it obeys the principle of progress, and moves on to new positions.

In studying the Puritan theology we are studying an intellectual statement of Christianity which has lost its sway over the modern mind. The theology of the

THE PURITAN THEOLOGY

Puritans was Calvinism. How the Puritans of England fell under the sway of Calvin is an interesting page of history. It was in 1534 that Henry VIII, by the Act of Supremacy, was declared to be head of the English church, and England's final break with Rome was consummated. Only two years later a young Frenchman, twenty-seven years old, brought out a volume of theology known as Calvin's Institutes. Exiled from Paris, the youthful theologian made his way to Geneva, where, for twenty-five years, with one brief interruption, he promulgated his ideas to the world. Whatever one may think of Calvinism, he is bound to acknowledge that John Calvin is one of the most remarkable characters of history. An emaciated semi-invalid, he worked with almost superhuman strength, stamping his ideas not only on Geneva but on a considerable portion of Europe. His eyes blazed with a piercing fire and his mind was as keen as a Damascus blade. Through the reign of Edward VI, Calvin was in correspondence with the leaders in English politics, and Cranmer and many others were mightily influenced by him. When Mary came to the throne, she, under the Roman Catholic influence of Spain, adopted a policy intended to bring England back under the power of Rome. It was the old policy of persecution. She began to burn at the stake those who resisted the Roman Catholic program, and in her short reign of five and a half years nearly three hundred Protestants were put to death. Thousands of Englishmen fled to the continent for their life, among them hundreds of clergymen. Many of these found their way to Geneva, where Calvin was now at the zenith of his fame and power. Sometimes he had a thousand students at his feet. The world has known few such teachers. He had a genius for building his ideas into the minds of those who listened to him. On

FOREFATHERS' DAY SERMONS

the death of Bloody Mary, the refugees returned to England, carrying back the theology of Calvin. It was the radicals who had fled to Geneva, and it was the radicals everywhere who had listened most gladly to the Calvinistic doctrines. It is noteworthy that all the Separatists were Calvinists, all the Presbyterians, all the Baptists, all the Independents and Congregationalists, all the Pilgrim Fathers, all the colonists of Massachusetts were steeped in the doctrines of John Calvin. There was something in Calvinism that made it congenial to ardent and liberty-loving hearts, but it also won converts in classes widely separated from the Puritans. Parker, the Archbishop of Canterbury, was a stubborn opponent of the Puritans and at the same time a Calvinist; so was Archbishop Grindall, and so also was Archbishop Whitgift, one of the most implacable of all the enemies of Puritanism and one of the stoutest defenders of Calvinistic doctrines. He was one of the authors in 1595 of the Lambeth articles, one of the stiffest pieces of Calvanism ever put forth as a symbol of faith. These facts, if borne in mind, will save us from a blunder often made, the blunder of identifying Puritanism and Calvinism. It has often been taken for granted that Calvinists and Puritans are one and the same people, that Calvinism is Puritanism and that Puritanism is Calvinism. The two are to be distinguished. Puritanism is a spirit, and Calvinism is a theology which Puritanism made use of in working out its destiny. Puritanism is a reform movement, and Calvinism is a weapon which the reform movement wielded in fighting its battles. But the two are distinct. All Puritans were Calvinists, but not all Calvinists were Puritans. The Puritan spirit was in the world long before Calvin was born, and this spirit remains after Calvinism has been discarded.

THE PURITAN THEOLOGY

The Puritans of the seventeenth century, however, were Calvinists and so were the New England Puritans of the eighteenth. The men who in 1646 formulated the Westminster Confession of Faith were uncompromising Calvinists. Two years later when the Congregational churches of New England felt the time had come to issue a declaration of faith, they wrote this in the preface of what is known in church history as the Cambridge Platform: " The Synod having perused and considered the Confession of Faith published of late by the Reverend Assembly in England, do judge it to be very holy, orthodox and judicious in all matters of faith: and do therefore freely and fully consent thereunto, for the substance thereof." The only points on which the Congregationalists of the New World differed from the Presbyterians of the Old World were points of church government. In all matters of doctrine they were one. In 1658 the representatives of one hundred and twenty Congregational churches of England met in the Savoy palace in London and formulated what is known as the " Savoy Declaration." This is one of the famous creeds of Congregationalism. It accepts the doctrine of the Westminster Confession, and then sets forth the Congregational ideas of church government. In 1680 the Boston Synod adopted the Savoy Declaration as the creed of our American churches. This position was reaffirmed by the Saybrook Platform issued in 1708. All through the eighteenth century and through more than half of the nineteenth century, Calvinism was the professed theology of the Congregational churches of America. Little by little, however, both ministers and laymen fell away from the old Calvinistic interpretations, and when, in 1865, the representatives of our churches met in Plymouth, Massachusetts, and put forth what is known as the

FOREFATHERS' DAY SERMONS

Burial Hill Declaration of Faith, it was deemed inexpedient to introduce into that declaration a statement recommended by the committee, to the effect that " our churches still adhere to that body of doctrines known as Calvinism." Allegiance to the past was expressed in more general and elastic phrases, making room in American Congregationalism for all those who were no longer Calvinists. When the committee of our National Council formulated the creed of 1883, the Calvinistic tone and complexion were completely wanting, and when in 1906, in the city of Dayton, a creed was agreed upon by the representatives of our own denomination and two others seeking a basis of union, there was in it of Calvinism not a trace. So far, then, as our denomination is concerned, the Puritan theology may be said to have passed away. We are living in a new age, and the new wine cannot be poured into the old skins.

When one picks up a volume of any one of the Puritan theologians, either Owen or Baxter or Howe, Edwards or Hopkins or Taylor, he is impressed first of all by the Biblico-argumentative character of the discussion. Puritan theology is a mixture of Bible sentences and logic. Every argument begins with the Bible. A principle announced in the Scriptures is seized upon and its contents are unfolded, by a process of reasoning rigorous to a degree. At certain points in the progress a pause is made for the contemplation of certain texts which prove that the movement is in the right direction and that it has the sanction of the Bible. When at last the conclusion is reached, another collection of proof texts is presented to demonstrate that the conclusion is none other than the mind of God. The structure is built by the reason, but it is all made to rest upon Scripture. The argument is unfolded in the strictest

THE PURITAN THEOLOGY

and most logical manner, and from the final decisions there is apparently no possible escape.

To understand the complexion of Puritan theology it is necessary to understand the sixteenth century and the three centuries which preceded it. The mediæval church subordinated both the Bible and the reason to the church, and by church was meant the hierarchy of Rome. Whatever the church said was truth, and was to be accepted without argument or question. The church claimed absolute authority over men's conscience and reason. Nothing could be preached which did not have the sanction of the conclave of ecclesiastics in Rome. No book could be given the world that did not have the approval of the ecclesiastical censors. No opinion in science or philosophy was tolerated that did not commend itself to the Pope. It was he who could determine what the Scriptures taught, and the laity were to accept their religious opinions at the mouth of the church without investigation. In this way credulity was made synonymous with faith, and all sorts of superstition were foisted on men in the name of religion. With the Bible closed and reason in chains Europe sank into degradation and darkness. When at last men were found brave enough to question the decisions of Popes and Councils and to defy the threats of the church, it was natural that they should fall back on the Scriptures and the reason. Calvin, especially, exalted the Scriptures, proclaiming them the authoritative declaration of God's will, and along with the belief in the Scriptures he had profound confidence in the ability of the enlightened Christian man to read the Bible for himself. The followers of Calvin built on these two principles, the authority of the Scriptures and the right of individual judgment. Wherever men accepted these two principles, they were always quoting Scripture, and were always reasoning about it as though the reason were a faculty not to be banished from the realm of faith. When Rome said, " Listen to the church," the Puritan said, " Listen to the Bible." When Rome said, " The church has all authority," the Puritan replied, " Our only authority is the Bible." When Rome said, " The church is infallible," the reply was, " There is no infallible authority but the Scriptures." When Rome said, " Take what I give and ask no questions," the Puritan said, " I cannot accept anything except as my conscience allows." It was in this way that the Puritans were driven into a conception of the Bible which got them into numberless embarrassments, and which has caused their descendants no end of trouble. One extreme begets another. Rome's exaggerated doctrine of the church forced the Puritan to accept an untenable doctrine of Biblical inspiration. Puritan theology is too confident of the trustworthiness of argument, and blunders constantly in its uses of the Scriptures.

A second characteristic of Puritan theology is its inwardness. It moves down deep in an inner world. It is morbidly introspective, abnormally analytical. The Puritan theologians were experts in analysis. Whatever they touched was divided and subdivided and then divided several times again. They had a fondness for tracing relations, and a passion for subtle distinctions. They saw that the decrees of God are of different kinds and they delighted in showing the distinction between different kinds of faith, and between various kinds of grace. The spiritual processes of salvation were traced with microscopic thoroughness, and every movement of the soul was labeled and catalogued. The differences between justification and conversion, and between conversion and regeneration,

THE PURITAN THEOLOGY

and between regeneration and sanctification, these were matters of cardinal importance to be unfolded in sermons and elaborated in books. Puritan theologians became specialists in metaphysics and dialectics. To dissect and classify all the contents of the soul was their joy. In this way they became fearfully prolix. There is no end to their writing. When we open their ponderous volumes we are appalled by their teeming amplifications and the stupefying luxuriance of their psychological diagnoses and fine-spun distinctions. To the modern mind the masterpieces of Puritan theology are insufferably dull.

This inwardness of Puritan theology was the result of the rebound of the human mind from the externalism of the mediæval church. From the fourth century onward to the sixteenth, religion had become increasingly a ceremony and pageant. The worship was made more and more elaborate and ornate. Rite was added to rite, form was built upon form, until Christian worship, once so simple, became gorgeously complex. Splendid robes, blazing candles, swinging censers, holy pictures, processions, crucifixes, relics, pilgrimages, bowings, genuflexions, prostrations, nothing so splendidly elaborate had ever been seen before upon the earth. It was ritualism run to seed, formalism grown rank and deadly. When the revolt came, it was certain to be extreme. Lutheranism was a revolt against the externalism of the Roman church, but Calvinism was a revolt more intense. Luther was born in a pious Catholic home, all his teachers were devout Catholics, and he himself for several years was a faithful monk in an Augustinian Monastery. He never quite escaped the education of these early years. There was much in Roman Catholic worship which he liked. He liked pictures and images, crucifixes and candles, and he could never altogether get away from

FOREFATHERS' DAY SERMONS

the literal interpretation of the words, "This is my body." He had a poetic nature. The mystical element in him was strong. It was impossible for him to feel toward Roman worship as did the French lawyer, John Calvin. Calvin looked upon Roman Catholic worship as an abomination. Everything about it was corrupt. It was only paganism intruding itself into the Christian church, and making on its forehead the sign of the cross. Looking on the whole mass of Roman ceremonies and observances, he said: "Take them away! They are tomfoolery. They are idolatry. When did Jesus and the apostles ever authorize such trumpery as this? Take them all away!" And away they were taken. Under the influence of Calvin, Christianity became severely intellectual and spiritual. The sensuous element in worship was cut out. No appeal whatever must be made to the senses. God is spirit and they who worship him must worship him in spirit.

It was thus that Puritanism plunged into the soul. The formal and the external had fascination no longer. The world of color and form was not to be compared with that inner world where the spirit of man communes with his Maker. The mind was turned in on itself. Men began to watch themselves, to analyze themselves, and to keep a record of their thoughts and feelings. Instead of elaborating ceremonies they now elaborated ideas; instead of amplifying things physical they now amplified doctrines; instead of taking delight in the pageantry of the cathedral they stood awe-struck in the temple of their own soul. Man is a pendulum, and swings between extremes. The church of the Middle Ages was too formal and external, the Puritans became too intellectual and retrospective.

The dominating ideas of Puritan theology are three: First, the sovereignty of God. On this everything else in

THE PURITAN THEOLOGY

Puritanism is built. From this everything else flows. The Puritan saw the Lord sitting on a throne, high and lifted up. He was a king, a monarch, a ruler. He issued decrees. Men were his subjects and he ruled them with a will that could not be changed. Whom he chose to save, he saved, whom he did not choose was lost. He was the God of the Old Testament. He was the high and holy God of Isaiah, the great and terrible God of Nehemiah, the God of the Psalmist who is angry with the wicked every day. The Puritans were driven to the Old Testament for direction in regard to the management of affairs of state, and it was thus that their conception of the Almighty was taken from the Old Testament rather than from the New.

The second dominant idea was the unworthiness of man. He is helpless. He is sinful. He is vile. He deserves nothing at the hands of God. The fall of man occupies a central place in Puritan theology. The depravity of the soul is one of the fundamental doctrines. The conception of man was taken largely from the Old Testament. Favorite Puritan texts were: " I abhor myself." " Woe is me, because I am a man of unclean lips." " I am a worm." " I am vile." " I was shapen in iniquity; and in sin did my mother conceive me." " From the sole of the foot even unto the head there is no soundness in it; but wounds, and bruises, and festering sores." Man, a sinner, lying helpless at the foot of God, that is the very core of Puritan theology.

One thing more, however, must be added, the greatness of the soul. Man is vile because he has fallen, he is helpless because he has sinned. But in the beginning he was created in God's image, and through God's will this image can be restored. Paradise was lost, but it can be regained. Man, therefore, has a great work to do. He is an instrument which the Almighty designs to use. He is a servant whom the great God sends upon his errands. He has, therefore, the protection of God, and God will see to it that his servant's work shall be accomplished. Man is accountable to God. To him he answers for his belief and for his conduct. Let priests, therefore, stand back. Let kings also stand aside. No matter who he is, every man has access to the King of kings and the Lord of lords and is responsible to him alone. It is here that you get Calvinism at its best. Calvinism lays hold of man and lifts him above the heads of priest, bishop, archbishop, cardinal, Pope, and leaves him face to face with God. It carries him above the heads of statesman, prince, king, emperor, potentate, and tells him he has to do only with God. With the coming of that vision modern liberty was born. It was the belief that every man stands alone before God that made the American Republic possible.

The Puritan theology has ceased to sway the mind of our churches. The theology of the twentieth century repudiates much that the seventeenth century held dear. We take our conception of God not from the Old Testament but from the New, not from Moses but from Jesus. Jesus believed that God is King, but he is a Father-King. He is omnipotent, but he has a father's heart. He is majestic, but it is the majesty of tenderness. He is august, but it is the augustness of compassion. God has many attributes but the deepest thing in him is his fatherhood. We are his children. He owes and gives us a father's love. Our God is the God and Father of our Lord Jesus Christ.

We get our conception of man also from Jesus. We believe that man is a sinner, but we do not believe that the deepest thing in him is his sin. He is by nature not a child of the devil but a child of God. When he comes to himself he arises and goes to his father. Sin, then, is an

THE PURITAN THEOLOGY

intruder. Transgression is unnatural. The roots of man's being are not corrupt. The essence of human life is divine.

We accept all that the Puritans believed concerning the greatness and worth of the soul, and we have a new apprehension of the worth of society. Calvinism was individualistic in its philosophy and we are increasingly socialistic. We are interested more and more in the social aspects of religion. It is not enough for a man to answer where he is, he must also give answer as to the whereabouts of his brother. It is not enough to love God, we are bound also to love men. The theology of Bunyan's Pilgrim's Progress has been outgrown. Christian started from the City of Destruction and his chief desire was to get himself into the City of God. He did not think of those around him. The modern Christian knows that he cannot get into the eternal city unless he takes some one with him. To Bunyan this world was a city doomed to destruction: to us it is the subject of redemption and is going to be transformed into the city of God. The world is not a wrecked vessel destined to go down, only a few elect individuals to be saved from the wreck, but the vessel, though wrecked, is to be saved and is to come into the harbor with a redeemed race on its decks. It is because of this new conception that the world is full of dreams and schemes of social betterment. Everywhere Christians are planning and working to make a better world. Never has the missionary movement been so mighty as it is today, and never before have there been so many Christians interested in social, political and industrial reform. Men are organizing against the saloon, against gambling, against oppression of the wage-earner, against militarism and war. We are coming to believe that this is God's world and that there is nothing evil in it which cannot be pulled down.

FOREFATHERS' DAY SERMONS

Our new theology is in part due to our new conception of the Scriptures. The Puritan idea of the Bible has gone forever. That idea was that the Bible is a solid book, made of a single piece, equally valuable in its every part. All its books are equally inspired and every sentence expresses the clear and final word of God. That idea has been driven out by the idea of development. We now see that everything progresses, including revelation itself. The illumination of the Hebrew mind was progressive. Prophets and lawgivers spake in divers manners and with different degrees of knowledge and authority. We do not reach the supreme light until we come to Jesus. He is the only one to whom we are to listen for the final word. All the moralities of the Old Testament must stand before the judgment seat of Christ. Everything contrary to his spirit is not according to the mind of God. And thus we are saved from the perplexities of our fathers. They were always defending indefensible things in the Scriptures, or apologizing for things which shocked the Christian conscience. We do not apologize for or defend these things. We simply drop them out. We care for them no longer. They are not God's word to us. We point to Jesus, saying: " Here is God's well beloved Son, hear ye him."

Has, then, the Puritan theology passed away? If by Puritan theology you mean the five points of Calvinism, the answer must be, Yes. Particular predestination, limited atonement, natural inability, irresistible grace, the perseverance of the saints, these are doctrines no longer preached from the pulpit, and if they were preached, no one would care to hear them. The intellectual forms of one age will never satisfy its successor. Every generation must formulate its own theology. The Puritans thought out theirs and we must think out ours. But the soul of

THE PURITAN THEOLOGY

Puritan theology can never pass away. The power of this theology lay in its three dominant visions: the vision of the majesty and holiness and sovereignty of God, the unworthiness and impotence and sinfulness of man, and the immeasurable worth and high destiny of the human soul. Calvinism in its fundamental doctrines has passed into the blood of the Christian church, there to remain forever.

It is easy to criticise the thought of men who lived three hundred years ago, and to make merry with their errors and their limitations, but before you jeer at the Puritan theology, remember the kind of men it made and the mighty victories it won. It passed like great drops of iron into the blood of men, turning their faces to flint and their weakness into the strength of Titans. It made Calvin and enabled him to convert the little Republic of Geneva into a School of Morals for all Europe. It made John Knox and enabled him to stand up against Queen Mary and to convert half-civilized Scotland into one of the ruling countries of the world. It braced the heart of William the Silent and made half-drowned Holland unconquerable by all the power of Spain. It filled the soul of Cromwell and made it possible for him to fling from the English throne a king who believed he had a divine right to govern wrong. It set up on the ruins of monarchy a commonwealth, and broke forever the power of the traditions of despotism on English soil. It sustained the hearts of the Christian fathers on their long and desolate voyage across the Atlantic, and it inspired them to write their immortal compact in the cabin of the Mayflower. The initial words are, " In the name of God, Amen." It was when that line was written that American history really began. It nerved men in the wilderness to believe that there could be a Church without a bishop and a State without a king. If it be true, as

FOREFATHERS' DAY SERMONS

Jesus says, that by their fruits we are to judge, then by the fruits of the Puritan theology we must conclude there was something in it more than error, and more than the idle speculations of narrow and benighted minds.

One of our greatest debts to the Puritans is that they taught us the value of clear thinking on the data of religion. They believed in theology and made it the queen of all the sciences. The queen it must evermore remain. It is a strange notion which has seized certain persons that it matters not what one thinks, and that life is not influenced by what one believes. The Puritans were incapable of entertaining a notion so preposterous. Everything in the long run depends on what men think. Ideas are forces, and they are the ruling forces of the world. The world's conduct is moulded by the world's belief, and the church's life is marred or strengthened by its theology. One of the weaknesses of the modern pulpit is that it is not theological enough. It does not deal sufficiently with the intellectual interpretation of the great facts of religion. It is not enough for preachers to expect men to read the Bible. Men must know what the Bible is, and why it is worth reading, and what reasons there are for thinking it contains a message which the human race would do well to heed. A man who thinks is bound to have a doctrine of inspiration. It is not enough to urge men to believe on Jesus, and leave the matter there. They must know who Jesus is, and why it is important to listen to what he says. It is not enough to persuade men to accept the fact of Jesus' death. Everything depends on the interpretation of that event. What connection had that death with you? In what relation does it stand to the race of men? What place has that death in God's government of this world? It is only by interpreting the fact of the death of Jesus that one gets

THE PURITAN THEOLOGY

out of it an energy to brace the heart in the days of trouble, and a force to curb the power and cleanse the guilt of sin. It is not enough to say, Do this, and Do that, for the soul is strengthened for the doing of difficult and dangerous duties only by being fed on truth. The men who have made and guided the Christian church are men whose minds have worked their way to clear-cut conclusions as to the significance of the events in the life of Jesus and the meaning of the phenomena which spiritual experience brings to view. It is one of the causes of our lukewarmness and inefficiency that we do not think enough about God and of our relation to him. If church members had clearer ideas of what God is and how God works, and what God wants, their hope and joy would be immeasurably augmented. The Puritan says to us: "Think! Use your mind in your religion. Make your way out to definite conclusions. Build up in yourself solid and vital convictions. Set your mind to work on the subject matter of revelation, and formulate a conception of God and man, of duty and destiny, which will satisfy the reason and both calm and invigorate the heart." It is one of the high distinctions of the Puritan that he had a theology, and one of the highest services he can render to our modern world is to induce us who profess to follow Jesus to work out a theology of our own.

THE PURITAN CONSCIENCE[1]

"I have lived in all good conscience before God until this day." — ACTS 18 : 1.

It was two hundred and eighty-nine years ago this very week that a little company of people landed on the coast of Massachusetts who have left a deep impression upon all the history of this Western World. These people were representatives of a large body of men and women differing from one another in many respects, but having certain fundamental things in common, living in different countries and known under various names, being called Huguenots in France, and the Reformed in Holland, and Puritans in England and Scotland. It has been my custom for a good many years to think with you on one of the Sunday mornings of each December about some trait of the Puritan mind and temper, some phase of the Puritan character and career. I have done this because I deem it highly important that we maintain living connection with the past, and that in these hurried days we take time occasionally to commune with the spirits of the mighty men of the years that are gone.

There are four groups of men who have in large measure created the world in which we are living. The first company is the Hebrew Prophets, those deep-eyed servants of God, who in the seventh and eighth centuries before the Christian era announced the ethical principles by which the civilized world has agreed to regulate its life. The second

[1] Dec. 19, 1909.

THE PURITAN CONSCIENCE

company is the Apostles — the men who in the first century laid the foundations of the Christian Church. The third group is the Reformers, the religious leaders who in the sixteenth century broke the spell of a lower interpretation of the Christian religion, and shattered forever the authority of an institution which had proved recreant to its trust. The fourth body of worldmakers is the Puritans, the men who, dominated by the spirit of the Reformers, carried new ideas into the political realm, reconstructing the constitution of the English State, and founding in the new world free communities which became in time a mighty factor in the building of the American Republic.

All these four groups of men were alike in two respects — they all were hated. The prophets were always the most unpopular men in Israel. The writer to the Hebrews was true to history when, in speaking of the religious leaders of his race, he said, " They wandered in deserts and in mountains, in dens and caves of the earth; they were destitute, tormented, afflicted." There was tragic truth in the words of Jesus addressed by him to the men of his time: " Your fathers murdered the prophets and you are whitewashing their tombs." The apostles, like the Hebrew prophets, were despised and rejected. To use an expression of St. Paul, they were " the offscouring of all things." All of them with a solitary exception met a violent death. Their names were held in execration. The Reformers also aroused the venomous hostility of the world. Luther and Calvin and Latimer and Knox were, during their lifetime, covered with mountains of calumny and abuse, and in the great libraries of the world there are scores of volumes in which these servants of humanity are held up to contumely and execration. The Puritans of the seventeenth century, like the Reformers of the sixteenth, were a target for the abuse

FOREFATHERS' DAY SERMONS

of their fellows. To many men then living they were savages or devils, and in many quarters the work of vilification has extended down to the present hour. All four groups of men were alike in this — they all wore crowns of thorns.

They were also alike in the fact that they all were mighty. They all left their finger-prints on the body of the world's life. The Hebrew prophets, Amos and Hosea, Isaiah and Jeremiah, drove their ethical ideas so deeply into the gray matter of the brain of the race that nothing can ever dislodge them. The apostles were giants who turned the world upside down and kindled a fire that still is raging. Wherever the gospel of Jesus of Nazareth is preached the names of the apostles will be mentioned with honor. They are satellites that will revolve forever around a sun that will never be extinguished. No matter what we may think of the Reformers we are bound to acknowledge that they created the atmosphere which we are breathing to-day, and that they turned the stream of history into the channel down which our little barks are sailing. The Puritans also were men of might. What vigor they had in them we may judge from the elongation of the hatred which has followed them. Men do not go back two hundred years and dig up the corpses of ninnies and nobodies. Only giants are dug up and gibbeted after they have been in their graves six generations. Nobody will hate us two hundred years from now. But the strength of the Puritans is best proved by the creations of their genius. They stamped the name *Puritan* upon measures and institutions which have survived to the present time. Men are still talking about "the Puritan theology." There was theology before the Puritans lived, but they gave it a new tone and vitality. They made it different from all the

THE PURITAN CONSCIENCE

theologies that had hitherto been. Puritan theology is the conceptions of God and man, duty and destiny, as those conceptions were fused and moulded in the hot fires of the Puritan mind. Men still speak familiarly of " the Puritan Sabbath." The Sabbath existed long before the Puritan age, but the Puritans gave it a temper which it had never had before. They laid their hand upon it and changed the character of it. The Puritan Sabbath had such vitality in it that even to-day some people are afraid that it may come to life again. Many volumes have been written about the Puritan home. Home was an ancient institution, but the Puritan created a new atmosphere for the home, so that " home " among English-speaking peoples has never been quite the same since the Puritans threw their halo around it. Men still discuss the Puritan conscience as though it was something quite distinct from all the other kinds of conscience which history has produced. We take it for granted that it is something unique, and that even now it is a factor in the world's life. The Puritan conscience — let us think about it this morning. Let us call the Puritans up before us and ask them to defend themselves. If you listen attentively you will hear them saying what Paul said when he was arraigned by his countrymen and compelled to defend himself: " We have lived in all good conscience before the face of God."

Whence came this conscience which was peculiar to the Puritan? It came from a reverent study of the Scriptures. In the Middle Ages there was no printing press. Bibles were the exclusive possession of the clergy and the rich. The common people had no books. But the Reformers, aided by the printing press, gave the Bible to the people. A certain class of the people seized upon the book with avidity; they pored over its pages day and night; they

FOREFATHERS' DAY SERMONS

devoured it. Out of the Bible they got a new conception of God. In the writings of the prophets and apostles they learned that God is holy love, that He has created man in His image, given him a piece of work to do and will call him to give an account of his stewardship on the last great day. It was this new conception of God that created the Puritan conscience. Man's moral nature thrilled with a new life. Under the fresh light that fell on it, man's moral sense rose to a new stature in the presence of a moral God. Conscience is ever dependent on one's conception of the Eternal. If the conception of God be high, then man's conscience has high standards of conduct. Wherever the idea of God is low, there the ideas of morality are loose.

This fact should warn us to beware of certain definitions of conscience which are current. For instance, it is often said that conscience is "the voice of God in the soul of man"—or that it is "a divine dictator in the soul, infallibly deciding what is right and what is wrong." All such definitions are erroneous, and being erroneous they are mischievous and may prove fatal. Conscience is not God's voice in the soul, nor does it infallibly tell us what is right and what is wrong. Conscience is a faculty of the mind, an organ of the soul—you can educate it, train it, cultivate it; or you can pervert it, dwarf it, starve it. God is in the moral sense, but the sense itself is not God. The voice of God is mixed with human feelings and opinions and traditions. A man's moral nature can be educated, and conscience therefore is a faculty the value of whose judgments depends upon its enlightenment and the state of culture to which it has attained. You cannot educate the voice of God, but you can educate the conscience. Conscience in different men may say a hundred different things,

THE PURITAN CONSCIENCE

but the voice of God speaks but one thing. Paul was always a conscientious man. He was conscientious even when he had Christians scourged ánd put to death. But his conscientiousness did not save him from regret and remorse, for when his conscience once became enlightened he saw that his past life had been a colossal blunder. When you see him with his face in the dust, if you go near enough to him to hear what he is saying, you will hear him exclaim that he is the chief of sinners and not fit to be called an apostle because he persecuted the Church of God. Englishmen had a conscience before the Bible was given to the people, but in the masses of men it was undeveloped, in many cases ignorant and defiled. For centuries the Bible had been lost. Because the Bible had been lost, men had lost the vision of Almighty God in Christ. The world was filled with the images of the saints, and Christians were instructed to pray to the holy men and holy women who in ages past had served God and blessed the world. Above the saints came the Apostles, and Christians prayed to the saints in order that they might influence the Apostles to secure for them the blessings which they craved. Above the saints came the Virgin Mary, to whom the Apostles prayed, and above the Virgin Mary stood Jesus, to whom the Virgin Mary spoke. And above the face of Jesus, completely hidden in the clouds, was the face of the Almighty Father, so far away that the common people did not dare to pray to him at all. They prayed to the saints, the saints prayed to the Apostles, the Apostles prayed to the Virgin and the Virgin prayed to Christ. It was through a long chain of intermediaries that the wishes of the people made their way to God. The result was a widespread degradation. When men lose the face of God they do not see clearly ethical distinctions. In a world peopled by the images of the saints men grew careless of the difference between right and wrong. But when men began to read the Bible and were brought into the presence of a holy God their eyes were purged and they began to ask the question, " Is this thing right? " They held every action up against a right God, and if it did not harmonize with God they would not do it. They would do only those things that they felt would be pleasing unto God. The distinction between pleasure and duty had well-nigh faded out. Indeed, duty had in many regions become a hollow name. But with this new conception of God came a new conception of duty: Duty is something owed to God, a debt that must be paid — and instead of being irksome it became glorious. The men who caught sight of God's face became interested in righteousness and devotees of duty.

The result was that little by little these people made themselves conspicuous. They refused to go with the crowd. The crowd was going in a certain direction, but these men said, " We cannot go with you because it is not right." The crowd was doing certain things, and these men said, " We cannot do them, because these things are not right." At first they became conspicuous in the Church. Parliaments and princes had decreed that certain things should be done in the Church. These men said: " We cannot do them because they are not right. Our conscience will not allow us to do them. We can do nothing contrary to the will of God." Making themselves conspicuous in the Church, they began at last to show the same disposition in the State. When kings gave their commands, these men said: " We cannot obey you, because you command what is not right. Obedience is impossible because it goes contrary to our conscience. We must answer to our conscience and to God, and not to man." It is at that point

THE PURITAN CONSCIENCE

that you find the explanation of the English Revolution of 1640, and also the explanation of the American Revolution of 1776. These men who were so particular about doing the thing that was right, and who ever strove to do their duty, excited the contempt and derision of many who passed by. One day somebody said, with a scoff, "Puritan!" It was a piece of mud flung at the head of a conscientious man, and the mud stuck. It was like another bit of mud flung at Jesus of Nazareth. Somebody said of him one day, "The friend of publicans and sinners," and the mud stuck. The rains of the centuries have not been able to wash it away. And that was like another piece of mud thrown at the followers of Jesus at Antioch. Somebody one day hissed after them as they went through the street, "Christians!" It was a piece of mud and it stuck. But strange to say all these bits of mud have been converted into crowns of glory.

But the Puritan conscience had the defects of its qualities. In a world like this it is impossible to cultivate any faculty without running the risk of overdoing. Many of us know the Puritan conscience best because of its eccentricities, its exaggerations, its perversions, its excesses. The Puritan party was made up of a large number of people, and there were different shades and grades of Puritans. A party as a whole always suffers because of the delinquencies or peculiarities of any of its members. More than once the republican party has suffered because of the folly or dishonesty of a group of prominent republicans, and not at all infrequently has the democratic party been obliged to pay a heavy penalty because of the rascality or foolishness of prominent democrats. The Puritan party has been subjected to constant misunderstanding and criticism because of the oddities and lapses of certain individual mem-

FOREFATHERS' DAY SERMONS

bers of that party. There were Puritans who carried their conscientiousness to unwarrantable lengths. Any virtue, no matter what, can be exaggerated into a vice. Justice is a virtue, but if you push it too far you become cruel. You ought to be generous, but if you are too generous you become a spendthrift. Economy is a virtue, but if carried too far it becomes parsimoniousness. A man ought to be brave, but if he is too brave he becomes reckless. Everyone ought to be prudent, but if he is too prudent he is cowardly. Frankness is a good thing, but if one is too frank he is boorish. We ought to be sympathetic, but if sympathy is overdone we are sentimental. We ought to be pious, but not sanctimonious. People who are too good are " goody." It is possible to have " too much of a good thing." Too much of a good thing is a bad thing. Whenever you pass beyond the appointed boundaries of a virtue you find yourself in the domain of a vice. A vice is a virtue gone to seed. We ought to examine ourselves — some of us ought to do this more frequently than we do — but self-examination carried too far leads to morbidness, and in some cases to insanity. A public speaker ought to be careful of his speech, but if he is too careful he mars it. A full-fledged grammatical error, mangling a sentence by taking hold of it awkwardly, dropping out an entire link in the argument, is not nearly so bad in the public speaker as a visible straining after nicety of expression, a finical and fastidious scrupulosity in the use of words. Education is a good thing, but it is possible to be overeducated. A man may whet his intellectual faculties until he becomes sharp as a razor, and like a razor he is good for nothing but to cut with. You all know people who are all edge. They cut everything and everybody to pieces. They never hear a bit of music that they do not cut it to pieces. They

THE PURITAN CONSCIENCE

never see pictures without cutting them to pieces. Sermons and preachers and public worship are all cut into shreds. The intellectual faculties have been overeducated. Just so it is possible to be too conscientious. A man may develop his conscience until it becomes a nuisance. He may be so conscientious that he may be miserable himself and make all his neighbors miserable, too. He may be so conscientious as to paralyze his power of action. There are people who are not willing to confess Christ because they are so conscientious. They have such a fine sensitiveness as to what one ought to be if he is a Christian that they refuse to obey one of Christ's plain commands. They are too conscientious to join the church. They have such a high idea of the obligations which a Christian assumes and such an exalted sense of honor as to what a church member ought to do that they simply refuse to obey one of the wishes of Christ. A man is always too conscientious if his conscience prevents him from doing things that Christ wants done. An overdeveloped conscience leads into all sorts of punctiliousness and pettiness and picayunishness. A man may coddle and pamper his conscience until it renders him contemptible. Christ poured his scorn upon those punctilious, pettifogging Pharisees who went into a patch of weeds in their garden and carefully picked out one tenth of the mint and anise and cummin because they were so anxious to render a tithe to God of all they possessed. Those were the men who strained at a gnat and swallowed a camel. It is well to be careful in one's eating, but if one is too careful he brings on nervous dyspepsia. One ought to be careful of his actions, but if he is too careful he becomes self-conscious and awkward. One ought to be careful in making distinctions between right and wrong, but if he falls into the habit of splitting hairs and making a great ado about trifles, it is evidence that his conscience has been developed too much.

An overdeveloped conscience also leads to boorishness and, it may be, to cruelty and tyranny. A high degree of conscientiousness and bigotry have often gone together. It was here that the Puritan most frequently failed. The Puritan was so sure that he was right that he found it difficult to be courteous to the man who had a different judgment. To many a Puritan the conscience was the voice of God in the soul. His psychology was defective, and because he identified his own moral judgment with the voice of God he had scant respect for the man who differed from him. For conscience to take off his hat to another conscience that differs from it, that is indeed a high and rare grace. It was one that the Puritans did not always possess. When, therefore, you hear people speak disparagingly of the Puritan conscience, they usually have in mind some overdeveloped conscience — a conscience that is exceedingly punctilious and excruciatingly scrupulous, a conscience that quibbles over trifles and finds supreme delight in splitting hairs. Or they have in mind a bigoted conscience — a conscience that says, "I am the voice of God, and every man who differs from me is wrong." But these are only excesses of the Puritan conscience. The Puritan conscience at its best is a conscience that has had its eyes purged by a new vision of God.

But a preacher in the twentieth century need not dwell on the danger of overconscientiousness, for the drift is in a direction entirely opposite. The danger of our day is not overscrupulousness, but unscrupulousness. The peril of our time is not exaggerated punctiliousness, but carelessness in the making of distinctions and blindness to high

THE PURITAN CONSCIENCE

moral ideals. Have you never heard a man say, with a chuckle: " He got there just the same, — there were many crooked things which he did, but he got there just the same. He did sundry things which he was rather sorry he had to do, but he got there "? Alas, he got there, but he was smirched. Which would you prefer to have said about you — he is clever, or he is conscientious? Many of you would prefer to have it said that you are clever. That would send you home smiling. You would smile to yourself every time you thought about it. To be clever is to be quite up to date. But to say that one is conscientious means that one is rather old-fashioned, and one would rather be up to date than old-fashioned. Would to God we had more conscientious men and women.

There are three kinds of conscience against which the Bible warns us. There is what Paul calls a " seared " conscience — a conscience seared with a red-hot iron. This does not mean a conscience that has simply been rendered insensible by rubbing over it a hot surface, destroying the delicate nerve pulp of the soul. Paul had in his mind's eye another picture. It was the custom in his day for slave-owners to brand the arms or backs of their slaves with a hot iron, so that when the slaves ran away they could be easily recaptured and brought back to their owner. What we do with cattle, slave-owners in the first century did with men. Paul says that there are men who have the conscience branded with a branding iron. They do not belong to God, the world has stamped its mark upon them. Thousands of Americans have this branded conscience; they care nothing for God. Their master is public opinion. Within the last ten years we have had one nest of rascals after another uncovered in this country, and what a squirming and wriggling we have seen when the unholy brood has been brought into the light; but so far as I have been able to see in the newspapers there has never been a solitary indication of remorse on the part of any one of the scoundrels because he had sinned against God. There has been a good deal of disgust and indignation because government has interfered and made things unpleasant, and in a few cases men have been quite overwhelmed with disgrace because their good name has been taken from them, but not a single miscreant, so far as I know, has ever beaten his breast and cried out, " God be merciful to me, a sinner! " There is no vision of God, there is no Master but the public. I have heard men say that things are in better shape now than they were a few years ago in this country, that because of the influence of President Roosevelt business men will not dare to do to-day what they were doing only a few years ago. That means that there are men who will go just as far as public opinion will allow them to go. They care nothing at all for the laws of God or the rights of humanity, but will do anything whatsoever if public opinion does not condemn it. Such men have a conscience seared with a red-hot iron. And until men have a desire to keep their conscience void of offense toward God, and also toward man, we have no ground to build our hopes for a prosperous or enduring nation.

There is also a " defiled " conscience against which we are put on our guard. The defiled conscience is always a flabby conscience, the heart of it having been eaten out by luxury and self-indulgence. It is the defiled conscience which is a menace to the strength and influence of the Christian Church. There are many church members whose conscience is evidently blunted or drugged. When Christians go with the crowd to read slimy novels, and when

THE PURITAN CONSCIENCE

church members go with the crowd to see a slimy play, and when church members do not obey the rules of their church, it is because their conscience is defiled. Instead of scoffing at the excesses of the Puritans, or chattering about the foibles of the tall-statured saints of God who made this world a better place to live in, we ought to pray heaven unceasingly that our conscience may be purged, and that we, living our life in the fresh vision of God in Christ, may be careful to distinguish between the right and the wrong and ever find our supreme delight in the doing of the things that we owe to him.

It is possible so to abuse one's conscience as to kill it. The moral sense may become so calloused by the rough treatment to which it is subjected that the day will come when it has no longer the power of feeling. There are men of whom it can be truly said, They have no conscience. They are ever ready to do whatever they want to do, and nothing which they do brings upon them a twinge of regret or a pang of remorse. Within the last week a tragic event has happened — a king without a conscience has gone into eternity to stand before the King of kings and Lord of lords. One is awestruck when he tries to picture to himself the meeting of an earthly king who had killed his conscience, standing in the presence of a holy God.

In a world like this, where we are beset by temptations on every side, and where it is so easy for the conscience to become seared or defiled or slain, let us ever and again turn our faces toward those intrepid servants of the Lord who, notwithstanding the scorn and opposition of an ungodly generation, endeavored to keep their conscience void of offense before the King of heaven; who were not free from foibles and defects, making mistakes neither insignificant

FOREFATHERS' DAY SERMONS

nor few, but who will stand out grand and massive through all the centuries as men who in a turbulent and licentious age had, in the words of Cromwell, "The fear of God before their eyes, and made some conscience of what they did."

XI

THE PURITAN AND THE HOME [1]

"The church in thy house." — PHILEMON 2.

On the Sunday in December which comes the nearest to the anniversary of the Landing of the Pilgrims it is my custom to draw my inspiration from some page of Puritan history. Readers of history are rapidly coming to the conclusion expressed long ago by Lord Macaulay that the Puritans were the most remarkable body of men which the world has ever produced. And undoubtedly the thing which made them so remarkable was their religion; for whatever we may say of their limitations, their shortcomings and their blunders — and all these they had, and that too in abundance — it cannot be denied that they were above all other men religious, keeping the fear of God before their eyes and making some conscience of what they did. And because they were religious their history becomes in a sense a sacred book — a huge and invaluable Book of Acts — as picturesque and as thrilling and as God-inspired as is that smaller book written by the beloved physician and bound up with the writings of the prophets and apostles.

We should bear in mind that the word Puritan is a wider term than we at all times recognize. We should not speak of the Puritans as though they were all men made after the same fashion, cast in the same mould. There were many grades and varieties of Puritans, some of them Anglicans, some Presbyterians, some Baptists, some Inde-

[1] Dec. 18, 1904.

FOREFATHERS' DAY SERMONS

pendents, some Quakers. Some of them were Calvinists, and others were Arminians. It is not right to identify the Puritans with any system of theology or with any polity of church government. As a matter of fact as Puritanism worked itself out in life, it became in the end predominantly Calvinistic, and the Puritans who are best known to history are the Independents of England, the Presbyterians of Scotland, and the founders of New England. But theology and church polity were only accidents and did not constitute the essential part of the Puritan movement. Puritanism is the name not of a theology or a system of church government, but the name of a certain temper, a certain outlook, a certain spiritual passion, a certain attitude to the Eternal. The Puritan first and last is the man who has a fresh vision of God, who has an abiding sense of God's sovereignty and God's holiness, and who allows this vision of the eternal almightiness and holiness to cleanse his heart and shape his life. Briefly stated, the Puritan is the man who sees God.

In his Sermon on the Mount our Lord declares that if we seek God first and his righteousness all necessary things shall be added to us. So it has proved in history. Men who saw God high and lifted up sitting on his throne gazed with such steadfast eyes upon the ineffable glory that when they looked to earth again their eyes were dulled to the importance of terrestrial distinctions. They could no longer recognize the contrast which the world had always made between the king and his subjects. Kings had for centuries been regarded as divine. No matter what they did their deeds were right. But men who had once seen the King of heaven and had come to feel their absolute dependence on his will and their accountability to him for their conduct, could now no longer accept the theory that

THE PURITAN AND THE HOME

kings have a divine right to govern wrong. This new vision working itself out in the realm of politics led first to the Civil War in England, and later on to the Revolution in America. Republicanism in government was born in the Puritan vision of God. The world had long made much of the distinction between the clergy and the laity. A layman was as nothing in the presence of his bishop. His bishop, no matter what his character, could issue laws, and the layman was under obligations to obey. A man who had gotten a fresh vision of the supreme head of the church could no longer recognize the authority of bishops who did not show in their lives the graces of the Master. They remembered how it had been written: " Call no man Master. One is your Master, even Christ; and all ye are brethren." And with these words ringing in their ears they proceeded to resist the authority which bishops claimed as all their own. This idea working in the realm of church government resulted first in Presbyterianism, which places authority in the hands of Presbyters, part of whom are clergymen and part of whom are laymen; and later on it worked itself out into the Congregationalism of New England, which puts supreme authority in the hands of the laity. Presbyterianism and Congregationalism were born in the Puritan vision of God. The world had always made much of the distinction between rich and poor, to the rich certain privileges belonged to which the poor had no rightful claim. The rich man's son could be educated while the poor man's son was doomed to ignorance. But the man who had once seen the King became blind to the distinction between rich and poor, and believing that every man, no matter who he is, is accountable to the King, the Puritans went on to say that every man must therefore read the laws issued by the King, and in order to read these laws

FOREFATHERS' DAY SERMONS

it is necessary that every man should have an education. And so wherever the Puritan spirit spread, new emphasis was placed on schools. Colleges were founded for the education of the ministers and common schools established for the instruction of all men's children, rich and poor. The Public School system of America was born in the Puritan vision of God. In the opinion of the world there had always been a vast difference between man and woman. From the beginning of the world in every land and in every time woman had been either the toy or the drudge of man. Such she had been in Egypt, and no more was she in Athens, and but little more was she in Rome. The husband had an authority over his wife and over his daughters, which in many instances resulted in degrading them to the level of slaves and things. But when men caught a fresh vision of the King and grasped the great idea that every soul is accountable to Almighty God, the old distinction between man and woman faded out, and both of them standing on the same level acknowledged their dependence on the Eternal and looked to him for strength in the doing of their work. Woman could no longer be man's drudge, for her soul, like his, was immortal; no longer could she be his plaything or his toy, for duty was now a greater word than pleasure. And out of this new conception of the dignity of womanhood there came a new conception of the Christian home. The home of our modern civilization was born in the Puritan vision of God. My subject this morning is the Puritan and the home.

It may be that to some of you my subject may appear somewhat somber and uninteresting. We are all ready to grant that the Puritans were mighty men of valor, fighting tremendously in battle. History makes it clear, likewise, that they were indomitable in the hall of debate.

THE PURITAN AND THE HOME

But while we are ready to grant that in public life they were worthy of all admiration, it may not be clear to all of us that they were praiseworthy men in their homes. The impression has gone abroad that the Puritan was glum and disagreeable, that he was a " severe and sour-complexioned man," that he spoke invariably through his nose, that he was very strict and exceedingly solemn — in short, that he was a disagreeable personage with whom to live. But we should not allow ourselves to be misled by the caricatures and exaggerations of the men who despised the Puritans because the Puritans overturned the things in which they delighted and believed. The foibles and peculiarities of the Puritans lend themselves easily to ridicule, and all sorts of jocose and sarcastic books have been written, holding their peculiarities up to scorn. Any man, no matter who he is, can be made ridiculous by a man who does not like him; and any age, no matter what, can be rendered disgusting by one who seizes upon its most superficial features, allowing all the deeper and lovelier elements to drop out of sight. There are papers published in New York City which give a totally erroneous idea of what New York life in the twentieth century really is. Should the people of five hundred years from now glance up and down the columns of those papers they would suppose that New York City in the twentieth century was a great aggregation of knaves and fools. It is not fair to judge a city by the flings and squibs of the most superficial of its papers. Nor is it fair to judge the men and the women of the sixteenth and seventeenth centuries from the funny things that are said about them by their foes. The man who takes the trouble to get into the real life of the Puritan period discovers that he is in a world warm and beautiful, filled with tenderness and sympathy and love. There were homes

FOREFATHERS' DAY SERMONS

then out of which joy and liberty had been driven just as there are such homes to-day, but the typical Puritan home was not a sour and gloomy place, but a place made warm and lighted up by the sweetest affections of the human heart. If you want to know of the Puritan as he really existed look at the picture of Colonel Hutchinson painted by his wife. How noble in temper, beautiful in disposition, upright in character and lofty in ideal, than whom there does not exist a more gracious and more courteous gentleman to-day! If you want to see what Puritan women were, look at the picture of Mrs. Wallington, as painted by her son Nehemiah, a woman in all respects up to the high level of womanhood painted in the Hebrew book of the Proverbs — so gracious and so modest, so industrious and so thoughtful, so simple and so human and so good that we every one should love her if we should meet her in our home to-day. And some of that sort of men and women, came across the Atlantic and laid the foundations of New England. It is not necessary to draw upon our imagination in order to form a conception of these people. The letters of John Winthrop to his wife have been preserved, and any one can read them who will. No one who reads them will assert that love of husband to wife, or wife to husband is more beautiful, tender or true to-day than it was at the very beginning of the history of New England. We can never hope to do the Puritans justice unless we remember that they were human, that they had their joys and sorrows, their ecstasies and despondencies, their triumphs and defeats, all of them very similar to our own, and if courtship is sweet to-day it was no less sweet then, and if man's love for woman re-creates the world to-day, filling it with glories that cannot be painted, love did as much among the Puritans. What love story written in our day

THE PURITAN AND THE HOME

can surpass in beauty and romance, and in glow and tenderness, the story of the courtship of Jonathan Edwards? We all know that he was a mighty theologian, we forget that he was first of all a mighty lover. When Longfellow tells the story of the courtship of Miles Standish he does not draw entirely on his imagination, for amid all the hardships of those old New England days there was the sound of music and of dancing, and human hearts were joyful and men's homes were happy then as now.

Indeed, the world never knew what the home can be until the Puritan created it. The way it came to be is full of interest to any one who likes to see the manner in which divine institutions grow. There were several forces which worked together to produce this, one of the finest of all God's creations, and among these forces the Bible must be reckoned first. It was a great day for England and the world when Bishop Bonner, Bishop of London, chained to the pillars of St. Paul's Cathedral six huge Bibles. The Bible was something new in England, and around these Bibles in St. Paul's Cathedral crowds hung all day long. A man with good, clear voice was immediately pressed into service and compelled by the crowd to read to them until he was exhausted. They had never heard such stories, never listened to such poetry and history. They hung spellbound upon the lips of the reader until the sun went down. But it was an equally great day for England and the world when a company of refugees driven out of England by the cruel hand of Bloody Mary brought out in Geneva in the year 1560 a new translation of the Scriptures which became known throughout the world as the Geneva Bible. John Calvin was the inspirer of it, and it was he who wrote the Preface to it. His brother-in-law was the chief of the translators, and this Geneva Bible had certain

FOREFATHERS' DAY SERMONS

excellences which no preceding Bible ever had. All its English predecessors had been large in form and so expensive the common people could not buy them. The Geneva Bible was comparatively a little book. It was rich in notes explanatory of the text. It had marginal readings after the fashion of our modern Bibles, and best of all the chapters were cut up into verses so that it was easy to find the place. This book became the family Bible of the English people, and such it remained for fifty years. Before the end of the sixteenth century one hundred and fifty editions of it were published, and even for a third of a century after the appearance of the King James version the Geneva Bible still held its ground. It is difficult for us to realize, no matter how vivid our imagination, what the Bible in the sixteenth century meant for England. It was a new book. For us the book is old, we have thumbed it over. Its sentences are commonplace. The freshness has disappeared. Its finest beauties no longer impress us. Its shining glories no longer fascinate and thrill the heart. But in the sixteenth century the Bible was a new book. Its sentences sounded like rich strains of music floating out through the open doors of heaven. Its pictures, greater than any other pictures in the world, filled men's hearts with awe and raised them to unwonted raptures. O that for a moment we could feel the power of a Bible absolutely new! And then the Bible was practically the only book in England. There were books in the libraries, but not in the hands of the common people. Imagine a world in which there was no fiction, no poetry except a few verses of Chaucer, no books of history, no books of science, no books of biography, no books of any sort whatsoever, no newspapers, no pamphlets, no religious papers, no missionary magazines, no tracts, no reports, none of the thousand

THE PURITAN AND THE HOME

publications which fill the mails and accumulate upon our tables. Just one book in the home and that book the Bible. No wonder it began to transform men's lives. It affected first of all their language, they began to talk in Biblical terms. We smile as we read their language, it sounds so stilted and so scriptural. It was natural for them thus to speak, for the books which a man habitually reads are the books whose phrases involuntarily slip into his speech. The book affected men's fashion of dress. It moulded their character, it directed their conduct — in short it re-created the world. It brought on reformations and revolutions, and the end is not yet. And one of its great works was the cleansing of the atmosphere of the home.

But the Bible was not the only treasure which the Puritan found. He not only found a book but he found a day. He found the Sabbath. The Sabbath had been lost in England. It had long ceased to be a holy day. For generations it had been a holiday, a festival and a day of sport. It did not stand out as the supreme day of the week, but it was only one of many holidays named after the saints, and on the Lord's day men had license to do many things for which they had no opportunity on any other day of the week. But as soon as men began earnestly to study the Scriptures, they read the fourth commandment, " Remember the Sabbath day to keep it holy. Six days shalt thou labor and do all thy work. The seventh day is the Sabbath of the Lord thy God: in it thou shalt not do any work." When the Prayer Book was compiled in the reign of Edward VI the English congregations after the preacher had repeated the fourth commandment were in the habit of saying, with bowed head: " Lord have mercy upon us, and incline our hearts to keep this law." Men repeated those words Sunday after Sunday, year after year until by and

FOREFATHERS' DAY SERMONS

by the commandment took hold of the conscience, and Christians began to say to themselves, we must keep this law. The fencer laid aside his buckler, the archer unbent his bow, the dancer removed the bells from his legs, and instead of playing, men began to read the book. It was in the year 1595 that an Anglican minister, Nicholas Bound, brought out the first edition of the book which was destined to have a profounder influence on the thought and life of the world than almost any other book of that century. The book had an extended title, the first phrase in which was, "The True Doctrine of the Sabbath." The book at once stirred up furious opposition. The Archbishop endeavored to suppress it, and many copies were burned, but in the year 1606 an enlarged edition was published and, in spite of the most furious opposition of the church authorities, the book was scattered everywhere and read with eagerness by all who desired to know the meaning of the fourth commandment. King James in order to counteract the Puritan influence had published a book of sports stating the various forms of recreation which were allowable on Sunday. And it was the republication of this book by Laud in 1633 that stirred the Puritans of England to new resistance, and sent other thousands of them across the sea. Ten years after its publication Laud's book was ordered burned by the common hangman, by the Puritans who had at that time come into power. In the first place then we have a home book, and in the second place we have a home day; a day for the book and a book for the day. A day and a book working together created an atmosphere in which new domestic graces burst into bloom.

When a man has the Bible and a free day on which to read it, he is sure to discover things which have hitherto

THE PURITAN AND THE HOME

escaped his attention. As soon as men studied the Bible with care it was borne in upon them that woman has a place in the divine plan which man had attempted to take from her. In the first place the Savior of the world was born of a woman. Throughout his earthly ministry he was attended by faithful women. It was to women that he spoke on the Via Dolorosa. It was to a woman that he spoke while hanging on the cross. It was to a woman that he appeared first after his resurrection, and in the apostolic prayer-meeting on which the Holy Spirit fell, women sat side by side with the men. Paul's great declaration to the Galatians seems to express the doctrine of Christianity in regard to women: " There is neither Jew nor Greek, bond nor free, male nor female, but all are one in Christ Jesus." And along with this new conception of woman men gained a new conception of themselves, they learned the beauty and the necessity of self-control. And thus, little by little, living in the fear of God woman became the queen of man's heart, and as soon as she became enthroned in his heart she became the creator of his home. Neither a doll nor a drudge can make a home, home is the creation of a queen. Puritanism finding the Bible and then finding the Sabbath, elevated woman to a position in which it was possible for her to give a new glory to home.

It is interesting to watch the home when once created, working its way out into literature and into art. The ancients never painted any pictures of home. There were artists in Egypt, Assyria, Babylonia and Greece, but no artist in either of those countries has left us a picture of the home. They painted gods and demigods, kings and warriors, but never did they create a picture of the home. Nor did the mediæval painters — those men of genius whom we are proud to call the old masters — take delight in picturing the home. There was only one family which had a fascination for their brush, and that was the Holy Family. There was only one mother whom they delighted to place upon the canvas, and that was the Virgin Mary. It was not until we come to Holland in the days of the Puritans that we find painters beginning to paint domestic scenes. Home life took on a new glory in Holland after it had broken away from the grip of Spain, and Dutch painters turning their back upon warriors and battles now began to vie with one another in portraying the quiet glories of home. From the sixteenth century until now the home scenes have been increasing until in all of our art galleries many of the best and most interesting paintings are those which give us the interior of the home. It has been working its way out into music. Many of our sweetest songs are those that tell us of home. I heard Patti at the noon of her fame and her power sing to an audience of five thousand people " Home Sweet Home," and there was scarcely a dry eye in the house. A man's heart is dead that does not respond to the memories and associations of home. The word has enshrined itself in the heart of many of our hymns. It has become one of the great words of religion. It was Puritanism that baptized it into the name of Christ. We have seized upon various names by means of which to express our idea of heaven, but the one word in all the language which seems best to satisfy the heart and to tell what we desire for all our loved ones is that little, dear word *home*. And when one we have loved leaves us and we want to tell where he has gone, the sweetest and most satisfying sentence which our lips can speak is, " He has gone home."

Will the Puritan home stand the disintegrating forces which are now arrayed against it? The home is subject

THE PURITAN AND THE HOME

to the greatest strain to which it has been subject since the world began. All sorts of forces seem to conspire together to wreck this, the foundation stone of our civilization. Our industrial system seems to be opposed to it. The multiplication of machinery appears to have a tendency to break it down. Our women, married and unmarried, are in ever increasing numbers being driven into gainful occupations. The expensiveness of living is constantly increasing, and in order to meet household expenses it seems to be necessary for women to become wage-earners. Children are more and more scattered in all directions in order that they too may earn an income. In the olden days father and mother, brothers and sisters all worked together under the same roof and on the same farm, but in our modern world father goes one way, mother goes another way, each child goes still another way, and thus throughout the day, separated and scattered, each one does his task, returning at night to a place that is not really a home but a place in which to sleep. City life is waging a tremendous warfare against the integrity of the home. The majority of people in all our great cities must of necessity live in rented houses. It is never possible to feel toward a house that is rented as one feels toward a house that he owns. Moreover the houses are in many cases so nearly alike along an entire street that it is hard to distinguish them except by the number that is painted over the door. Houses do not have that individuality which endears them to the heart and around which the affections can entwine themselves. Tens of thousands are obliged to live in apartments, the apartments being piled one on top of the other, each apartment being almost the same as every other, and as much alike as so many pigeon-holes into which human beings are thrust over night. And moreover the multiplication of clubs and societies and organizations of many varieties and names use up the evenings, allowing husbands and wives little time together, and parents no time with their children. Fashion also is working with both hands against the home. There seems to be an increasing tendency among the so-called upper classes for mothers to get rid of their children as soon as they can. On coming into the world the children are handed over to the nurse, later on they are passed over to the care of the governess. They are sent at the earliest moment to the kindergarten, and then after a short season in school they are hurried off to some academy or boarding-school, the chief desire of many fathers and mothers being to roll the responsibility of bringing up their children on to somebody else's shoulders and to get out of the trouble and responsibility which the training of children involves. There are thousands and tens of thousands of young men and young women growing up in this country who have been practically denied the very greatest privilege which it is in the power of heaven to bestow. They have never from their infancy known the meaning of home. And this is a loss which is not only incalculable, but it is a loss which can never be made good. Good things may come to us in the later years, but nothing so good can ever come as home. The man and the woman who were denied a home in the days of their youth are men and women who are forever maimed. There are certain things which one learns at home which can be learned nowhere else on earth, and if they are not learned at home in the days of one's youth, they are never learned at all. There are virtues and graces the very sweetest which the human spirit can put forth which do not blossom anywhere else except in homes made warm and fragrant by parental love.

THE PURITAN AND THE HOME

And it is because our home life is breaking down that we have an increasing number of divorces. The divorce evil is one of the most alarming phenomena of our day, and unless it can be checked America is doomed. We already have a worse record than that of any other nation in the civilized world. We seem to be growing worse with the years. It was the dissolution of the marriage tie that was largely responsible for the fall of an empire that called itself eternal, and we need not expect the republic founded by Washington and saved by Lincoln to withstand the virus of a sin which proved fatal even to Rome. Men and women in increasing numbers seem to marry for every other reason than love — for fortune, for place, for convenience, for society, out of whim or caprice. They live together for a little time, then they discover there is a difference of taste or a difference of ideal, or one is not altogether congenial to the other, or a longing for the old freedom of unmarried life comes back. The result is separation, and a new drop in the cup of our national infamy. The Christian church must set itself against this evil with all the energy of deep conviction and unsparing indignation. It must be counted, except in the rarest instances, the greatest disgrace to be divorced, and men and women who promise before God and in the sight of men to take one another for better or for worse, for richer or for poorer, and to live together until God does them part, must not be allowed recklessly to trample upon the most sacred vows which human lips can take and human hearts can promise, and still hold their heads up in society which is decent.

We must guard the home with all diligence, for out of it are the issues of life. It is the nursery in which immortal souls are formed, it is the fountain from which the streams

FOREFATHERS' DAY SERMONS

of national life proceed. It is the foundation of the school, the foundation of the state, the foundation of the church. There is no problem which cannot be settled provided we have a nation of Christian homes. There is no evil which cannot be discomfited and routed provided we have a nation of families bound together by the ties of faith and love. "The church in thy house." That is the church to be prized and reverenced above all others. It is there that your worship to Almighty God must be most sincere, and most complete. If the church in thy house is not a church then we can have no church anywhere. But if the church in thy house is full of the spirit of Christ, if God's commandments are the law of its action, and if Christ's promises are the music of its days, and if Christ's ideals are the inspiration of its ambition and its effort, then we shall have a church which on the Lord's day in the house of prayer will be able to render praise acceptable to the King. And then shall we have a nation against which the gates of destruction shall not prevail.

There are two pictures of home which are preeminent above all others in English literature, both of them pictures of a Puritan home. The first is Robert Burns' "Cotter's Saturday Night." Burns was not a Puritan in his living, but he was a man of keen insight, and he saw that the Puritan home was the source of Scotland's strength and the foundation of her greatness. As a distinguished English critic has said, the lines of this poem fall on the heart like strains of slow and solemn music.

"The cheerfu' supper done, wi' serious face,
They round the ingle form a circle wide;
The sire turns o'er, wi' patriarchal grace,
The big ha' Bible, ance his father's pride:
His bonnet rev'rently is laid aside,
His lyart haffets wearing thin an' bare;

THE PURITAN AND THE HOME

Those strains that once did sweet in Zion glide,
He wales a portion with judicious care;
And 'Let us worship God!' he says, with solemn air.

They chant their artless notes in simple guise;
  They tune their hearts, by far the noblest aim:
Perhaps ' Dundee's ' wild warbling measures rise,
Or plaintive ' Martyrs,' worthy of the name:
  Or noble ' Elgin ' beats the heavenward flame,
The sweetest far of Scotia's holy lays:
  Compared with these, Italian thrills are tame;
The tickled ears no heartfelt raptures raise;
Nae unison hae they with our Creator's praise.

The priest-like father reads the sacred page,
  How Abram was the friend of God on high;
Or, Moses bade eternal warfare wage
  With Amelek's ungracious progeny;
  Or how the royal bard did groaning lie
Beneath the stroke of Heaven's avenging ire;
  Or, Job's pathetic plaint, and wailing cry;
Or rapt Isaiah's wild, seraphic fire;
Or other holy seers that tune the sacred lyre.

Perhaps the Christian volume is the theme,
  How guiltless blood for guilty man was shed;
How He, who bore in heaven the second name,
  Had not on earth whereon to lay his head:
  How his first followers and servants sped;
The precepts sage they wrote to many a land:
  How he, who lone in Patmos banished,
Saw in the sun a mighty angel stand;
And heard great Bab'lon's doom pronounced by Heaven's command.

Then kneeling down, to Heaven's Eternal King,
  The saint, the father, and the husband prays:
Hope ' springs exulting on triumphant wing,'
That thus they all shall meet in future days:
  There ever bask in uncreated rays,
No more to sigh, or shed the bitter tear,
  Together hymning their Creator's praise,
In such society, yet still more dear;
While circling time moves round in an eternal sphere."

The second picture is Whittier's "Snowbound." It will live as long as there are men upon this earth who love their home. The old house which it describes is standing still.

FOREFATHERS' DAY SERMONS

with the open fireplace and much of the furniture as they were in the olden days. Standing under that humble roof one can realize afresh the secret of New England's greatness. From the beginning until now New England has been the land of homes. Much of her soil is barren, her skies through a large portion of the year are inclement, but from the beginning until now it has been to many hearts a Garden of Eden because to them it has been home. The reason, I think, why we find it difficult to pity the early founders of New England and to believe that their life was hard, the reason why we do not shudder when the poets and historians tell us about the terrible winters, the fearful beasts and the bloodthirsty Indians is because all those early days are filled for our imagination with enchantment, because we see the firelight dancing on the walls, and hear the flames of the great logs roaring in the chimney. It could not have been so cold and dreary — we keep saying to ourselves — with such loving people sitting around the open fire!

> " So all night long the storm roared on:
> The morning broke without a sun;
> In tiny spherule traced with lines
> Of Nature's geometric signs,
> In starry flake, and pellicle,
> All day the hoary meteor fell;
> And, when the second morning shone,
> We looked upon a world unknown,
> On nothing we could call our own.
> Around the glistening wonder bent
> The blue walls of the firmament,
> No cloud above, no earth below, —
> A universe of sky and snow!
> The old familiar sights of ours
> Took marvelous shapes; strange domes and towers
> Rose up where sty or corn-crib stood,
> Or garden-wall, or belt of wood;
> A smooth white mound the brush-pile showed,
> A fenceless drift what once was road;
> The bridle-post an old man sat

THE PURITAN AND THE HOME

With loose-flung coat and high cocked hat;
The well-curb had a Chinese roof;
And even the long sweep, high aloof,
In its slant splendor, seemed to tell
Of Pisa's leaning miracle.

As night drew on, and, from the crest
Of wooded knolls that ridged the west,
The sun, a snow-blown traveler, sank
From sight beneath the smothering bank,
We piled, with care, our nightly stack
Of wood against the chimney-back, —
The oaken log, green, huge, and thick,
And on its top the stout back-stick;
The knotty forestick laid apart,
And filled between with curious art
The ragged brush; then, hovering near,
We watched the first red blaze appear,
Heard the sharp crackle, caught the gleam
On whitewashed wall and sagging beam,
Until the old, rude-furnished room
Burst, flower-like, into rosy bloom;
While radiant with a mimic flame
Outside the sparkling drift became,
And through the bare-boughed lilac-tree
Our own warm hearth seemed blazing free.
The crane and pendent trammels showed,
The Turks' heads on the andirons glowed;
While childish fancy, prompt to tell
The meaning of the miracle,
Whispered the old rhyme: '*Under the tree,
When fire outdoors burns merrily,
There the witches are making tea.*'

Shut in from all the world without,
We sat the clean-winged hearth about,
Content to let the north-wind roar
In baffled rage at pane and door,
While the red logs before us beat
The frost-line back with tropic heat;
And ever, when a louder blast,
Shook beam and rafter as it passed,
The merrier up its roaring draught
The great throat of the chimney laughed,
The house-dog on his paws outspread
Laid to the fire his drowsy head,
The cat's dark silhouette on the wall
A couchant tiger's seemed to fall;
And, for the winter fireside meet,
Between the andirons' straddling feet,

FOREFATHERS' DAY SERMONS

The mug of cider simmered slow,
The apples sputtered in a row,
And, close at hand, the basket stood
With nuts from brown October's wood.

What matter how the night behaved?
What matter how the north-wind raved?
Blow high, blow low, not all its snow
Could quench our hearth-fire's ruddy glow.
O Time and Change! — with hair as gray
As was my sire's that winter day,
How strange it seems, with so much gone
Of life and love, to still live on!
Ah, brother! only I and thou
Are left of all that circle now, —
The dear home faces whereupon
That fitful firelight paled and shone.

Henceforward, listen as we will,
The voices of that hearth are still;
Look where we may, the wide earth o'er
Those lighted faces smile no more.
We tread the paths their feet have worn,
   We sit beneath their orchard trees,
   We hear, like them, the hum of bees
And rustle of the bladed corn;
We turn the pages that they read,
   Their written words we linger o'er,
But in the sun they cast no shade,
No voice is heard, no sign is made,
   No step is on the conscious floor!
Yet love will dream, and Faith will trust,
(Since He who knows our need is just,)
That somehow, somewhere, meet we must.
Alas for him who never sees
The stars shine through his cypress-trees!
Who, hopeless, lays his dead away,
Nor looks to see the breaking day
Across the mournful marbles play!
Who hath not learned, in hours of faith,
   The truth to flesh and sense unknown,
That Life is ever lord of Death,
   And Love can never lose its own!

XII

THE PURITAN SABBATH AND OURS[1]

"Remember the Sabbath day to keep it holy.' — Exodus 20 : 8.

The Puritans liked to call their day of rest the "Sabbath." Sometimes they called it the "First Day." This was the expression employed in the Gospels. More frequently they called it the "Lord's Day." They had authority for this in the first chapter of the book of the Revelation. But their favorite name was "Sabbath." This was the word which Moses had used, and David, the sweet singer of Israel, and all the Prophets, and it was, therefore, presumably the favorite of Heaven. The word "Sunday" they would not use because it was not to be found in the Bible. It was a word of pagan origin, meaning Sun's Day, just as Monday means Moon's Day, and any word coined in a heathen mint could not be applied to a divine institution. Scriptural sanction was essential for all their religious names and customs, and, therefore, "Sunday" was among them a name tabooed.

In dealing with the Puritan Sabbath, we are dealing with a familiar theme. We have all our life heard about it, and have come to feel that we know quite well just what it was. For more than two centuries it has been a subject to make merry with. No other Puritan institution has been made the butt of so many jokes, upon none other has been poured such abundant and hilarious ridicule. Satires in prose and verse have been written on the theme, and English and American writers have emulated one another

[1] Dec. 18, 1910.

FOREFATHERS' DAY SERMONS

in making the Sabbath observances of the Puritan grotesque and laughable. Mirth-provoking articles on the subject have not yet ceased to appear, and many a volume has been filled with droll narratives of the ways in which our forefathers endeavored to keep the Sabbath holy.

It has also been a theme for scorn and indignation. For many, the subject has been too serious for a smile and has brought forth only lightnings of condemnation. The Puritan Sabbath has to these persons been anything but a joke. They have found in it a tyranny and a scourge, an engine for darkening and maiming the life of the world. The sufferings of the children crushed by the Puritan Sabbath have called forth passionate commiseration, and the cruelty of the fathers and mothers who endeavored to banish from the first day of the week every trace of gaiety and enjoyment, making the day a day of gloom to every one but religious enthusiasts or fanatics, has been often dwelt upon and held up for wrath and execration. There are some who feel that the Puritan by his policy of Sabbath observance made a vast and unpardonable subtraction from the sum total of human joy, and that no institution of the Puritan world is so deserving of endless maledictions as the Puritan Sabbath.

When humor and scorn combine to exploit a thing, they carry the memory of it far. All the world knows that there was once such a thing as the Puritan Sabbath, and it knows quite accurately what sort of a thing it was. It knows that the Sabbath of the Puritans was a stiff and straight-laced day, very solemn and very somber, a burden to the boys and girls and an intolerable yoke to the man of the world. People who scarcely know who the Puritans were, whence they came, what they achieved, or at what date they van-

THE PURITAN SABBATH AND OURS

ished, are well posted in regard to the way in which they observed the Sabbath. There are men in this congregation, who, born in homes in which the Puritan traditions still lingered, have lively recollections of the interminable length and indescribable tediousness of the Sabbath in their boyhood, and one often meets persons who have given up all interest in religion because — as they say — of the way in which as children they were obliged to keep the Day of Rest. John Ruskin in his autobiography humorously intimates that he might have become an evangelical clergyman if he had not been obliged when a boy to eat cold mutton for his Sunday's dinner. His father and mother and aunt were Puritans.

The Puritan Sabbath has passed away, but in many a quarter there are fears that it may come back. Herod was not more fearful of the return to earth of John the Baptist than is many an American of the return of the Sabbath of the Puritans. When from time to time an effort is made in any of our cities to curtail somewhat the encroachments of those who would make all days alike, a shriek of terror rends the air, and in many a paper, in startling headlines, the public is warned of the peril of reinstating the Puritan Sabbath. From time to time certain stories are rehearsed to give the new generation a vivid idea of the kind of men the Puritans were. The bachelor preacher who refused to baptize a baby because it happened to be born on Sunday, is as sure of deathless renown as Cæsar, Charlemagne and Napoleon, and the Boston man who kissed his wife one Sunday morning on his own front doorstep on his return home after a three years' absence, and was set in the stocks for two hours as a penalty for his misdemeanor, is also an heir of immortality. Wherever the story of the Puritans is related, the

FOREFATHERS' DAY SERMONS

tale of that man's kiss and its consequences will be told as a memorial of them.

But before we break into laughter or give way to indignation over the Puritan Sabbath, sundry observations should be made. Bishop Butler said many wise things, but he never said anything much better than this: "Let us remember that we differ as much from other men as they differ from us." It is easy to forget this. We look with wonder upon a man who differs from us, lamenting the immense distance he is away from us, and we forget that he is also astonished at the distance which we stand from him. We laugh at him and forget that he is laughing at us. We think his opinions erroneous or silly, and that is just what he thinks of ours. In our heart we call him a fool, and in all probability that is what he is calling us. It is well to remember that the laugh is always on both sides, and that both men look equally funny to the other. We smile at the fashions of the Puritans. They were so odd. We gaze on the old pictures of their lords and ladies, and we wonder how such styles of dress could ever have been counted beautiful or in good taste. But what would the Puritan think if he could look at us? Probably our styles would stir him to laughter and cause him to wonder what had become of high standards of taste. There is no doubt that the people of three hundred years from now will laugh equally loud over the styles of the sixteenth century and those of the twentieth. We read of the cold churches of the Puritans with amazement. We cannot understand how people could desire to glorify God by making themselves uncomfortable. To sit in a cold room for two or three hours with no other heat than that which came from the sermon, that strikes us as something incomprehensible. But what would the Puritan think if he came back to our

THE PURITAN SABBATH AND OURS

world, and saw thirty or forty thousand people sitting out in the open air on a bleak November day, their noses purple because of the icy wind and their teeth chattering from the cold, looking intently for two hours at a lot of college boys tumbling over one another on the ground in frantic efforts to push a little leathern ball a few feet nearer to two poles erected at one end of a field? He might wonder at the curious freaks which human nature takes and at the queer ideas which mortals hold of having a good time. We pity the poor church members of the seventeenth century who would sit and listen patiently to a sermon two hours long, and cannot understand how after finishing one sermon they should want in the afternoon to hear another. But what would the Puritan think if he saw a twentieth century Christian buried in a Sunday newspaper, poring over its pages for two long hours, convinced that he is spending his time profitably? The longest of the Puritan sermons never went, I believe, beyond the twenty-eighthly, whereas, I am told, the Sunday paper often extends to the thirty-secondly and occasionally to the sixty-fourthly.

Our estimate of a thing always depends upon our degree of interest in it. To a person who cares nothing for golf what is outwardly more silly than that popular game? A full grown man in possession of his senses, solemnly takes his place in the presence of a little ball two inches in diameter, and after mature deliberation and a great flourish with a club, knocks the ball, if successful, several hundred feet through the air; whereupon he walks to where the ball is supposed to be, and spends sometimes ten or fifteen minutes in looking for it, if it has gone into the grass or into a stone wall or into a body of water, all for the privilege of hitting it again. There is nothing more absurd than

FOREFATHERS' DAY SERMONS

golf — to the man who does not care for it. And so it is with sermons. If a man does not like a sermon nothing is more tedious and stupid. If a man is not interested in religion, then religion is to him an unmitigated bore. A man who cares nothing for religion has no right, however, to assume that men who devoted one day in seven to religion were of necessity having a dismal time. Much of the gloom with which we have surrounded the Puritan is the creation of our own uninstructed fancy. We can never do justice to men of former times unless we possess a vigorous imagination. We must put ourselves in their place. We must look out upon the world through their eyes, and fit ourselves into their environment. The world in which the Puritans lived was not our world. They had no magazines or weeklies or daily papers. They had no lectures or theaters or operas. Like all human beings they needed stimulus and inspiration, and for these they were obliged to look to the pulpit. What is now done by the editor, the author, the lecturer and the actor was then done by the preacher. It was necessary for him to do four men's work, and had we lived in those days, many of us would have wanted two sermons every Sunday and every sermon two hours long. If you remember what the meeting house was in early New England days, you will see that it was far from a gloomy place. The people were in many cases obliged to walk long distances to the church. In winter time they waded through the snowdrifts, making their way toilsomely through the forests, over treacherous streams, the man carrying his musket on his shoulder, the mother carrying the baby in her arms, and when at last they reached the meeting house it was to them a place of refuge, a garden of Eden in which they caught once more the breath of the flowers of paradise, a glorious feast re-

THE PURITAN SABBATH AND OURS

minding them of the rest which is prepared for the children of God. No wonder they tarried long, and counted the hours spent within its walls the most precious of the week!

Moreover we must take into account the Puritan emphasis upon the necessity of religious instruction. Without instruction in religious matters they believed that every state and civilization must deteriorate and perish. It was necessary — so they thought — for both adults and children to be painstakingly instructed in those things which God had revealed through the prophets and apostles, and in order to do this work thoroughly they began the Sabbath at sunset Saturday evening and in some places at three o'clock Saturday afternoon. We have quite other ideas in regard to the importance of religious education. Some of us think that it can safely be made an elective. It is not a feature of our public schools. Even the colleges planted by the Puritans do not put the Gospels among the studies which are prescribed. Pagan authors are given a foremost place, but the evangelists and prophets, if they have any place at all, are among the electives, and boys are bidden to take or leave them as they choose. In many a Christian home there is no religious instruction, and in many a Christian church there is no Bible school such as the community needs, because Christians in such large numbers fail to fit themselves for Bible teaching and refuse to make the sacrifice which instructional work demands. But it is too early yet to laugh at the Puritan because he believed in catechisms, and asserted that religious education is essential for the health and growth of a nation, and that the chief work on the Lord's Day is the prosecution of moral and religious instruction. Let us not laugh just yet, for we do not know how we are coming out. There are stormclouds along the horizon, and what the future holds is hidden from our eyes. It may be that some day the world will discover that on this subject of religious instruction the Puritan was right and that we were wrong.

And then we must not allow ourselves to be gulled. We have all heard of the "Blue Laws" of Connecticut, and some of us have been ashamed of such an exhibition of Puritan tyranny and folly. One of these blue laws read thus: "No woman shall kiss her child on the Sabbath." Another one ran: "No one shall play on any instrument of music, except the drum, trumpet, or jewsharp." It is that sort of legislation which has given foes of the Puritans occasion to jeer. But the next time you hear some one railing at the blue laws of Connecticut, say to him: "What a gullible creature you are! Do you not know that that code of laws was fabricated in the brain of a Tory refugee, who was driven out of New England near the close of the Revolutionary War?" Mr. John Fiske calls him a "Baron Munchausen," but a severer name has often been employed. Samuel Peters went back to England disgruntled, and he took delight in seeing the Englishmen open their eyes on the recital of the queer doings of the Americans. It was his object to make them out fanatics and fools, and so in 1781 he published the alleged "Blue Laws of New Haven." Those who have read but little history and who get their notions of the past from rumor and hearsay, have taken the blue laws of this Tory mischief-maker as authentic and literal history. These laws were only a part of that huge joke in which the world has indulged at the expense of the Puritans.

I do not say that the Sabbath legislation of Colonial New England was not in spots both tyrannical and fantastic. Many of those early regulations strike the modern mind as mischievous and childish. Their incessant inter-

THE PURITAN SABBATH AND OURS

ference with personal liberty would not be submitted to by Americans now living; no, not for a day. Nor can it be said that there were never any blue laws of any sort in New England. All laws are blue laws to the men who transgress them. The law against stealing gives a thief the blues after he finds himself behind the bars. The law against racetrack gambling has made many a New York gambler blue. Early New England had numerous statutes which contained not a little of the spirit which Samuel Peters hit off in his famous code. But after the worst has been confessed, it still remains true that the Puritan Sabbath was not so awful as it has sometimes been painted.

At this point let us define the Puritan Sabbath. It embodied two fundamental principles. It was a day of rest and it was a day of religion. The two supreme prohibitions of the day were: " Thou shalt not work," and " Thou shalt not play." Works of mercy and of necessity were of course permitted, but " necessity " was interpreted narrowly. For instance, no cooking was allowed because the cooking could all be done on Saturday. No dishwashing was countenanced, because dishes could be washed on Monday. Every sort of work except that imperatively demanded, was banished from the Puritan Sabbath, and so also was every sort of play. John Cotton, in his " Milk for Babes," expressed the general conviction: " We should rest from labor, much more from play." In 1712 Increase Mather laid it down with authority: " Children must not be allowed to play on the Sabbath." There were no games for children, no sports for men on the Lord's day as observed by the Puritan. In his conception the day was a day for the improvement of the soul. On the first day of the week it was one's privilege to turn his thoughts toward God, and to meditate upon the things which had

FOREFATHERS' DAY SERMONS

been written for man's guidance here and to secure his blessedness hereafter. A day for rest and spiritual upbuilding, this in a word was the Sabbath of the Puritan.

If you ask whence came the day, the reply is they found it in the Bible. The Puritan read his Bible with a hunger and devotion of which we know but little. To him it was a new book. For centuries the Bible had been the possession of the clergy only. The common people could not have it; first, because books before the invention of the printing press were enormously expensive; secondly, because most of the people could not read; and thirdly, because it was the conviction of the leaders of the church that the Bible could not safely be entrusted to the hands of laymen, but must be read and interpreted only by the priest. With the coming of the printing press and the Reformation a mighty change took place. The Bible passed almost at once into the hands of the common people. They found in it the voice of God. They searched it for condemnations of what the mediæval church had taught and practiced. When Catholics said, "Listen to the Pope," the Protestants replied, "Listen to the Bible." When one side said, "The Pope is infallible," the other retorted, "We have an infallible Book." When priests asserted that it is the church which tells men what they ought to do, the Protestants declared that men must be guided solely by the Scriptures. With this conception of the Bible it was natural that one should begin with Genesis. The whole Book was inspired, every syllable was straight from heaven, no paragraph or sentence could be safely neglected. And so men began with the first verse of the first book and read straight on for guidance and consolation. In the Book of Exodus they found this: "Remember the Sabbath Day to keep it holy. Six days shalt thou labor and do all thy

THE PURITAN SABBATH AND OURS

work; but the seventh day is the Sabbath of the Lord thy God, in it thou shalt not do any work, thou, nor thy son, nor thy daughter, thy manservant, nor thy maidservant, nor thy cattle, nor thy stranger that is within thy gates." It was all straightforward, unambiguous, explicit, clear and complete. There could be no misunderstanding of the words. Men said: "This is God's law. We are bound to obey it. All men must obey it or suffer." They read the next book and the book which followed, and in these three books they found how this fourth commandment among the Jews was applied. No fire could be kindled on the Sabbath. Picking up sticks on the Sabbath was prohibited. No one was permitted to move out of his place on the seventh day. All of this was from God and all everlastingly binding on the consciences of men. In the year 1595 there appeared a book entitled: "The True Sabbath and the New Testament." Its author was Dr. Nicholas Bownd, a reasoner of great ability and a writer of unusual clearness and force. His book had a remarkable popularity and exerted a prodigious influence on the thought of his age. The book was so mighty that the government attempted to suppress it, but when its re-publication was prohibited its pages were copied by hand, and the manuscripts were industriously circulated from house to house. The book had a greater influence in the creation of the Puritan Sabbath than any other dozen books ever written. The author foundationed the Sabbath on the fourth commandment. He gave it an Old Testament atmosphere, and his interpretations were similar to those of the Jewish rabbis. The Sabbath was made not a feast but a fast, and numerous examples were given of the dire consequences which had overtaken persons who had in one way or another desecrated the Holy Day. The Puri-

FOREFATHERS' DAY SERMONS

tans of Scotland and England read the book with avidity and awestruck hearts, and among the makers of the New England Sabbath Nicholas Bownd must be given high place.

Starting with the idea that the day must not be desecrated by sport or toil, it is interesting to note how the idea stiffened and hardened under the attacks to which it was subjected. We always prize most highly the treasure we are in danger of losing. We seldom think of our health so long as we have it. But when it threatens to slip away from us its value becomes inestimable, and we count it the chief of our blessings. It is the thing which we fight for which looms large in our eyes. The Puritans were obliged to struggle for their Sabbath, and it was because of this struggle that it became more and more their most highly prized possession. When Henry VIII tore England from the See of Rome he remained in many ways a Catholic and so did a majority of his people. They liked the Catholic candles and vestments and many of the ceremonies and also the Roman Catholic Sunday. Elizabeth was like her father, and had a fondness for many of the features of the Church of Rome. When James I came to the throne he sided with the Catholic party in wanting a Sabbath which was not too strict. The Catholic church had from early times made Sunday not a holy day but a holiday. Catholics were expected to attend Mass in the morning, but after that they were at liberty to do what they pleased. As it was possible to attend Mass early, practically the whole of Sunday could be devoted to amusement. Dances were held on the green, men baited bulls and bears, and others practiced at archery, theatrical plays — called Interludes — were acted, and the whole day was given over to frivolity and fun. Against this degradation of the day the Puritans

THE PURITAN SABBATH AND OURS

entered a fiery protest. But James was determined that many of the Sunday games and sports should go on, and writing a declaration to this effect it was published in what was called the "Book of Sports," and through the Archbishop this Book of Sports was ordered read in all the pulpits. Many Puritan ministers refused to obey the mandate and were driven forthwith from their churches. One of the causes, then, of the quarrel between the Anglican church and the Puritans was this Sabbath question. The thrusting of that Book of Sports upon the Puritan preachers was one of the most exasperating of all the acts of tyranny of which the Anglican church was guilty. Stung to desperation Puritans began to find their way to Holland, but even there the Sabbath was shamefully disregarded, and one of the reasons why the Pilgrim Fathers came to the New World was because they wanted the liberty to keep the Sabbath in accordance with what they thought to be the will of God. When, after the anchoring of the *Mayflower*, Miles Standish and his little company started out to reconnoiter, they came on Saturday to an island, now called Clark's Island, and although the long-looked-for mainland lay full in sight and every man was eager to put his foot upon the beautiful and promised shore, they would go no farther, because it was the Sabbath, and they would not begin their life in the new world with any profanation of God's holy day. It was in that spirit of loyalty to the Sabbath that the history of New England began.

In such an atmosphere and with such a history behind them, it is not difficult to understand how Sabbath observation and legislation developed as they did. The day was hedged round jealously and guarded with almost frantic zeal, so fearful were they that this precious inheritance should suffer outrage or dishonor. What happened among

FOREFATHERS' DAY SERMONS

the rabbis in Palestine long before, came to pass again in New England. Men became fussy in regard to Sabbath observance, punctilious and fanatical, and the day, with many, lost much of what rightfully belongs to the Lord's Day, because of the legal atmosphere through which it was studied. A tone of severity passed into it, it was made too sober and constricted. There was not enough in it of the joy of the Lord. But we can see how it all happened. Life in those days was grim and hard. The early settlers had a tremendous struggle. At their door were wild beasts and savage men, and on the other side of the Atlantic were implacable enemies constantly plotting their destruction. How fearful was the situation can be seen from the fact that it was over a century after the discovery of America before a permanent settlement was made on the New England coast. Not till the Puritans came were men found of sufficient stamina and grit to wage successfully the bitter and harrowing warfare. Isolated and harassed, it is not to be wondered at that their views of life were not always well balanced, and that something of the severity of their fight for existence passed into their interpretations and religious practices. The New England Sabbath was not the product of normal conditions, but developed in a time of strain and stress, when it was easy for earnest and God-fearing men to become morbid in their conscience and to go to extremes in their efforts to find and live the truth. We can admire and reverence the men even while we are unwilling to accept in all respects their conception of the Lord's day and refuse at many points to follow their example.

The Sunday problem is still alive. It could not be settled in the seventeenth century for the people living now. The Puritan solution is clearly inadequate, and we have not yet formed a satisfactory one of our own. The

THE PURITAN SABBATH AND OURS

problem seems to grow more difficult all the time. It bristles with perplexities. Nowhere is it more complicated and baffling than in a great American city like New York. Our city is an aggregation of the representatives of many nations and races, holding various and conflicting traditions, and apparently incapable of being brought into any unity of opinion or practice in regard to a Sabbath. When two great religions meet each other, one holding that the seventh day, and the other maintaining that the first day is the heaven-appointed Day of Rest, it is not easy to work out a scheme of public policy which will do justice and mercy to all. The works of necessity have increased amazingly since colonial days. The lives of men under the influence of inventions and the progress of democracy have become wondrously intertwined, and our lives are bound up together more tightly now than in any preceding age. Our civilization is of such a nature that it is absolutely impossible for all men to drop their work on any one day of the week. The area of necessary labor has been enormously expanded, and to draw the line between works necessary and works unnecessary is a difficult if not impossible task. There are thousands of steamships on the oceans, and these cannot on Saturday night put out the engine fires and drift until Monday morning. Steamships are obliged to plow straight on through the week. Transcontinental trains, with their passengers and freight, cannot well stop at Saturday midnight wherever they chance to be, and resume their movement twenty-four hours later. The policemen in a city cannot on Saturday evening lay down their sticks and badges and take them up again on Monday morning. Police protection is necessary seven days a week. The members of the fire department cannot lock up the engine house at the end of the week and report for duty a day later. Fire is no respecter of days, and cities are as likely to burn down on Sunday as on any other day of the week. The apothecary must keep his door always open, for people get sick and medicines are needed on Sunday. The plumber must be always on call, for a water pipe may burst Sunday morning, and unless immediately repaired measureless damage will follow. In the great manufacturing districts fires must be kept in the furnaces and men must look after these fires no less on Sunday than on Saturday or Monday. A host of cooks and waiters must toil on the Lord's day, for tens of thousands of city people are living in hotels or in apartment houses dependent on hotels, and it is no longer possible to do all of the cooking on Saturday and all of the dishwashing on Monday. Where will you draw the line between what is necessary and what can be dispensed with? A day without labor is in our times an impossibility.

If toil is encroaching on the Sabbath, so also is recreation. Within the last generation the world has received a new gospel, the gospel of play. Men from the beginning have played when they could, but play in past ages was from impulse. Men now play not only from impulse, but because science teaches that play is a part of man's duty. All work and no play is not according to the intentions of the God who created the human body. But when are men going to play if, obliged to work six days in the week, they have no leisure but on Sunday? Our forefathers knew nothing of two systems which our civilization has created, first the factory system under which tens of thousands of men and women are crowded together in factories and mills, where from Monday morning until Saturday night they labor amidst the clank and roar of machinery, and often in an atmosphere in which human beings cannot get the

THE PURITAN SABBATH AND OURS

oxygen which the blood demands; and second, the office system under which thousands of men are stowed away in great office buildings, each one shut up in a little pigeon-hole of a room, to be released, in many cases, only at the end of the week. What are these men going to do on Sunday? If recreation is essential, and if it is not possible on six days of the week to get it, there is likelihood that the Sabbath will be made more and more a day of play. Moreover we have a wider conception of human nature than men had two centuries ago. We see that there are many other faculties in the soul besides the praying faculty and the faculty which sings songs of praise. There is a recreation of the eye and of the ear and of the intellect, and also of the lungs and the heart and the muscles, and a value is now given to pictures and music and literature and out-of-door life which had not come into the Puritan's ken. But when you begin to travel in this direction, where are you going to stop? At what point will you draw the line in the following list of possible sources of innocent enjoyment on the Lord's day? Will you open the public libraries of the city seven days in the week? Many persons have no books at home, and others cannot consult rare or costly volumes in the library except on Sunday. Shall the libraries therefore be open on the Sabbath? But if the libraries why not the art galleries? Many persons like pictures better than books, and get more inspiration from them. What will you do, then, with the pictures owned by the city: draw a curtain over them one day out of every seven, as the father of John Ruskin always did over his, or will you expose all your works of art on Sunday that everyone may look who will? If the art galleries are open on Sunday, why not the music halls? Music is to many far more uplifting than either books or pictures, and why should

FOREFATHERS' DAY SERMONS

not the lovers of music be given what they want on the Day of Rest? Why not let all the singers sing and all the lovers of music listen and thus contribute to the cultivation of the musical taste of the city? If, however, the music halls are to be open, what do you say as to the theaters? Some people like speaking better than singing. A play means more to them than a concert. A drama is a sermon, whereas a song is a nuisance. If good singing is wholesome why is not also good acting, and why should not everything that is wholesome be sanctioned on the Day of the Lord? There are many, however, who care little for music or acting, but who are enthusiastic over out-of-door games. They like baseball and football and polo and rowing and wrestling and running. Such exercises are invigorating to those who take part in them, and exhilarating to those who look on. They take place in the open air, which has advantages over the theater and music hall, and if you are going to give books to those who like books, music to those who appreciate music, pictures to those to whom pictures appeal, theatrical productions to those who are fond of the drama, why not give games to those who have a taste for athletic sports? Where are you going to draw the line? On what grounds will you draw it? Horse-racing is also enjoyable to many worthy and law-abiding citizens, and if men may run races on Sunday, why not horses also? There are many tastes and many minds and many needs in the population of a great city, and where are you going to draw a line between the things which may wisely be permitted and the things which must inexorably be forbidden? The subject is so perplexing that many excellent people have fallen down in a fit of helplessness and confessed that they are incapable of dealing with so complicated a problem. So far

THE PURITAN SABBATH AND OURS

as they can see the only way out is to let everybody do on Sunday what he pleases. Make it a day of liberty, they say, and do not attempt to bind it round with restrictive regulations. All Sunday legislation, they assert, is Puritanic, and therefore antiquated, and consequently to be abolished. A free Sunday for free Americans, this is the conclusion to which many a man reared in a Christian home has been driven by the complexity of the Sunday problem.

But however confusing the question, there are a few things which every one of us should see clearly and lay hold of with both hands. The Day of Rest was made for man. God made it, and he made it for man because man needs it. We are to keep one day out of every seven free from our customary toil, not simply because of what is written in the Fourth Commandment, but because of what is written in the structure of man's body and mind. Sabbath observance must not be foundationed solely on any sentence in the Bible, but on the law of God as expressed in the human constitution, and as revealed in human history. Moses did not invent the Sabbath. It was old before Moses was born. It did not begin with the father of the faithful. It existed thousands of years before Abraham. It has been traced by the scholars through the centuries back to the world's far-off morning. It is a human institution, probably as old as humanity. It has always had its enemies, but they have not been able to destroy it. At the time of the French Revolution the National Convention voted to abolish Sunday from France. The experiment was tried and failed. In a few years the penitent nation came back and picked up again the discarded day. No people can dispense with it and prosper. Disraeli did not exaggerate when he declared that the Sabbath is the corner-stone of civilization.

FOREFATHERS' DAY SERMONS

If the Sabbath belongs to man, then every human being should be permitted to possess and enjoy it. No one should be allowed to rob him of it. It is man's birthright, and to lose it leaves him poor indeed. All men cannot rest on the same day, but society should make it possible for every man to have one day out of every seven free from toil. I have seen it stated that two million people in England are obliged to labor seven days out of every week. If that be true, it is a terrible arraignment of the Christian civilization of England. The case is worse, I presume, in the United States. A committee appointed not long ago to investigate the situation in our own city, reported that three hundred thousand men and women in Greater New York never have a day of rest. In order to hold their positions at all it is necessary for them to labor seven days a week. This is a damning blot on the fame of our city. It is an outrage on humanity, a sin against Almighty God. Every Christian should burn with indignation in the presence of a wrong so cruel and so inhuman. A man who must work seven days out of every week is a drudge and a slave. Society has reduced him to a galling and degrading bondage. Working seven days at the same task every week, he cannot be the man that God intended him to be. So long as there is in the world one human being who is deprived of his weekly day of rest, there is a wrong to be righted and a tragedy to be brought to an end. The pulpit has no clearer duty than thundering God's law upon this point into the ears of every generation. The work of the church of Christ will not be ended until every man is in secure possession of a Sabbath day.

There is no reason why any of us should be ashamed of the Sabbath as it was observed by the Puritans. They

THE PURITAN SABBATH AND OURS

stood for a divine principle, and however mistaken they may have been in the application of it, they saw with clearness the divine character of the Day of Rest. We may smile at the multitudinous thorns of the hedge which they set about the Sabbath, but we must not forget what lovely things grew and blossomed inside the hedge — flowers whose perfume, wafted on all the air, has made this a sweeter world. Take up some day Henry Ward Beecher's novel, "Norwood," and read again his chapter on the New England Sabbath. Beecher departed far from the Puritan at many points, but his eyes were never dim to the glory of the New England Sunday, and his heart was sensitive to the numberless blessings which the New England Sunday brought. Ralph Waldo Emerson departed farther from Puritanism than did Beecher, but to the end he revered the Puritan for what he had done for the Sabbath. Sunday is the core, he used to say, of our civilization. When De Tocqueville visited our country eighty years ago he was profoundly impressed by the extraordinary influence of New England. When he came to write his masterly book, "Democracy in America," he said: "The principles of New England spread at first to the neighboring states; then they passed successively to the more distant ones, and at length they imbued the whole confederation." No one familiar with American history can question that much of this New England influence was due to the tone of mind created and to the principles developed on the day that was kept holy to the Lord.

Beautiful, life-giving and glorious day, never more needed than now, and never in more imminent peril, let us, as Christians, do what we can to keep the day unspoiled, and to hand it down to our children as a rich legacy. Let us each one build our example into a bulwark, protecting

FOREFATHERS' DAY SERMONS

the day from the forces which are arrayed against it. Holland is saved by her dykes. The North Sea, voracious and pitiless, pounds at them incessantly, trying to wear them away. There is an ocean of frivolity and lawlessness and greed everlastingly dashing itself against the first day of the week, and it is Christian men and women who are the living material which must be built into the dykes which shall save from destruction one of humanity's divinest and most indispensable possessions. Be careful, then, of your example. Show by your conduct that you love and prize the day. Make it different from all the other days. Adorn it. Make it the jewel of the week. Keep the purple in the day. Do not let it fade. Treasure it. Consecrate it. Make it glorious. Read on the Sabbath only the best books. Think only the highest thoughts. Nourish only the noblest feelings. Let it be a day without a thorn. Release yourself from toil, and also from downward looking thoughts and worry. Banish the gloom. It is the day of the Sun of Righteousness. Get into the depths of the meaning of it. Climb to the tops of the truths embodied in it. Be in the spirit. Say to yourself and to others: " This is the day which the Lord hath made; we will rejoice and be glad in it."

XIII

CONGREGATIONALISM [1]

" Look unto the rock whence ye were hewn and to the hole of the pit whence ye were digged." — ISAIAH 51 : 1.

That exhortation has on it the earmarks of the Hebraic spirit. A Hebrew preacher was never so much at home as when he was dealing with the past. It was his delight to carry his countrymen back over the road along which they had traveled and to revive the memories of the experiences through which the nation had come. He loved the past not because he was the victim of that morbid sentimentalism which loves to brood over scenes which have vanished, but because he was so intensely interested in the future. The Hebrew preacher felt himself called of God to make the future glorious, and in order to do this he was obliged to use the past. He dealt with a people who were easily discouraged and in order to brace their drooping spirits he held up before them the glowing record of God's dealings with their fathers. By unrolling history he showed them how through all the centuries every night had dawned into a broader day, and every crown of thorns had been transfigured into a crown of glory. When his hearers grew faint-hearted and approached great duties with fear and doubtings he heartened them and drove them forward by urging them to take one good long look backward. The vision of what had been made it easier to believe in the things which were to be. When men saw bygone centuries stand behind them each one jewelled with

[1] Dec. 15, 1901.

the mercy of the Lord, they faced the future with untroubled faces assured that He who had begun a good work in them would perform it until the final day. The vanished generations were colaborers with the preacher, driving into the hearts of living men strong reasons for expecting new revelations of God's grace. And so it was well-nigh impossible for a Hebrew preacher to preach without bringing into a sermon a bit of Hebrew history. He never wearied of recalling Abraham and Isaac and Jacob: he was never more eloquent than when relating the wonders of deliverance wrought by God through Moses. It was difficult for a Hebrew poet to write a poem without weaving into it some reference to the goodness with which God had crowned the years. The Hebrew leaders were always saying: Look unto the rock whence ye were hewn, and to the hole of the pit whence ye were digged.

But there was a still deeper reason why the Hebrew preacher made such constant use of history. The Hebrews were dominated always by the conviction that they were a peculiar people, intrusted with a unique mission and appointed to a glorious destiny. From the very earliest times it had been borne in upon them that to them was given what was given to no other people and that through them all the nations of the earth were ultimately to be blessed. To men possessed with such a belief all experience must become sacred. Everything that happened to the Hebrews was supposed by them to have a divine significance. Every event was a guide post pointing the direction in which the people ought to move, every experience a window opening out upon the Eternal. Their history was their Bible. It was the food upon which they reared their children. It was the literature which was read in the synagogues, it was history which the Levites sang in the

FOREFATHERS' DAY SERMONS

Temple service. Indeed our Bible is little more than a book of history. The majority of its books are historical, and the others are adorned and illumined by quotations from the historians. If we have ears to hear we can hear the old book saying to us: " Look unto the rock whence ye were hewn, and to the hole of the pit whence ye were digged. Look unto Abraham your father, and unto Sarah that bare you!"

Indeed the history of every nation is to that nation a Bible, a book which ought to be studied with unfailing enthusiasm and religious care. In the experience of a people God's character is revealed and his will concerning that people is made increasingly clear. Every nation will be strong in proportion to its willingness to gather up the lessons which preceding generations have worked out and to drink in the spirit of the mighty men who have made the nation what it is. I wonder if we Americans are studying our history as we ought to study it? Do we earnestly teach it to our children in our homes, does it hold the place in our schools which it ought to hold, is it used in the Christian pulpit as frequently and effectively as it ought to be used by the men who are the ordained leaders of a people who like the Hebrews are also a peculiar people and to whom God has entrusted a mission to mankind?

If some boy should ask why not preach every Sunday from a sentence taken from a United States history, the answer is that while the history of every nation is in the deepest sense a Bible, there is a value to the Hebrew history which no other history can match. The Hebrews had a capacity for religion quite exceptional in the history of the world. They had an insight into spiritual laws and processes and a genius for interpreting spiritual phenomena

FOREFATHERS' DAY SERMONS

given to no other people. Because of their moral sensitiveness and their responsiveness to the movements of the Eternal Spirit, God was able to work out through them wonders which he could do through no one else. Out of that race he could bring a man in whom it was possible for the Godhead to dwell, and who could reveal to all the world both the disposition of God and the possibilities of man. For this reason the Bible, though largely a book of history, is exalted above all other books. To it is given a name which is above all other names, and to it belongs a power which no other book can claim. In the reading of American history, therefore, the Bible is a lamp to our feet and a light to our path. We will count our history sacred, but we will hold it up in the light which streams upon it from the Book of Books, that in this light we may read in our own national experiences the wondrous messages of God.

December may be fairly counted the most historical month in the calendar. It is the month when Americans are most inclined to look unto the rock whence they were hewn, and to consider the wonderful way in which the Lord God Almighty has led us. It is the month of New England dinners. The December air is made warm with the breath of orators who tell again the deathless story of the Pilgrims. The old poems are recited, the old hymns are sung, the old memories are freshened and ten thousand hearts are cleansed and strengthened by remembering Abraham our father and Sarah who bare us. In harmony then with the spirit of the time let us think this morning about that branch of the Christian church with which most of us are identified, for by thinking of it we shall be carried into the very heart of our national history. Our subject is:

CONGREGATIONALISM

Congregationalism, its Origin, Principles, and Mission

In order to grasp the significance of Congregationalism we must first master the meaning of Puritanism. What is Puritanism? Whence did it come, what did it do, when did it vanish? These are questions which ought to have answers in the mind of every intelligent American citizen. Puritanism in its essence is a zeal for purity, in doctrine, worship and conduct. This zeal has always been in the world. Every land and time has produced its Puritans. There were Puritans among the Hebrews. Elijah was one, Isaiah another, Ezra another, John the Baptist another. From the first century of Christian history until now there have been men who have resisted the corruptions of their day, and hungered and thirsted after righteousness. The deeper the corruption the hotter has been the desire to consume it. In the fourth and fifth centuries of our era the Christian church fell into the hands of a company of Roman politicians who converted the simple Gospel of our Lord into a cumbrous and mysterious thing which only ecclesiastical experts could understand. The faith once delivered to the saints was wrapped round with many so-called traditions and curious interpretations, the simple worship of early days was elaborated into a gorgeous ceremonial decked out with rites and features taken from the pagan temples; the simple government of the early churches was developed into a vast system along lines suggested by the structure of the Roman Empire, officials rising, one order above another, in a compact and mighty hierarchy, at whose top there sat the august Bishop of Rome. Under the sway of this hierarchy the virtues and graces of the Christian life in many places drooped and died, clergymen in appalling numbers became dissolute and idle, while the masses of the people floundered in ignorance and super-

FOREFATHERS' DAY SERMONS

stition. From the very first there were men who protested against the encroaching tyrannies and who endeavored to stem the devastating tide. From the eighth century to the thirteenth there were isolated companies of Christians who uttered their protest against prevailing wrongs, and strove to reproduce the pure and saintly life of Christ. In the fourteenth century an English priest, John Wycliffe, cried out against the usurpations and tyrannies of Rome with a voice that shook the universal church. He was hated by the hierarchy, and had it not been for powerful defenders he would have been promptly silenced. After his death his body was taken from its grave, burned to ashes, and the ashes were strewn in the little brook which flowed in front of the church in which this intrepid servant of God had fired the hearts of Englishmen by telling them the old, old story of Jesus and his love. In the fifteenth century a Bohemian professor, John Huss, following the example of Wycliffe, protested against the Roman abominations, and for this he was seized and burned, and his ashes were scattered in the river Rhine. At the close of the same century an Italian priest, Savonarola, enraged the hierarchy by his flaming thunderbolts, and he was strangled, and his body burned. Near the beginning of the sixteenth century a German priest, Martin Luther, uttered a protest so loud and thrilling that Northern Europe rose to its feet in revolt against the corruption of the Roman church. A few years later the English King, Henry VIII, wrenched England out of the clutches of the Bishop of Rome, and this gave opportunity for the forces which had been working since the days of Wycliffe to manifest themselves in efforts for a thorough reform. These efforts held in check by the conservative king became more radical and vigorous under Edward VI. The movement was checked by

CONGREGATIONALISM

Bloody Mary, but gained fresh momentum in the reign of Elizabeth. It grew in volume and might through the reigns of the first two of the Stuarts and reached its consummation in the days of the Commonwealth. Puritanism then, as that word is used by English-speaking peoples, is the movement for purity in doctrine, worship and life which began in the reign of Henry VIII, as a protest against prevailing corruptions, which became a political force in the reign of Elizabeth, and which came to its coronation in the protectorate of Oliver Cromwell.

The Puritans were the English men and women whose hearts were hot for release from Roman bondage, and who struggled to bring the Christian church back to the simplicity and purity of the Gospels. We ought to take a close, long look at these men, for they have been often misunderstood and flagrantly misrepresented. They were hated and resisted by many of their neighbors while they were alive, and have been caricatured and lampooned by their enemies even to the present hour. In the mind of many intelligent persons now living the Puritans were a bigoted and benighted race, a set of sour faced, crabbed hearted Christians who were unhappy themselves and made it uncomfortable for everybody else. According to the popular conception all Puritans talked with a nasal twang, dressed in uncouth and outlandish ways, and took delight in stripping life of almost all that makes life worth living. Their foibles and eccentricities have been so magnified that some of us have lost sight completely of what the Puritan really was. He has seemed so odious and ridiculous we have not cared to ascertain what he actually did. The mention of his name has called up before us a sour, narrow, inhuman individual from whom we have hidden our face, and a thing is " Puritanic " — so some people

FOREFATHERS' DAY SERMONS

think — whenever it is intolerant, unreasonable, and gloomy.

But we must not allow ourselves to become the victims of an uninstructed imagination. We must study history and make ourselves acquainted with the facts. It is not safe to trust for guidance either caricatures or lampoons or scurrilous forgeries. If we are willing to do a little honest reading we discover that the Puritans were men of like passions with ourselves, quite sensible and practical and altogether human. They loved and married and brought up children just as we do; they bought and sold, made money and lost it just as we do; they laughed and cried, played and worked like mortals of every land and time, and enjoyed to the utmost the rich, glorious privilege of living. They differed from one another just as men differ from one another now-a-days. It is not fair to reduce the Puritans to one common type of disposition, or to set up any one individual and say: "See there, that is Puritanism!" Men of the same church or party differ widely from one another. Roman Catholics are not all alike, neither are Protestants, nor Republicans, nor Democrats. There were Puritans who were glum and morbid, narrow and superstitious, but there were others sunny-hearted and the most liberal men of their generation. When we condemn such men as Nehemiah Wallington we must not forget Sir Harry Vane, genial and open-minded, one of the noblest characters in English history. If we dislike John Endicott with his narrow ideas and cruel interpretations we must remember John Winthrop, charitable and liberal, beautiful and sane, one of the very noblest figures in the history of our Republic. Of course there were *little* Puritans, morbid and fussy, but let us never forget the great ones. There were Puritans who shone in the firmament of their times

CONGREGATIONALISM

like stars of the first magnitude; others flickered and sputtered like tallow dips, and it is one of these tallow dips which the prejudiced critic of today seizes on and holds up to scorn, saying, " Here is the best which Puritanism could produce," while all the time he is living in a country flooded by the light which streamed from God into a darkened world through the great souls which had been cleansed and glorified by the Puritan spirit. Puritanism infused into the greater natures which it mastered, so says an English scholar whose religion differs widely from that which the Puritans professed, a solemnity and a power such as have but once or twice been equalled in the whole history of mankind. When therefore you hear the jocose critic pouring contempt upon the Puritans, ask him if he has ever heard of John Knox, one of the greatest giants who ever from a Christian pulpit shook the hearts of men with the sweet thunders of the Gospel. Ask him if he has read John Milton, the author of the greatest poem in English literature, and one of the mightiest geniuses who ever enshrined deathless thought in immortal verse. Ask him if he has heard of John Bunyan, the man who wrote the greatest allegory ever written in any language. Ask him if he has heard the name of Oliver Cromwell, the strongest man who has sat on the English throne since the days of William the Conqueror. These are only a few of an immortal company of saints and heroes who stopped the mouths of lions and turned to flight the armies of the aliens.

And as for what the Puritans did who can tell the completed story? When your mole-eyed critic has finished his jibes at the nasal twang and the boorish manners, remind him of a few of the great things which the Puritans accomplished. When kingship under the Stuarts was

FOREFATHERS' DAY SERMONS

climbing up the rounds of power seeking to reproduce on English soil a despotism like that of France and Spain, it was Puritanism which boldly faced the conquering usurper and trod him into the dust. When the English church was exercising an authority which Christ never gave it, and when church officers like William Laud were cutting men's ears off and slitting their noses and branding their cheeks because they refused to conform to ecclesiastical customs which the church had decreed, it was Puritanism which rebelled against the great usurpation and won for organized Christianity the liberty which is our pride and glory. In an age when Catholic Spain ruled the seas, and Catholic Rome was making desperate efforts to regain the lordship of the lands, it was Puritanism which shattered the fleets of Spain and paralyzed the armies of the Emissaries of Rome. It was the Puritan spirit which braced the hearts of twenty thousand Englishmen to face the dangers of the ocean and the greater perils of an unknown land, which twenty thousand pioneers have done more to shape the structure of our institutions and to fix our moral and political ideals, and to mould the temper and disposition of our people than any other twenty thousand men and women who have ever crossed the sea. Mr. John Fiske in the finest piece of historical writing which ever came from his pen, has traced with a master's hand the great drama in which the political center of gravity was shifted from the Tiber and the Rhine to the Thames and the Mississippi, and in his opinion the most significant event of all the events which prophesied the final triumph of the English over the Roman idea of nation building was the migration of English Puritans across the Atlantic ocean to repeat in a new environment and on a far grander scale the work which their forefathers had wrought in Britain. In

CONGREGATIONALISM

the mightiest contest ever waged on earth between two contradictory ideas Puritanism was the tremendous militant force that determined the issue.

But it is not only in Church and State that we are to look for the conquests of the Puritan spirit. It was pointed out long ago by Charles Kingsley that even in the world of fashion the Puritans have conquered, and that they have determined for the modern English speaking world the canons of taste. In the seventeenth century the men of fashion wore their hair in graceful curls hanging over their shoulders. It seemed to the Puritans that a man should cut his hair short. In derision they were called " roundheads." But every man to-day is a round-head. O Puritan thou hast conquered! The gentlemen of the seventeenth century dressed in gaudy colors. They loved red and green and blue. It seemed to the Puritans that more sober colors were becoming. And here again the world has come round to where the Puritan took his stand. When we dress in brown and drab and black we confess that the Puritan was right. Three centuries ago it was customary for men to bedeck themselves with jewelry, ribbons and laces, against which the Puritans rebelled. To them a man was dressed in taste only when he dressed plainly. In the matter of dress and manners the Puritan triumph has been complete. We no longer count him a gentleman who was counted such in the days of Shakespeare. The English gallant of those days seems to us a dude or fop. His pockets were filled with cards and dice, his mouth was filled with oaths, and his ideas of morality had not come to him from the New Testament. This perfumed, ruffled, swaggering dandy was offensive to the Puritan upon whom a nobler ideal of manhood had dawned. And here again the Puritan has conquered. Even the facetious people who make

FOREFATHERS' DAY SERMONS

fun of the Puritans have accepted the Puritanic conception of a gentleman.

Upon every department of our life these mighty men have left the prints of their hands, and it is becoming in us to render them the homage which is their due. We cannot rightly interpret history until we understand these men, for in the words of John Richard Green " the whole history of English progress on its moral and spiritual side has been the history of Puritanism." The unprejudiced scholars of all countries and parties agree with Macaulay in saying " they were the most remarkable body of men, perhaps, which the world has ever produced." We belittle ourselves whenever we attempt to belittle them. We show ourselves either ignorant or biased whenever we refuse to acknowledge the debt which the world owes them. The men of the seventeenth century were excusable for their unjust judgments upon Puritan conceptions and conduct, for they were obliged to look at them through a distorted atmosphere filled with prejudice and rumor. But we need not be thus blinded. We can see them through the clear atmosphere which God throws round a century out of which the life has gone: we are far enough removed from them to view them in the right perspective, and to catch the true proportion of their lives and deeds. We are indeed ungrateful and contemptible if we ever allow ourselves to think or speak disrespectfully of the men who bought for us with agony and bloody sweat our dearest rights and privileges, and who with tears and blood laid the deep foundations on which have been reared the fabric of our liberties.

Out of the heart of Puritanism Congregationalism came. In times of reform men go to different lengths. How far a man will go depends on his temper, education, insight, and the combination of his faculties. Some men by the

CONGREGATIONALISM

momentum of hereditary forces must be radicals, others must be conservatives. The men of the sixteenth century who started out to reform the church stopped at different points. There were four revolts. Each one more radical than the one which preceded it. First came what we may call the Episcopal revolt. There were Englishmen who were devoted to the English church and who loved its polity and forms of administration but who wished to purge it of its corruptions and to cut it loose from some of the usages and traditions with which the church of Rome had bound it. These men clung to the sacraments, the creeds, the Episcopacy, and the general structure of an established national church. Freed from the Pope all they asked was that certain features of the Roman paraphernalia might be dispensed with. Bishop Hooper, sometimes called the Father of Puritanism, may stand in our mind as a representative of this class. He made war on Romish ceremonies, and because of this he was one of the first to be burned at the stake by Bloody Mary.

But other Englishmen went farther than Hooper went. There were men who were not content with simply cutting off the Pope; they insisted that the Bishops must go too. The Bishops had for centuries been tyrannical in their temper and had claimed and exercised prerogatives which the New Testament did not give them. There was no peace or freedom for the church of Christ — so many Englishmen felt — unless the bishops should be driven out and the ecclesiastical authority be placed in the hands of a body of presbyters, part of them clergymen and the other part laymen. Here we come to a fuller recognition of the rights of laymen than the church had known since the days of the Apostles. Christians who preferred to be ruled by presbyters became known as Presbyterians.

FOREFATHERS' DAY SERMONS

They retained the sacraments and the creeds, and like the Episcopalians were stout defenders of a state church. Thomas Cartwright may stand before us as an illustrious champion of the Presbyterian position.

But there were Englishmen not so conservative as Thomas Cartwright. They were afraid of ruling Elders no less than of Bishops, and claimed that as the faith was once for all delivered to the saints so also ought supreme authority in the church to lie in the hands of the people. They believed that presbyter was only priest writ large, and that men could never enjoy the freedom wherewith Christ had made them free until every congregation of faithful men was a democracy exercising complete control over all its affairs. This meant of course that the Act of Supremacy was a mistake, for Jesus Christ and not Elizabeth was the head of the church. It also meant that the Act of Uniformity was a usurpation, for every congregation of faithful men had a right to worship God in ways which seemed to them best. These radicals were known as Separatists, and were hated of all men. They were feared and shunned by Romanists, Episcopalians and Presbyterians alike, as traitors to their country and ecclesiastical anarchists bent on shattering the church of God to fragments. Six of them were seized and hung during the reign of Elizabeth, and many others suffered many things at the hands of state officials. The Episcopalians had placed power in the hands of the Bishops, the Presbyterians in the hands of the Presbyters, the Separatists in the hands of the People, but in the sixteenth century to trust the people was both treason and blasphemy. John Robinson was one of the bravest and brainiest of these Separatists. He was the pastor of the church a portion of whose members landed at last on Plymouth Rock.

CONGREGATIONALISM

But to certain Englishmen John Robinson was a conservative. There were men who insisted on going farther. The Separatists had cast off Pope, Bishop, Presbyter, and State Church, but they clung to the sacraments and the clergy and the creeds. Why should not these also be cast off? Why not make Christianity wholly spiritual, burning up every sign and symbol which could suggest to the mind the ancient tyranny and the age-long corruption? God's voice in the soul of man, this, so these men asserted, is enough, and anything beyond this is both unscriptural and dangerous. These radicals became known as Quakers, and George Fox stands in history as their father.

Here then we reach the extreme limits of the Puritan movement. Beyond this it was not possible to go. One set of men threw off the Pope, the second set threw off the Bishops, the third set threw off the Presbyters, the fourth set threw off the clergy, sacraments and creeds. And thus the splendid Roman Catholic Church with her awe-inspiring hierarchy and her elaborate and magnificent ceremonials stands at one extreme, while at the other extreme we have only a little company of plainly dressed, earnest faced people waiting in silence for the movement of God's spirit. Roman Catholics and Quakers are separated from one another by the entire diameter of Christian thought. Under the influence of Rome the church of the carpenter of Nazareth was arrayed in gorgeous and multitudinous robes. One robe after another was torn from her by the hands of devoted reformers until at last, without clergy, sacrament, or creed, she stood naked, listening not to Parliament or council, Pope or King, but to Him who although not seen is loved.

But it is the Separatists with whom we are just now concerned. They did not agree among themselves and divided into two bands, the first calling themselves Baptists, the second becoming known as Independents. These Independents on reaching the new world became known later on as Congregationalists. The Baptists and Independents agreed on all points save two, the mode of baptism and the proper subjects of baptism. To the Independents the form of baptism was not essential, various forms having been used in Bible times, and therefore any one of these is valid. To the Baptists there was no valid baptism unless the entire body was submerged. The Independents, following the unbroken tradition and practice of the entire church for over a thousand years, claimed that children of Christian parents are proper subjects for baptism, whereas the Baptists limited this sacrament to those who were able to make a personal confession of faith in Christ. But in their general conceptions of church polity, and in their root ideas of God and Christian privileges and freedom, the Baptists and Congregationalists have ever been at one. All Baptists in church government and administration are Congregationalists, that is, they agree with us in vesting final authority neither in officials nor in councils, but in the hands of the local congregation of believers.

What is the root idea of Congregationalism? The right of every Christian to immediate access to the throne of God. Out of this basal idea everything else flows. Unless this first truth is admitted, then everything else in Congregationalism is without defense. From the days of Robinson downward we have steadfastly believed in the priesthood of believers. Every believer is a priest and has the right to enter the holy of holies and commune with the Eternal. To every seeking child of God is given directly wisdom, guidance, power. This was vehemently denied by the Church of Rome. Her teaching was that souls must come

CONGREGATIONALISM

to God through the church. By the church was meant priest, Bishop, Cardinal and Pope. Outside the church there was no salvation. Through the clergy and through the clergy alone came absolution, guidance, favor with God. Our forefathers brushed aside with one magnificent sweep the whole hierarchy from bottom to top, saying: "We are all priests unto God, and each one of us must stand for himself before the judgment seat of Christ."

After Henry VIII freed England from the yoke of Rome the English government attempted to usurp the place which the Roman hierarchy had filled. King and Parliament claimed the right not only to select church officials, but also to determine the forms of worship. The tyranny of Rome was superseded by the tyranny of Canterbury and Whitehall, and our forefathers rose in swift and determined rebellion. Elizabeth claimed the right to say by what forms all her subjects should worship God, and this right the Separatists denied. She hung a few of them and imprisoned many, but conquered none. James I with more pomp than wisdom declared that he would compel these men to conform to his church laws or he would harry them out of the land. It was to escape his wrath that the Pilgrims fled into Holland. Charles I was still more despotic than his father. Finding Parliament unwilling to be his tool, he ruled for eleven years without a Parliament. Through a large part of this period William Laud was practically head of the English church, and so merciless were his measures to bring non-conforming Christians into subjection that within these eleven years twenty thousand English Puritans crossed the Atlantic to make their home in New England. These men were determined that no one — be he even Pope or King — should stand between the soul and God.

FOREFATHERS' DAY SERMONS

But if it be true that every Christian has a right to go straight to God and is capable of receiving from him wisdom in every time of need, then upon the shoulders of every Christian is rolled a burden of responsibility. If the Christian has rights he also has duties. If he has privileges he also has obligations. If he can become a partaker of the divine life then he may be safely trusted. He may be relied on to take a share in conducting God's business on earth. He may be entrusted with church administration. In other words a company of Christian believers, every one of whom has immediate access to the mind and heart of Christ, can be trusted to manage their own church affairs without interference from Bishop or Pope, Council or General Assembly. If Christ is present wherever two or three are assembled together in his name, then his cause will not suffer if left entirely to those among whom he dwells. The congregation of believers has the right to rule, and Christ alone is head. It is for this reason we are called Congregationalists: we believe that the congregation, rather than the Presbyters, or the Bishops, or the Pope, can be trusted to decide what it ought to do. A church must have a form of worship. Who shall decide what it shall be? We say let the congregation decide it. Why not? Who shall write the confession of faith? Let the members of the church do it. They are instructed of Christ. Who shall choose the minister, and the other church officials? The congregation certainly. Who shall determine who shall be admitted into the church, and who shall be cast out as unworthy, and what shall be the methods of church activity? Why not let the people decide all these questions! If every Christian can go straight to God who gives liberally and upbraids not, surely a company of faithful men may be trusted to carry on church life and work to the glory of

CONGREGATIONALISM

God. Trust the people, that is our message to the world. We are ecclesiastical democrats. We believe in government of the people, by the people and for the people. That is our platform in politics, that is our creed in religion. The people may make mistakes, but their blunders will not be more numerous nor fatal than those made by selected bodies of church officials, or by national or international assemblies. This then is Congregationalism: the right of every local body of believers to fix their own forms of worship, to phrase their own creed, to choose their own officers, and to administer without outside check or interference their own church affairs.

It is in this local independence that we differ from the other branches of the Christian church. The Episcopal church believes in uniformity of worship. That idea is an inheritance from the days of Elizabeth which it has never been willing to cast off. Every Episcopal church throughout the country must accept at the hands of the General Council a prescribed form of worship and this must not be departed from by any congregation in the entire Episcopal communion.

We Congregationalists do not believe in binding men so. Human beings differ in temperament and taste, in aptitudes and culture, and forms which are edifying to one company of Christians are only wearisome to others. We Congregationalists say let every congregation worship in the way which best satisfies its needs and promotes its growth in holiness. The little congregation in a mining town in the shadow of the Rocky Mountains might not want a service like the one we have in Broadway Tabernacle, and we might not care for the one most helpful to our distant Western friends. Let the Tabernacle worship in its own way, and let the little Western town direct its

FOREFATHERS' DAY SERMONS

worship as it chooses, and let neither body of believers tyrannize in these matters over the other, for Christ has made us free. That is Congregationalism.

From the Presbyterians we differ in our government. The Presbytery, Synod and General Assembly are councils with judicial powers: the councils of Congregationalism have advisory functions only. What the General Assembly decrees all loyal Presbyterians must obey: what our national council advises all good Congregationalists will do, so far as the advice commends itself to their best judgment. Under one form of government the restrictions are external and legal, under the other the compulsions are interior and spiritual. By the action of the General Assembly one creed is binding on all Presbyterian preachers and churches: Congregational churches phrase their own creeds, each church for itself. The present creed of the Presbyterians is an inheritance of the seventeenth century. In the judgment of many Presbyterian leaders this creed is antiquated and in certain parts unchristian and false. But no matter how widely thousands of Presbyterians may dissent from their creed and how vigorously individual leaders may attack it, it remains the authorized confession of faith of all Presbyterian clergymen and churches until the General Assembly has modified it or cast it away. No Congregational church can be obliged to subscribe to any creed which is not acceptable to the majority of its members.

From the Methodists we differ in our freedom in the choice of ministers. According to the theory of Methodism, pastors are chosen by the Bishop, and the appointment of the Bishop is final. The members of the church may vigorously protest and the preacher himself may be reluctant to go, but if all are loyal Methodists they will abide by the decision of the Bishop no matter what it may be.

CONGREGATIONALISM

Congregationalism submits to no such bondage. We believe that the members of a church know better than any outside officials what man can most acceptably meet their needs, and build them up in righteousness. No man can become the pastor of any Congregational church without receiving a majority vote of all the members who care to express their preferences in choosing a leader.

From the Catholics we differ at almost every point. With them the hierarchy is supreme, with us the people. It is the Catholic clergy who determine the entire policy of the church and fix every detail in its administration: in a Congregational church nothing of moment is done without the consent of the laity. According to the Roman idea the clergy constitute the church: according to the Congregational idea the church is made up of the Lord's followers.

What then has been the mission of Congregationalism? It has taught the world new lessons in freedom. It has demonstrated that the people may be trusted. By admitting laymen into new liberty it has developed the sense of individual responsibility and produced a body of Christian people who have profoundly influenced the temper and methods of the entire Christian world. There is not a denomination which does not bear on it the marks of our influence. We have radiated the spirit of liberty into every branch of the Christian church in the new world. The Roman Catholic church in the United States is widely different in temper and ideals from the same church in any other land. Catholic laymen have in many instances rebelled against the tyranny of their ecclesiastical superiors, manifesting an independence and determination to secure their rights which remind one of the spirit which has from the beginning dominated our Congregational churches.

FOREFATHERS' DAY SERMONS

We have above all others contributed to the creation of that atmosphere of democracy under whose continuous and irresistible influence all American institutions have taken their present shape. Because of the strength and independence of our leaders we have been able to be the advance guard in many a noble cause. In the great work of education we have always been in the forefront. We founded the first college established in the new world, and planted the idea out of which our public school system has developed. If men are to be trusted they must be educated. To those who rule in state and church knowledge is indispensable. Bowdoin and Dartmouth, Amherst and Williams, Harvard and Yale — all founded by Congregationalists — are witnesses to our unfaltering belief that neither state nor church is secure unless the people have knowledge. Streams of influence have flowed from these New England colleges across the land, causing colleges and academies and schools to spring up, helping to shape the life of communities and to fix the temper and ideals of our civilization. First in education, we were first also in the work of home and foreign missions. We sent the first Christian workers among the Indians, and organized the first American society to carry the gospel to foreign lands. We are the light brigade in the Lord's great army, and can dash ahead and seize strategic points and hold them until the heavier battalions come up. We did this in the days of slavery. We pushed our work into the South and while other churches held aloof we preached the rights of black men under the eaves of southern meeting houses in which the worshipers had forgotten that a negro was the child of God. Our freedom gives us room to act and that at once. While Radicals and Conservatives in the national councils of the other branches of the church wrestle with one another, the latter constantly holding the former back from attempted reformations, we are free to plunge at once into whatever great work the Lord assigns, and can keep abreast of the most advanced thought and most efficient methods of the times. If any Congregational church is ever a laggard in the day of progress or ever a recreant to present duty, it is not because it is handicapped by denominational machinery, but because its pastor and members are blind to opportunity and unwilling to come to the help of the Lord against the mighty.

But we have given more than our spirit to our sister denominations. We have assisted them in their work by lavish contributions of men and money. Many of the giants of Presbyterianism were born in Congregational homes, and Episcopacy owes not a little of its strength to the men whose torches were lit at our fires. The greatest Episcopal preacher which America has produced was given to that denomination by a Congregationalist mother, and the successor of Bishop Brooks was reared and trained within our denominational fold. Run through the churches of the metropolis, and you will be surprised to find what a large proportion of the effective preachers, and the faithful and influential laymen, have on them the marks either of Congregational ancestry or Congregational training. Our polity has produced a type of Christian which is prized and utilized in every branch of the Christian church. Of our money we have given so freely to outside causes that our own enterprises have often been crippled by deficits resulting from our indiscriminate generosity.

If we have given we also have received both in brain and treasure from every branch of the Christian church. We have not lived alone, nor have we worked alone. Whatever is excellent in the methods and labors of other Chris-

FOREFATHERS' DAY SERMONS

tians we claim the privilege of using. All things are ours because we belong to Christ. As a branch of the universal church we prize and use whatever treasures have been given to preceding generations. Everything that belongs to Christianity belongs to us, and from every branch of christendom we have taken ideas and interpretations which have enriched our denominational life. To the Presbyterians we have been bound by ties especially close and tender, freely exchanging ministers and laymen, and for many years working together in home and foreign missionary labors.

Indeed our hospitality to all members of the great household of faith and our willingness to cooperate with all who call upon the name of the Lord have been our crowning characteristics. We are not sectarian nor exclusive. We dwell more upon the points on which we agree with our neighbors than upon the points on which we differ. So seldom do our ministers preach on Congregationalism that thousands of our people do not know our history and cannot state the distinguishing principles of our denominational life. So slight is the emphasis placed on denominational loyalty that our members on moving from one locality to another pass readily into whatever communion happens to be nearest to them. Congregationalists above all others are sought after by those soliciting money for needy causes, so great is their reputation for willingness to help whatever movement promises to advance the Kingdom of our Lord. We have no quarrels with anybody. Claiming the right to worship God in our own way, and to do our work as seemeth to us best, we give to every body of Christians the rights which we claim for ourselves. If some Christians prefer incense and candles, let them have them; if others like an elaborate liturgy, let them enjoy it; if others like

CONGREGATIONALISM

Bishops or Presbyters, or Presiding Elders, or baptism by immersion only, it is their privilege to have what they desire. We deny to no man the freedom with which Christ has set us free. We are willing to cooperate with all branches of the church so far as they will let us. We strive to live at peace with all our neighbors. While we do not believe in the uniformity of the church, we do believe most heartily in its unity, and our constant aim is to keep the unity of the spirit in the bond of peace. With all true Christians everywhere we join with Christ in his high priestly prayer that all his followers may be one. The Broadway Tabernacle is a Congregational church, but she does not parade her denominational name in her legal title. She is true to the best spirit and tradition of our denominational history when she writes as the first article in her creed these catholic and fraternal words:

"As a church of Christ, associated in accordance with the teachings of the New Testament, for the public worship of God, for the observance of gospel sacraments and ordinances, for mutual edification and encouragement in the Christian life, and for the advancement of the Redeemer's kingdom, we declare our union in faith and love with all who love our Lord Jesus Christ."

XIV

THE CONTRIBUTION OF CONGREGATIONALISM TO EDUCATION [1]

"Remember the days of old, consider the years of many generations." — DEUT. 32 : 7.

It would not be possible for me to allow this day to pass without reminding you that it is the anniversary of one of the cardinal events in human history. No phenomenon of the Christian centuries is more deserving of our earnest study than the Puritan movement of the sixteenth and seventeenth centuries, and in all that mighty movement of thought and action no event is of deeper or more lasting significance than the landing of the Pilgrims on Plymouth Rock two hundred and eighty-two years ago.

We Americans, I fear, do not deal seriously enough with the past. The present is so fascinating and so absorbing we have neither the time nor the inclination to give ourselves to the men who have lived and the years that have been. And that is a pity. To neglect the past is to impoverish and weaken our life. We are not isolated creatures, unrelated to yesterday; we are members of a vast society, cells in a complex organism, our blood carries impulses and instincts formed by the experiences of a thousand generations. The forces which drive the ship on which our fortunes are embarked blow like winds out of the vast cave of the Past. The swell of the sea over which we glide is due to convulsions which took place generations ago. Our world was built up bit by bit by men and women who vanished

[1] Dec. 21, 1902.

THE CONTRIBUTION TO EDUCATION

from the scene of their labors before we came upon the stage. Our atmosphere, intellectual, social, political, religious, is the creation of men whose hands have vanished and whose voices are still. How then can a man appreciate his age unless he knows the ages of which his age is the latest born child? How can he interpret his times unless he understands the times out of which the present world has been evolved? Our distinguished fellow townsman, Mr. Howells, has of late been giving advice to young women in regard to books and reading. Although a novelist himself, he places fiction last and history first. Young women, he says, should read history for perspective. And this advice is good for men also, both young and old. Without true perspective we cannot place correct valuations on either characters or events, nor can we measure the relative importance of the forces combining to create the dangers and the problems of our modern world. How can we understand the industrial crisis which is on us if we are not familiar with the world's history since the days of the French Revolution? And how can we correctly interpret the life and duty of the Christian church unless we have mastered church history from Reformation times down to our own?

Thus to the superficial and uninformed observer denominationalism is a hopeless enigma or a rock of offence. That the Christian church should exist under different forms of government and with divers types of worship seems to him fresh evidence of the enormous range of human folly, and of the constant activity of the devil. "Why," he exclaims impatiently, "should there not be one church, with one worship, one creed, one head?" But to one who looks more deeply into the universe which is our home, it is no surprise that the Christian church should exist in many branches. God does indeed love unity, but he seems

FOREFATHERS' DAY SERMONS

to love it in variety. There is a unity in every landscape, but hill and valley, shrub and tree, moss and flower, rock and brook are some of the many forms which nature chooses by which to express her loveliness. Humanity is one, but God breaks it into races, giving to each race a specific work to do. He has made of one blood all the nations, but how widely they differ from one another! The same race becomes a different thing under different skies, the Anglo-Saxons preferring one form of government in England, another in Canada, another in the United States, and still another in Australia. Why should it be surprising if the Church of God, like a mighty tree whose leaves are to be for the healing of the nations, should throw out many branches, each branch producing a special variety of fruit? Or if the church of Christ is indeed an army, why should it not like other armies be organized into regiments, brigades, divisions, and corps, all of them under the leadership of the Captain of the world's salvation? And just as in an army efficiency is promoted and courage is increased by each regiment developing among its men an *esprit de corps*, by the treasuring of its memories, by the hallowing of its traditions, by the recital now and then of the experiences through which it has come with tattered flag and broken bayonet and garments rolled in blood, so it is a good and wholesome and Christian thing for each regiment in the Lord's army to preserve and hallow its traditions, to recount occasionally the battles in which it has played a part, and to ponder the significance of the miracles of grace which Christ through it has wrought in the history of his church. That we may be stronger Christians and more forceful men, let us think this morning about the contribution which that branch of the Christian church to which we belong has made to the cause of education.

THE CONTRIBUTION TO EDUCATION

The Puritan flood reached the shores of the new world in two streams. The first and smaller stream came by way of Holland and struck the coast of New England at Plymouth in 1620. The *Mayflower* brought 102 passengers, the *Fortune* 35, the *Anne* and the *Little James* 96, making a total of 233, an immortal company to be known forever as the "Pilgrim Fathers." But the colony which these men founded grew but slowly. At the end of seven years Plymouth had only 267 souls, at the end of twenty-five years only about 3,000. The "Old Colony" did not produce a great preacher, a famous scholar, or an influential statesman. It never planted a college. Not even a public school was established in Plymouth during the first half century of her history.

The fame of the Pilgrim Fathers rests not on what they themselves achieved but what they led to. These men were stepping-stones for others. As Bradford put it, " Out of small beginnings great things have been produced, and as one small candle may light a thousand, so the light here kindled hath shone to many, yea, in some sort, to our whole nation." The fire they kindled at Plymouth made it easier for other Puritans to cross the Atlantic. In 1628 John Endicott came with a company of 60, the following year Francis Higginson arrived with a company of 400, in 1630 John Winthrop came, and with him 1,000 others. In twelve years 20,000 came and then the flood of immigration ceased. Among these twenty thousand Englishmen an unusual proportion were clergymen, and most of these were men of university training. Fully three-fourths of the university men were from Cambridge. Among these men were John Cotton, a "walking library," according to his learned biographer, and Richard Mather, father of a president of Harvard College, and grandfather of one of

FOREFATHERS' DAY SERMONS

the most learned men of his day, and Thomas Shepard, the friend of Cromwell and Milton, and John Davenport, one of the three Americans invited to sit in the Westminster Assembly, and John Eliot, the first man to put the Bible into the Indian language, and John Norton, the author of the first Latin book produced in Massachusetts, and Thomas Hooker, whom Cotton Mather and others have called " the incomparable," and who was foreordained to become the author of " the first written constitution known to history, that created a government." With such leaders we are not surprised to read that a school was established in 1635, and that a college was founded in 1636. Two years later a young minister — John Harvard — about to die, left to the college one-half of his estate and his entire library consisting of 260 books, and from him the college took its name. The founding of Harvard College was an event the glory of which will never fade. Historians have loved to dwell upon the heroism of the little community which at the very beginning of its life, torn by dissensions within and beset by dangers on every side, was willing to set aside a sum of money equal to the entire taxation of the colony for the support of an institution of learning. Before these men had built their own homes or had made the necessary bridges and roads, their minds turned to the education of the young men who were to take their places after they themselves had passed on. Hostile Indians in their rear and a threatening government beyond the ocean had no such terror for them as did the fear that the church of God might be left without an educated ministry. Knowing that ignorance is the mother of superstition, they were ready to make every sacrifice necessary to establish in their midst a college which should do for the new world what Oxford and Cambridge had done for the old. It was

THE CONTRIBUTION TO EDUCATION

not the first time in history that a people by their representatives had founded a place of education, but never before had men so circumstanced as these given so generously of their substance for the maintenance of an institution in which their children might pursue the courses of the higher learning. The story of the first hundred years of Harvard's struggles is most fascinating. It was no easy thing for a college to live through those troubled and almost desperate times. Had it not been for constant sacrifice and patience the feeble school would have surely died. It was supported in large measure by the free offerings of the people. One man gave a sheep, another a piece of cotton cloth, another a silver spoon, another a fruit dish, sacred heirlooms which had been rescued from the homeland and borne through the storms of the sea, but which though precious in the eyes of their owners were cheerfully surrendered that the college might survive. From year to year collections were taken among the farmers of Connecticut, for they too could send their sons to Cambridge and reap the blessings which learning has to give. For fifty-seven years Harvard was the only college in America. Not till 1693 did the Episcopalians of Virginia, after a series of disappointments and delays which would have vanquished the hearts of less heroic men, succeed in establishing a college to which was given the name, William and Mary.

Of the twenty-three colleges founded in the eighteenth century five were established by Congregationalists. The first of these both in time and in importance was Yale, the year of its birth being the opening year of the century 1701. John Davenport had dreamed of such an institution for the young men of Connecticut, but he had died with his dream unfulfilled, bequeathing it to a generation which was able to give it a local habitation and a name.

FOREFATHERS' DAY SERMONS

Like Harvard, Yale was conceived in the heart of a Congregational minister and it was Congregational ministers who laid the foundations of its greatness. The ten ministers, all but one graduates of Harvard, who met at Branford in the closing year of the seventeenth century and who made a contribution of forty volumes from their library " for the founding of a college," were weak in resources but mighty in their faith. From the day when the legislature granted a charter vesting the governing power in the hands of ten Congregational ministers down to the present time, the majority of the governing body of Yale University have been Congregational ministers, and with the exception of President Hadley all the Presidents have been Congregational ministers, too. Yale began with a single student and in two hundred years the one has become three thousand. The acorn has grown into an oak.

One of the many men whose hearts were kindled by the great revival of George Whitefield was Eleazer Wheelock. In 1754 he opened a school for Indians in the northern extremity of old Lebanon in Connecticut, and this school, carried into New Hampshire, was enlarged and opened in 1770 under the name of Dartmouth College. Its first President, Dr. Wheelock, was a Congregational minister, as have been all its other presidents but one. The College of Vermont was founded in 1791, Williams College in 1793, and Middlebury in 1800, all three through the enthusiasm and energy of Congregational ministers and laymen.

But the time would fail if I should attempt to tell you of Bowdoin (founded in 1802) with its line of distinguished presidents, all of them Congregational ministers; of Amherst (founded in 1821) and the stream of men who have left her halls to teach and inspire and bless the world; of

THE CONTRIBUTION TO EDUCATION

Mt. Holyoke (founded in 1837), and its heroic founder Mary Lyon, who at a time when the world did not yet believe in the higher education of women dared to stand for principles which are now the commonplaces of our civilization, and left an impress on the spirit of her school which the years have not effaced; of Wellesley (founded in 1875), and the generous Congregational layman, Henry F. Durant, who made the village of college buildings on the shores of lovely Waban possible; of Smith (founded in 1875), and the consecrated Congregational woman, Sophia Smith, who by her generosity called into existence one of the greatest of all existing colleges for girls. These are the works of our hands in New England. None of these schools are in the strictest sense denominational. When their names are mentioned no one thinks of connecting them with any particular branch of the Christian church. Harvard swung away from Congregational authority a century ago, and the University of Vermont has never been a Congregational institution. In none of them are the principles of our denominational life expounded or enforced. They are simply Christian schools ministering to the higher life of the nation. Their aim is not to make Congregationalists, but men and women. But although we do not claim them as being in any narrow sense our own, we should feel grateful to the Giver of all good that he inspired the hearts of our Congregational fathers to leave behind them such monuments of their wisdom and devotion, and that men and women whose hearts have been kindled at our altars have been permitted through the grace of God to render so great a service to our Republic and the world. Our fathers labored, planting the tiny seeds, laying toilsomely the deep foundations, and other men of many different communions have by contributions of money, thought and

FOREFATHERS' DAY SERMONS

prayer, entered into their labors, expanding and strengthening what the men of other days began. But let it not be forgotten that the pioneers in the great work, the heroes in the opening of the battle, the men who bore the burden in the heat of the day, were the spiritual brethren of Cromwell and Milton, men who believed it possible to have a church without a bishop and a state without a king.

Harvard, Yale, Dartmouth, Williams, Bowdoin, Amherst, Mount Holyoke, Wellesley, Smith, what the nation owes to them who can measure or declare? How many lustrous names can be culled from the roll of their 76,000 graduates? Preachers, lawyers, doctors, editors, teachers, merchants, soldiers, statesmen, the men who have moulded America have in large numbers been moulded in the schools of New England. There is scarcely a town under our flag in which there is not at least one representative of one of these schools shaping by his life the thought and ideals of the community. Year after year through many generations a mighty stream of young life has flowed into New England from every section of our country, there to remain until drenched with the New England spirit and then returning to its former places to leaven the entire national life. And although our country stretches three thousand miles to the Pacific, and although there are in every section of the Union great and honored institutions of learning, rich in resources and teaching skill, this tide of life sweeping toward New England still continues unabated and is to-day one of the most remarkable and inspiring phenomena of our age. There are to-day over ten thousand students in these six colleges for men, and over twenty-five hundred young women in these three colleges for women, and of the 12,500, over 5,600 or 45 per cent. belong to regions outside of New England. In these nine institutions, all of them

THE CONTRIBUTION TO EDUCATION

founded by men and women of our communion, and all of them still retaining the Congregational atmosphere, are one-twelfth of all the college students of our Republic. Through the work of these nine institutions the spirit of Congregationalism has entered into the very blood and bone of the American people, and no account of our national greatness is fair or complete which does not recognize the vast service rendered to American democracy and Christianity by these nine Christian schools.

I have lingered thus long on New England because New England has been the fountain from which have flowed the streams of our denominational life. But Congregationalism is not an interpretation of the religion of Christ good for only one corner of a nation, it belongs to the entire continent, it is good for the world. And what it has been in New England it must be in every region which is willing to give it room to display its power and do its work. It was only a half-century ago that a few of our leaders, among whom was the pastor of this church, Dr. J. P. Thompson, broke down the barriers which had kept the polity of our fathers local, and taught men to see that we have a mission coterminous with the boundaries of the world. Within these fifty years we have been sowing colleges and schools beside all waters. We have belted the Gulf of Mexico with a line of schools, all but one of them for the uplifting of the people whom Abraham Lincoln set free. Rollins in Florida, Atlanta and Green in Georgia, Talladega in Alabama, Tougaloo in Mississippi, Straight in Louisiana, Tillotson in Texas, these are names which ought to be familiar to every boy and girl in our Sunday Schools throughout the land. And to these should be added Fisk University in Tennessee, and Howard University in Washington City, and also Hampton Institute in Virginia, for

FOREFATHERS' DAY SERMONS

Hampton was the outgrowth of forces which our American Missionary Association set in motion. No matter with what race we attempt to deal, we feel that without academies and schools we can do nothing.

And what we have done in the South we have done still better in the West. As early as 1833 we founded Oberlin, and one year later Marietta, and one year later still Illinois. If you inspect your map you will see we have belted the continent with our schools. In the northern chain are Olivet, Beloit, Ripon, Carleton, Fargo, Redfield, Yankton, and Whitman. In the central chain are Oberlin, Wheaton, Illinois, Grinnell, Tabor, Wilton, Gates, Doane, Forest Grove, and Pacific. In the south central chain are Marietta, Berea, Drury, Fairmount, Washburn, Kingfisher, Colorado, and Pomona. And thus in every way we are endeavoring to bind our nation by chains of schools around the feet of God.

But our line is gone out through all the earth, and our words to the end of the world. It seems well-nigh impossible for a Congregationalist to carry the Gospel to any land whatsoever without his endeavoring sooner or later to establish a school. The men who touch us become filled with the same enthusiasm and are fired by a like ambition. A bright Japanese boy, Joseph Neesima, comes to this country, goes through three of our schools, and before he has completed his course he is burning with a desire to establish a school in his own land. He is permitted to do this, and the Doshisha is founded at Kyoto. At Tungcho and Foochow in China, at Aintab and Harpoot, Marash and Marsovan, Smyrna and Constantinople in Turkey, at Pasumalai in India, at Samokov in Bulgaria, at Batticotta in Ceylon, at Madrid in Spain, we have planted institutions in which the intellect is trained and Western learning is

THE CONTRIBUTION TO EDUCATION

imparted under the influences of the religion of Christ. It was a Congregationalist, Dr. Daniel Bliss, who largely built up the Syrian college at Beirut, and it was another Congregationalist, Dr. Cyrus Hamlin, who built up Robert College in Constantinople and gave it a fame which circles the globe. What mighty results shall follow the faithful teaching done to-day by our foreign missionaries scattered across the lands we cannot even dream; we rest content with the assurance that work done in the Lord is never done in vain.

This then from the beginning has been the special form of work which God has given us to do. In this direction we have always travelled by what seems a divine thrusting on. The love of study and the love of teaching run strong and hot in the Congregational blood. A typical Congregationalist never feels that he has finished his course or kept the faith unless he has made a contribution to knowledge. Dwight L. Moody was a layman without the advantages of early school training. He became the mightiest Evangelist of his generation, and although unlettered was the hero of college students, and counted it the greatest work of his life to found two schools, one for boys and one for girls, on opposite banks of the river which flows through the lovely town in which he was born. General O. O. Howard, for many years an illustrious soldier in the United States army, and for a still longer period a faithful soldier in the army of the Lord, felt his life to be incomplete until he had raised a substantial endowment for Lincoln University at Cumberland Gap, Tennessee. Dr. Frank W. Gunsaulus, one of Chicago's busiest pastors, feels led of the Spirit to take upon his mind and his heart the additional burden of the management of a great technical school. We have supplied the world with teachers and professors

FOREFATHERS' DAY SERMONS

and college presidents. Dr. Gilman of Johns Hopkins, Dr. Angel of Michigan University, Dr. Northrop of the University of Minnesota, Dr. Adams of Wisconsin University, Dr. Thwing of the Western Reserve University, are only a few of a long list of men who have stood in recent years foremost in our Denominational Household of Faith and also in the great cause of American Education.

Because of our absorption in the work of instruction we have not grown numerically as have many of our neighbors. The Methodists and Baptists have been the great evangelizing churches of American Christendom. They have blown the bugle and beat the drums and enlisted recruits for the army of the Lord as no other bands of Christians in America have done. And they have their reward. They can point with pride to vast armies, millions strong, of men and women who march to-day under the banner of the cross as the result of their herculean efforts. We too have had our work, and have done it. If it is a work not so conspicuous or picturesque as that of others, it is a work no less necessary and no less substantial in its service to mankind. We Congregationalists number in the United States only 650,000 and in all the world we are only 1,200,000. But our mission has not permitted us to take delight in numbers. We have had a deeper and a more quiet work to do. We have never been sectarian, claiming that we alone constitute the true Church of God. Ever have we minimized all external rites and badges and enthroned the principles which lie at the centre of life in Christ. We have been content to create an atmosphere in which all Christian bodies might do more effective work, to build up a temper by which the world might come into closer sympathy with the ideals of our Lord himself, to introduce into all life a leaven, which, working silently and gradually,

THE CONTRIBUTION TO EDUCATION

shall by and by leaven the whole lump. No section of the modern world has escaped the touch of our spirit; every feature of our Republic bears the prints of our hands. We have fed the democratic spirit on both sides the sea, and with truthfulness we can say, To this end were we born and for this cause came we into the world to bear witness to the worth and supreme importance of an enlightened mind.

If you ask why we above all others have laid such emphasis on education and intellectual culture, the answer is to be found in the Puritan conception of the human soul. Our entire American system of education is the outgrowth of a religious idea. According to the Puritan, the human soul is great. The individual man, no matter where or who, is God's own creation, and this man answers to God and to God alone for his thoughts and actions. He has a right to read the Bible and to reach his own conclusions. He will listen of course to his religious teachers, but he will test the truth of what they say. He will not believe every spirit, but will test them and see whether they are of God. But how can a man be trusted with such weighty matters unless he is informed? How can he prove all things and be able to hold fast the good unless his mind is trained to observe, discriminate, and search below the surface for the truth of things? If a man is to be trusted with the Bible, then he must know how to read it. He cannot read it without an education. If church government is to be handed over to the freemen in Christ, then they must be intelligent, and how can intelligence grow unless fostered by schools? And if the government of the state is likewise to be entrusted to the hands of the people, then education is a debt which the state owes to her citizens. Without schools it is not possible to have a church without a bishop or a state with-

FOREFATHERS' DAY SERMONS

out a king. Schools then are a logical outcome of the Puritan conception of the soul. A deal of time has been spent in trying to find out to whom belongs the glory of introducing into this country our public school idea. Some have claimed it came by way of Holland and others have asserted with equal assurance that it was an importation straight from England. The fact is that wherever Calvinism took root, there sprang up a demand for schools. In France, in Switzerland, in Holland, in Scotland and in New England the same forces began to work, and popular education became a dream of the leaders of the church. Fifty years before the landing of the Puritans at Boston, John Knox in his book of discipline had demanded a school in connection with every church, and before the Pilgrims left Holland the Synod of Dort had given expression to the same demand. As Fiske says, "One of the cardinal requirements of democratic Calvinism has always been elementary education for everybody." It matters little therefore whether this school idea came by Cape Cod or by Sandy Hook, nor does it matter where or when the first school on American soil may have been established. What is certain beyond all successful contradiction is that it was in New England among the English Puritans that the idea was most fully developed and worked out into a system which in the course of time became the system of the entire American people. There was a public school in Boston as early as 1635, but it was not till 1647 that the General Court of Massachusetts passed a statute making it obligatory for every township having 50 householders to support a primary school and for every township having 100 householders to support a grammar school in which boys might be fitted for college. "By this law of 1647," says Edward Eggleston, "the Puritan government of Massa-

THE CONTRIBUTION TO EDUCATION

chusetts rendered probably its greatest service to the future. From that quaint act has been slowly evolved the school system that now obtains in the United States." The law adopted by Massachusetts in 1647 was adopted by Connecticut three years later, and in both colonies the reason given for the law was that men might have a better understanding of the word of God, "it being one chief project of the old deluder Satan to keep men from the knowledge of the Scriptures." Although education had its stalwart friends in Virginia and the very first Assembly in 1619 favored the erection of a proposed university and college, yet for various reasons all educational schemes dwindled and halted, so that when fifty years after the founding of Jamestown, the English Commissioners for Foreign Plantations asked for information on the subject of education from the Governors of Virginia and Connecticut, the former replied: "I thank God there are no free schools or printing presses and I hope we shall not have any these hundred years;" while the second reported: "One-fourth of the annual revenue of the Colony is laid out in maintaining free schools for the education of our children." It was the development of a complete system of education in New England which made it possible for Harvard College to attain a prosperity and supremacy which William and Mary College never reached, and which produced in New England a civilization in comparison with which the civilization of the South at a later day was found inferior. If we did not discover the idea of popular education, we at least developed it until all men were ready to establish it as one of our fundamental American institutions.

We may justly claim then that our contribution to the cause of education has been a large one. In these days

FOREFATHERS' DAY SERMONS

when the educational movement is the most popular as well as the mightiest of all, when in a single year the rich men of our nation are willing to give over one hundred million dollars that the interests of education may be advanced, when men are beginning to realize that no position outranks in importance the position of a teacher, and that no institution offers larger returns for the money invested than a well equipped Christian school, let us not forget the heroism and wisdom of our foresighted Congregational fathers, who, when "exiles in a wilderness," to use Macaulay's phrase, recognized the great principle that the state should take upon itself the charge of the education of the people. We do not claim we have done it all. We are not unmindful of the magnificent work done by brethren at our side. We claim simply a place in the very foremost ranks of the educational leaders and toilers of the world. We were the first to plant a college on these shores. We were the first to establish here a system of graded schools. We were the first to open college doors to women as well as men on equal terms. We were the first to establish a college for the higher education of women. We were the first to establish schools for the education of the freedmen of the South. We were the first to found institutions of learning in many foreign lands. We have been first, in proportion to our numbers, in supplying both men and treasure for the education of the world. And to God shall be the glory now and forevermore. And if his will concerning us for the days which are to come can be gleaned from the way along which he has led us through the centuries which are gone, then it would seem that we are ordained to minister especially to the human mind, and that along educational lines we are to seek and expect our coming victories. If this be so, then let us project the foundations

THE CONTRIBUTION TO EDUCATION

of additional schools for boys both in the East and West, and make certain of the strength of the pulpit in every college town, and let us be so generous with our gifts that no one of our existing schools or colleges shall ever for lack of money perish from the earth.

XV

FUNDAMENTAL TRAITS OF PURITAN CHARACTER AS ILLUSTRATED BY JOHN MILTON [1]

"*There was a man sent from God whose name was John.*" — JOHN 1 : 6.

The man whom the writer holds in his mind's eye is John the Baptist, the man of whom Jesus of Nazareth once said that no greater man had ever been born of woman. When the Evangelist thinks of John's wonderful gifts and his extraordinary influence and of how finely he fitted into the needs of his land and time, he is convinced that this John the Baptist did not come into the world by accident, but that he came as the servant of some one higher than himself, his advent being a part of the all-comprehending plan of Deity.

There is something thrilling in this Hebrew way of looking upon great men as messengers sent from God. The Hebrew was always linking the earth with the heavens. It was an ancient adage in Palestine that the spirit of man is the candle of the Lord, or in other words that human personality is the point at which the divine energy bursts into flame. With this conception of the relation of the human spirit to God, great men became to the Hebrew the revealers of the divine nature, the promulgators and defenders of the heavenly plan. It was for this reason that biography became the basis of the Hebrew system of education, and the life of the nation was organized around a few radiant and mighty names. Abraham, Isaac, Jacob, Moses, David,

[1] Dec. 27, 1908.

FUNDAMENTAL TRAITS

and Elijah, these and a few others became talismanic, and around these names not only the tenderest memories but also the fondest hopes were twined. Around these mighty personalities Hebrew parents gathered their children, awakening their hearts and invigorating their spirits by bringing them into contact with the men by whose genius and consecration the past had been made glorious and the nation been lifted to renown. To these men each succeeding generation went reverently back to light its torch, and from these men as from so many fountains there flowed vital streams by which the Hebrew world was kept strong and resolute in working out the destiny to which it had been called. It was out of a nation thus taught and guided that there came in the fulness of time the man of men, the one Perfect Man — Jesus of Nazareth.

If this was the method adopted by the most spiritually gifted nation which has ever played a part on the stage of human action, it is a method not without suggestion to nations which have still their career to run. God never leaves himself without a witness, but in every land and time great men and true arise to reveal the eternal purposes and to make plain the paths in which men's feet should walk. No form of atheism is so blind and mischievous as that which confesses God's presence and power in one particular nation and which fails to see him outside this narrow circle, which hails with gladness his operations among an ancient people, but which refuses to believe he was working yesterday and is working still to-day. It is the teaching of our religion that God is the same yesterday, to-day and forever, and if we have rightly caught the spirit and teaching of our Scriptures, we shall make the study of biography one of the highest functions of both school and church, and shall not hesitate to do in our time what John the Evange-

FOREFATHERS' DAY SERMONS

list did nineteen centuries ago, proclaim that men who usher in bright ages and make glorious the ideas by which the soul lives, are anointed by the Most High God and sent into the world by Him. Why should we not say with assurance and great gladness: "There was a man sent from God into the nineteenth century whose name was Abraham Lincoln," or "There was a man sent from God into the eighteenth century whose name was George Washington," or "There was a man sent from God into the seventeenth century whose name was John Milton"? It is this seventeenth century servant of Jehovah of whom we are to think this morning.

The world has been filled with voices during these recent weeks praising the name of Milton. It was impossible that the three hundredth anniversary of his birth should come and go without stirring the hearts of men profoundly. Poems have been composed in his honor, eulogies have been pronounced, essays have been written, orations have been delivered, and in divers ways and with various degrees of reverence and appreciation the English-speaking world has been induced to contemplate for a season the genius and achievements of England's greatest religious poet. Most of what has been said and written has had to do with Milton as an artist in the realm of words. And this is natural. It is indeed an attractive theme, and poets and essayists and literary critics will never grow weary of telling how this London poet spoke our language with a new accent and called out of it harmonies which had never been heard before. He was indeed a wizard, compelling the refractory adjectives to fall each one into its own predestined place, commanding the sentences to climb to unprecedented and unimaginable heights! What a magician he was in the mastery of tones, framing out of

FUNDAMENTAL TRAITS

them celestial harmonies which have fallen on the world like an unescapable and indescribable enchantment. But Milton the poet is not my theme. Nor do I care to deal with him at this time either as a patriot, or a thinker, or a controversialist or a statesman. He played in his day many parts, and the various acts which made up the tragedy of his life have a fascination when rightly told which clutches the attention and stirs the heart. But all this interesting history I must pass over with only here and there a glance, because my subject is Milton the Man. It is not to his style — called by Matthew Arnold the finest illustration in English literature of the great style — but to his character to which I would turn your eyes. The Grolier Club of this city has now on exhibition three hundred and thirty pictures of Milton — the largest number ever collected in one place at one time — but it is not his personal appearance in which I am interested. I wish to hold up before you the picture of his soul. It is not Milton the poet, or Milton the defender of liberty, or Milton the Latin Secretary of the Council of the English Commonwealth, but Milton the man, who is best worthy of our study. Let us examine the texture of his spirit, let us note the dominant traits of his mind and his heart.

It is when we deal with his character that we deal with that part of him which is imperishable. Much that he thought has long since become obsolete, much that he wrote has no longer interest except for antiquarians. The world cares nothing for what he thought on the subject of divorce, and only a little for his ideas in regard to education. His notions on political science have long ago been superseded, and his cosmogony, which he embodied in the greatest of his poems, belongs to a world which can never return. His conception of the stellar universe as a sphere

FOREFATHERS' DAY SERMONS

with a hard crust, suspended from the floor of heaven, in which crust there is an aperture near the top not far from the gate of heaven, through which both angels and demons can find access to our world, all this belongs to an order of thought which is as foreign to the men of our day as are the things which existed before the flood. Even his style of writing is antiquated. It is gorgeous and stiff as cloth of gold, but it is not the style to which men of our day are willing to listen. We examine it and admire it, just as we marvel at the elaborately carved old bedsteads and other pieces of furniture which have been handed down to us from preceding generations. His style of speech is as old-fashioned and antique as the fantastic lace collar he used to wear around his neck. But there is something about the man that can never die. That is his character. The world passes by his scientific and political and theological ideas with an indifferent eye, but it stands admiring and awestruck in the presence of the Man. He is a burning bush and men take off their shoes before him, knowing that in his presence they stand upon holy ground. Teachers of language have often brought their pupils to his style, feeling that faults of diction would be purged away by the flame of his burning words. I would bring the young men of America into his presence, sure that many a weakness will disappear and many a vice will wither, if only they are willing to stand for a season within reach of the heat of his flaming soul. Behold, Milton the Man!

Remember that you are face to face with a Puritan. Macaulay in his famous essay says he was not a Puritan, but in this statement the great English essayist departed from the facts. There was a reason. Macaulay did not like the Puritans, and as Milton was his idol, he did not wish to stigmatize him by identifying him with a set of men

FUNDAMENTAL TRAITS

against whom so many railing accusations had been brought. We will agree with Macaulay, however, when he says: "In his character the noblest qualities of every party were combined in harmonious union." But this does not prove he was not a Puritan. If he was not a Puritan, who was? He was a Puritan in education. When a boy he attended a church in whose pulpit there stood a Puritan preacher; when he went to school he sat at the feet of a Puritan instructor. When the time arrived for him to go to college he was sent to Cambridge, the hotbed of Puritanism, the university of John Harvard and Thomas Hooker and John Cotton, of Francis Higginson and John Winthrop and Roger Williams. He was a Puritan in his ideas. His attitude to the Bible, and his conceptions in theology, and his opposition to the Papacy and to Prelacy were all puritanic. When only a boy of fifteen he was turning the Hebrew Psalms into English verse, and to the day of his death he began every morning with a chapter of Scripture. If you want the Puritan theology full-toned, read Paradise Lost. He was a Puritan in his temper. He was intense, vehement, volcanic, furious. He struck hard and without mercy at everything which in his judgment was antagonistic to the will of God. He was a Puritan in his affiliations. He was the Latin Secretary of the Council of the Commonwealth, a council composed entirely of Puritans, whose work was the guidance of a Puritan state. His work was the work of a Puritan. He was the defender of the Puritan faith. He was the champion of the Puritan party and hurled thunderbolts against those who attacked either Puritan leaders or Puritan principles. If Knox is the preacher of Puritanism and Cromwell its soldier, then Milton is its defender and poet. He stood side by side with Cromwell, one fighting with his pen, the other with his sword, for the overthrow

FOREFATHERS' DAY SERMONS

of those who had wrecked the liberties of England. His contemporaries all thought he was a Puritan, and his enemies attacked him as one. As a Puritan he was thrown into jail on the accession of Charles II, and as a Puritan author his books were burned by the hangman, and as a Puritan he was hated by every Royalist, because he had defended the execution of Charles I and had made despotism odious among all whose faces were toward the light. He lives in history as a Puritan. The world has had only two supremely great religious poets, one a Roman Catholic, the Italian Dante; the other a Puritan, the English Milton. If he was not a Puritan, no Puritan has thus far existed on the earth. He was in fact a Puritan of the Puritans, a Puritan in every fiber of his being, a Puritan to the marrow of his bones, a Puritan by the foreknowledge and predestination of God, and no man shall ever be able to take away his crown.

But even to this day there are those who are reluctant to confess that Milton was a Puritan. He seems too good and great to be a Puritan, because in many circles a Puritan has been pictured as a creature quite contemptible and mean. The popular opinion has often made the Puritan a sour and crabbed bigot, talking through his nose, looking askance at every innocent enjoyment, bent always on reducing life to universal gloom. He has been pictured a sworn enemy of the drama, a hater of beauty, a despiser of pictures, a destroyer of art, one who has no ear for music, no eye for loveliness, no heart capable of feeling any of the higher pleasures which belong to cultured or even civilized men. If to be all this is to be a Puritan, then a Puritan Milton certainly was not, for he was a steadfast and enthusiastic lover of the drama. He began his literary career by writing a play — Comus — and he ended it by writing

FUNDAMENTAL TRAITS

another —Samson Agonistes. All his life long he praised the masterpieces of the great dramatic poets as having power to elevate the spirit and purge the heart of baser passions. He was a lover of music. He was born in a home filled with sweet sounds. His father was an organist and also a composer of considerable skill and repute. Milton was taught as a boy to sing, and in his opinion no education can be counted complete in which music has been neglected. He adored the beautiful. To a friend he wrote: "God has instilled into me, if into anyone, a vehement love of the beautiful. It is my habit day and night to seek for this idea of the beautiful through all the forms and faces of things." So sensitive was his soul to every form of loveliness that he has often been called the High Priest of Beauty, his highest function being to minister in her holy temple. He was not a narrow or crabbed man. On the contrary, he was generous and liberal beyond most of the men of his generation, carrying his idea of liberty beyond the bounds set for it even by the boldest friends of freedom, and enjoying the world even when he was blind, and old, and hated. If this man, then, be a Puritan, we must correct and enlarge our conception of the Puritan character. That there were men of the Puritan party who had no ear for music and no taste for art and no sympathy with the drama, is a well-known fact of history. But this does not prove that these limitations are an inseparable part of the Puritan character. The unlovely dispositions which the history of Puritanism discloses were only incidental, one might say accidental, and did not constitute an integral part of Puritan character and life. They were for the most part the product of chilling and dwarfing circumstances, the creation of an uncongenial environment. There was much in Puritanism which was only transitory and superficial, only foam floating on the surface of a great deep. When men pick up the malformations and freaks, the deformed and twisted specimens of human nature which a great historic movement brings to the front in time of storm, they should be reminded that every political and religious party has a right to be judged not by its worst but by its best, and that it is not in the exceptional or eccentric, but in the normal and abiding elements of life and character that the secret of power is to be sought and found. If you want to know what are the fundamental traits of Puritan character, do not look for them in some stunted individual whose life was crushed out of shape by the hostile forces of a narrowing environment, but come rather to a man who was planted in a large place and who was permitted to bring the Puritan virtues and the Puritan graces to a refreshing bloom and fragrance. Look at Milton!

What then are these fundamental traits as exhibited by England's foremost Puritan poet? First of all comes the sense of life as a gift of God to be used for God's glory. This is basal in all Puritan thought and feeling. As soon as you enter the Puritan world you feel that the heavens are over you and that they are influencing the earth. Man belongs to God, the Puritan asserts, and to God he is accountable for the use of his gifts. This was the old Hebraic idea, and in this idea every Puritan child was early established. Man must live a consecrated life. How early Milton accepted this idea we do not know. Judging from the picture of him, painted by a famous Dutch artist when he was only ten years of age, one would think that even then the boy was aware that he must be about some high and serious business. He tells us that from the age of twelve he hardly ever went to bed until midnight, so eager was he to store

FUNDAMENTAL TRAITS

his mind with the treasures which the books contained. It was in 1620 that a hundred Puritans started on the *Mayflower* for America. It was in that very year that the London boy of twelve embarked on a still wilder sea, and steered boldly into a still more mysterious West. At sixteen he was at Cambridge, burning with a desire not only to furnish his intellect but to perfect his character. At twenty-three he wrote a sonnet in which he declared his desire to do everything as in the " great Taskmaster's eye." At twenty-eight he wrote to his friend Diodati from Horton: " I am pluming my wings for a flight." By this time he had come to the conclusion that God wanted him to be a poet, and that it was his mission to write something which the world would not willingly let die. But to write a great poem, he said, the poet himself must be a poem. No man, he was sure, could write of praiseworthy thoughts and actions unless these excellent things existed first in himself. From an early age then this thought was uppermost: " I must live a dedicated life." This made him serious. It led to isolation. In Wordsworth's words: " His soul was like a star, and dwelt apart."

It was out of this abiding sense of accountability to God that there grew up the idea of duty. It was an old idea and had been in the world from the beginning, but never was duty so lustrous and sovereign as to the Puritan. It was something he owed to God. Milton from early years was under the sway of this potent conception. He must ever do what it was his duty to do. At the age of thirty he was traveling in Italy. His plan was to go on to Sicily and Greece. Just then word came that the conflict between the King and Parliament was coming to a crisis, and that in all likelihood the King would take up arms against his Scottish subjects. Milton at once made preparations to return

FOREFATHERS' DAY SERMONS

home. To see Greece had been one of the ambitions of his life, but " I thought it base," he said, " to be traveling for amusement abroad while my fellow citizens were fighting for liberty at home." Returning home he found England on the verge of revolution. The clash came. The King was dethroned. The King was beheaded. A commonwealth was established. This commonwealth needed defenders. Milton felt that he must come to its defense. He gave up his plans. He laid aside his ambition to write a great poem. He turned his back on the life of seclusion and meditation for which, both by temperament and culture, he was best fitted. He entered the dusty arena of controversy. He rushed to the defense of the men who were called murderers and impostors. He did it because it was his duty to do it. He could not do anything else. Like St. Paul, he cried: " Woe is me if I do not do this! " He heard a voice of rebuke ever saying to him: " Thou hadst the diligence, the parts, the language of a man, if a vain subject were to be adorned or beautified, but when the cause of God and His church was to be pleaded, for which purpose that tongue was given thee that thou hast, God listened if He could hear thy voice among His zealous servants, but thou wert dumb as a beast." He made the great surrender because it was his duty. In a sonnet to a friend he says: " What supports me, dost thou ask? The conscience, friend! " Behold the Puritan!

Of all the duties which lay upon the Puritan conscience the duty of virtue came first. The Puritan was first of all an advocate of purity. Hence his name — Pu-ri-tan. He hated vice, he detested immorality, he loathed uncleanness. Probably the deepest thing in Milton was his love of purity. While at college he was called " The Lady," possibly because of the beauty and refinement of his face, but most

FUNDAMENTAL TRAITS

probably because he did not care to take part in the debaucheries by which college life in those days was disgraced. His first ambition as a poet was to speak a ringing word against unchastity and to extol and glorify the idea of virtue. It is his very soul which you hear in lines like these:

> " Mortals who would follow me,
> Love Virtue; she alone is free.
> She can teach you how to climb
> Higher than the sphery chime;
> Or if Virtue feeble were,
> Heaven itself would stoop to her."
> ("*Comus.*")

After a spotless youth at home he spent a year in foreign travel. The most of that year was lived in Italy, at that time a fiery furnace of unbridled lust. But in the midst of the fire the English Puritan walked unscathed. On his return to England in August, 1639, he adds this sentence to his account of his journey, a sentence with which his biographer, Masson, closes the first volume of his monumental work: "I again take God to witness that in all these places, where so many things are considered lawful, I lived sound and untouched from all profligacy and vice, having the thought perpetually with me that, though I might escape the eyes of men, I certainly could not the eyes of God." Milton was as handsome as Goethe, as sensitive, inflammable, and passionate as he. How the great German dwindles in comparison with this English Puritan. Milton never betrayed a woman. There was no blot on his scutcheon. Behold the Puritan!

If there was any passion in the nature of our hero stronger than the passion for purity, it was his passion for liberty. His love of freedom was one of the elemental forces of his soul. Here again we strike that which is deep in every genuinely Puritan heart. A Puritan is a man who has so

FOREFATHERS' DAY SERMONS

clear a vision of God that he will not allow himself to be lorded over by any of the potentates of earth. Milton's father had intended his son to become a clergyman, and that was also the boy's first intention, but when the time came for him to prepare for the church, he drew back, on the ground that he was unwilling to write himself down a slave. The ministry was at that time so bound round by prescriptions and regulations that no man who loved liberty could become a preacher. Milton was twenty when William Laud became the Bishop of London, and it was only five years later that the Bishop of London was made Archbishop of Canterbury. Laud was a typical ecclesiastical tyrant. He slit men's noses and cut off their ears and threw them into loathsome dungeons if they would not bend to his autocratic will. It was impossible for Milton to think of the ministry under the administration of a man like that. He gave up the church and turned to poetry. Because of his ardent love for freedom he turned from poetry to prose. The finest of all Milton's prose writings, and the only one which now has any considerable number of readers, is his "Areopagitica," or "Speech for the Liberty of Unlicensed Printing." In the history of the development of freedom this work of Milton has a place from which it can never be dislodged. It is only when the heart is burning with fierce emotions that the tongue becomes eloquent and that words corruscate and flash. What must have been the temperature of the heart that pushed the blood to the finger-tips of the man who wrote "Areopagitica"? There are sentences in that argument which burn with a flame so intense, so clear, so beautiful it seems that it must have been kindled at the very altar of God.

So intense was Milton's love of freedom that it rose at

times to the fury of a mania. He became beside himself, frenzied, crazed. It is in his attacks on despotism that we come to what, in the judgment of many, is one of the deepest blots upon his fame. In defending liberty he became vituperative, furious, bitter. He perfected himself in the art of vituperation, not only indulging in it to surprising limits, but defending himself in the use of it, claiming that vituperation is the only weapon suitable for dealing with controversialists of a certain type. We stand amazed at this man's use of epithets. All the pointed and sharp-edged and jagged adjectives of our English speech were at his command, and he wove them into a scourge of scorpions with which to lacerate the backs of his opponents. It was a rude and wild age, and men of all parties used words as ruffians used daggers. In endeavoring to judge Milton two things must be remembered. We do not face to-day the enemy with which he was called to contend. The bishops of our day are amiable, harmless individuals whose power for working mischief has been curtailed by the growth of the democratic principle, both in church and state, and moreover our statesmen are so bound round by law that they can neither molest us nor make us afraid. We too would no doubt flame with wild wrath if we could see the outrages which Milton saw. And then we must bear in mind that great souls have passions of which lesser souls cannot dream. We do not see the beauty of liberty as Milton saw it, nor do we comprehend the immeasurable havoc wrought in the human spirit by the suppression of thought or speech. Like one of the old heroes in the Book of Judges he fought in fierce and lawless times, and when we see him reeling from the field, his body covered with mire and blood, whatever condemnation we may pass upon him, let us remember that the battle was tremendous and

FOREFATHERS' DAY SERMONS

that he fought an uncompromising and victorious fight. He was a warrior battling for liberty. Behold the Puritan!

A man on fire with passion for a noble cause is always ready to sacrifice. Willingness to sacrifice is a trait of the Puritan character. A man who bows before the sovereignty of duty cannot avoid a sacrificial life. Milton gave up little things like going to Greece, he gave up greater things like devoting his life to poetry. What this latter sacrifice meant to a man like Milton can be appreciated only by one who has Milton's love of solitude and Milton's ambition to do an immortal piece of work. But there was a greater sacrifice which he was called upon to make. It was necessary for him to give up his eyesight. When Salmasius, the famous French scholar of the university at Leyden, brought out a book defending the policy of Charles I and laying down principles which would destroy the foundations of free government everywhere, Milton felt that the argument must be answered. Salmasius was the literary dictator of all Western Europe, a counselor of princes and kings, and to allow his volume to go unanswered would jeopardize the cause of liberty throughout the world. Milton's eyes had already given him trouble. His physicians warned him to be careful. "If you go on with your writing," they said, "you may lose your eyesight." He went on, and paid the awful price. It is a price great for any man to pay, immeasurably greater, however, for a man who loves and lives in books. A recent writer has said: "Why should he, who penned L'Allegro, whose liberal soul was invited to give to England an epic such as he could write but did not, on Arthur, involving the whole cycle of Arthurian or ancient British legends; why should he, even in the name of God, truth, liberty, and country, doff his singing robes for the draught work of old Noll and his gloomy council of ministers?" Such writing as that is not only ignorant but low. The man who wrote that does not know the value of liberty. He is incapable of making any tremendous sacrifice for freedom. He does not know at what a fearful price our liberties have been bought. That kind of talk is like the talk of a man who would say that if the three hundred Greeks who died at Thermopylæ had only stayed in Athens and studied poetry they might have equalled the odes of Pindar or the tragedies of Æschylus. It is like saying, If the men in blue who fell at Gettysburg had only stayed at home they might have made money and founded colleges. It is like saying, If a certain woman had not married and brought up a family she might have won distinction as a player on the piano. Not only is such writing low but it is ignorant. That man does not know that Paradise Lost could not have been written had not Milton passed through a fiery furnace heated seven times hot. There are things which God communicates to no one except the soul that suffers. Without the trial and the tribulation of twenty years, Milton could not have created the poem which makes the whole world rich. He gave up his plans, his ambitions, the best years of his life, his eyes, and in return God gave to him an epic poem. Milton was ready to give up anything, everything for the glory of God! Behold the Puritan!

But in suffering the Puritan becomes mighty. He has in him the consciousness of unconquerable strength. Milton was a man whom no combination of forces was able to bend or break down. I have called him serious, but gloomy he was not. There is not a trace of gloom in any of his writings. You can hear the blowing of trumpets proclaiming victory all the way. From L'Allegro, where the flutes are playing and heaven and earth are dancing, down to the majestic strains of Samson Agonistes, the sun is always huge and glorious in the heavens by day and at night the quiet stars look down upon a world which God has made and rules. Nothing could daunt this intrepid man. Listen to him saying: " It is not necessarily a misery to be blind: the only misery is not to be able to endure blindness." He wrote a sonnet one day on his blindness in which he mentions certain musings which have been passing through his soul. He sees the King of heaven on his throne and watches his servants posting in all directions over land and ocean, and then he thinks of himself standing impotent, unable either to run or even walk, incapacitated by his blindness for doing the large things which the world needed to have done, but even this does not break him down. He consoles himself with a thought which he has expressed in a line more frequently quoted than any other line he ever wrote:

" They also serve who only stand and wait."

As his life went on the darkness deepened. The Commonwealth established by Cromwell was unable to ride through the storm. Charles II ascended the throne. The nation plunged at once into a wild season of recklessness and pleasure. Many of Milton's friends were thrown into prison. The principles dear to his heart were derided and overthrown. The cause to which he had given his life was brought to the dust. The heads of Cromwell and Bradshaw were exposed for public execration. His highest hopes were disappointed, his fondest dreams fell in ruins. Poor, disgraced, deserted, he sat alone and blind amid the wreckage of his country's liberties and the ruins of the great plans which he and others had formulated for the

FUNDAMENTAL TRAITS

English people, but his great soul soared on eagle's wings above the darkness and the storms of earth, kindling its undazzled eyes as of old "at the full midday beam." It was in these awful days that his mind turned to the old, blind hero of Israel — Samson. The Hebrew could not be conquered, neither could the Englishman. From first to last his soul was tuned to this high note:

> "I argue not
> Against Heaven's hand or will, nor bate a jot
> Of heart or hope, but still bear up, and steer
> Right onward."

Behold the Puritan!

What was the secret of this man's victorious strength? He wrestled not against flesh and blood but "against the principalities, against the powers, against the world rulers of this darkness, against the spiritual hosts of wickedness in the heavenly places" and came off more than conqueror because he had put on the whole armor of God, and had learned the secret of prayer. Milton stands unique among English men of letters for the boldness and frequency with which he prays. In the greatest of his prose writings he mounts from the crest of his reasoning into the region of prayer. We follow him in his massive argument, and lo! before we are aware of it, he is pleading not with us but with God. His greatest poem has in it many marvelous pictures but not one more awe-inspiring and self-revealing than that of the author in prayer. Milton had no doubt of the existence of the "Eternal Spirit that can enrich with all utterance and knowledge and that sends out his Seraphim with the hallowed fire of his altar, to touch and purify the lips of whom he pleases." Sure of God he throws himself upon God's strength and mercy at the very beginning of his immortal poem:

FOREFATHERS' DAY SERMONS

" O Spirit, that dost prefer
Before all temples th' upright heart and pure,
Instruct me, for thou know'st; thou from the first
Wast present, and with mighty wings outspread
Dove-like sat'st brooding on the vast abyss,
And mad'st it pregnant: what in me is dark
Illumine, what is low raise and support;
That to the height of this great argument
I may assert eternal Providence,
And justify the ways of God to men."

A recent Italian writer — Pietro Raveggi — has said that there is an apocalyptic splendor and mystery in Milton's invocations. "The language has the grandeur of poetry and the sweetness of the voices of Paradise. As we listen we are caught away and transported to the visions of the everlasting life." Veit Dietrich, having listened in secret to the prayers of Martin Luther while he was staying at Coburg, afterward confessed: " My soul, too, burned within me with a strange passion while he spoke so familiarly, so solemnly, so reverently with God." If you would learn the secret of the strength of this English Samson, listen to him while he prays. Behold the Puritan!

This then is the man Milton, the greatest man in the long line of English singers. No one would for a moment think of comparing Milton with Burns or Byron, or Shelley or Edgar Allan Poe. As a man he towers above Swinburne and Coleridge and Arnold and Tennyson and Browning. In manhood he outranks the great Shakespeare. As a poet Shakespeare stands first, but as a man he surrenders the palm to Milton. Shakespeare as soon as he made money enough to keep him in comfort turned his back on the world, retiring to his native village, where he spent the closing years of his life in the easy occupations of a gentleman farmer. In his dramas he acted on the principle which he puts into the mouth of Hamlet. To him the end of playing is " to hold, as 'twere, the mirror up to nature;

FUNDAMENTAL TRAITS

to show virtue her own feature, scorn her own image, and the very age and body of the time his form and pressure." In his genius for holding the mirror up to nature, Shakespeare has never had an equal. He gives us the world as he saw it. He is the most impersonal, the most impartial of all the poets. You can quote him on both sides of almost every question. He pictures Falstaff with as evident a relish as he paints the portraits of Imogene and Hermione. He does not take sides. He is not a prophet. He is not a soldier of God. He does not struggle for righteousness. Milton on the other hand was a warrior, a prophet, a defender of the faith. Like holy men of old he bore the burden of the Lord. Like prophets and apostles he wrestled with a world in rebellion against God. Vice was loathsome to him, virtue alone could win the plaudits of his heart. In that long line of shining singers who have filled the world with music from Geoffrey Chaucer to Robert Browning, there is not one so tall of stature and so noble in the regal traits of manhood as John Milton. Macaulay in his most famous essay has written sentences which the world has never been willing to change:

" There are a few characters which have stood the closest scrutiny and the severest tests, which have been tried in the furnace and have proved pure, which have been weighed in the balance and have not been found wanting, which have been declared sterling by the general consent of mankind, and which are visibly stamped with the image and superscription of the Most High. These great men, we trust, we know how to prize; and of these was Milton. The sight of his books, the sound of his name, are refreshing to us. His thoughts resemble those celestial fruits and flowers which the Virgin Martyr of Massinger sent down from the gardens of Paradise to the earth, distin-

FOREFATHERS' DAY SERMONS

guished from the productions of other soils, not only by their superior bloom and sweetness, but by their miraculous efficacy to invigorate and to heal. They are powerful not only to delight, but to elevate and purify. Nor do we envy the man who can study either the life or the writings of the great poet and patriot, without aspiring to emulate, not, indeed, the sublime works with which his genius has enriched our literature, but the zeal with which he labored for the public good, the fortitude with which he endured every private calamity, the lofty disdain with which he looked down on temptation and dangers, and the deadly hatred which he bore to bigots and tyrants, and the faith which he so sternly kept with his country and with his fame."

William Wordsworth, the greatest poet in the first half of the nineteenth century, spoke for the England of his day in a sonnet addressed to our Puritan poet. It was not the poet but the man to whom Wordsworth was looking when he wrote:

> " Milton! thou should'st be living at this hour:
> England hath need of thee: she is a fen
> Of stagnant waters: altar, sword and pen,
> Fireside, the heroic wealth of hall and bower,
> Have forfeited their ancient English dower
> Of inward happiness. We are selfish men;
> Oh, raise us up, return to us again;
> And give us manners, virtue, freedom, power."

On the ninth day of the present month in the City of London, at the celebration of the three hundredth anniversary of Milton's birth, a poem written by the world's greatest living novelist, George Meredith, was recited. George Meredith is eighty years of age and he knows the world as few men do. He knows England and he knows the great men whom England has given to the world. Listen to his words:

FUNDAMENTAL TRAITS

> "Were England sunk beneath the shifting tides,
> Her heart, her brain, the smile she wears,
> The faith she holds, her best would live full-toned
> In the grand delivery of his cathedral speech."

And then contemplating the present condition of mankind, cursed and torn by Mammon, who has become a monstrous, inveterate Moloch, the twentieth century novelist repeats the cry of the nineteenth century poet — "We need him now!" This is the tribute which the world pays to the Puritan.

It was two hundred and thirty-four years ago last month when on a Sunday evening the old blind poet left our earth. The world has greatly changed since that November evening. The London of Milton's day has disappeared. A new London is now the metropolis of the world. The house in which Milton was born was licked up by the flames of the great conflagration of 1666. The house at Horton in which he spent six happy years was torn down over a hundred years ago. All his London residences have one after another succumbed to the tooth of time, the last one disappearing thirty-one years ago. The intellectual house in which he lived has also been obliterated by the rising tide of modern knowledge. The scientific conceptions and the religious dogmas in which he made his home have been swept away never to come back again. We live in a new world with new notions and a new vocabulary, but Milton abides with us and will abide forever. He is a force in our politics, a power in our religion. His spirit is an indestructible part of the life of humanity. His fame is secure. In the words of Tennyson:

> "O mighty mouthed Inventor of harmonies,
> O skilled to sing of Time or Eternity,
> God-gifted organ Voice of England,
> Milton, a name to resound for ages."

FOREFATHERS' DAY SERMONS

Though dead, he yet speaks. And so long as the human heart in times of stress grows faint and seeks inspiration by gazing into the faces of those who have suffered and have overcome, so long as the human spirit casts its crowns at the feet of those who have fought the fight and kept the faith, will men in every land and in each succeeding generation, travel back to the old blind Puritan who sang in the night an immortal song, in quest of strength with which to meet and vanquish the foes of God which the soul encounters along the difficult and perilous way.